OXFORD STUDIES IN ANALYTIC THEOLOGY

Series Editors
Michael C. Rea   Oliver D. Crisp

Analytic Theology utilizes the tools and methods of contemporary analytic philosophy for the purposes of constructive Christian theology, paying attention to the Christian tradition and development of doctrine. This innovative series of studies showcases high quality, cutting-edge research in this area, in monographs and symposia.

D1593089

RITUALIZED FAITH

Central to the lives of the religiously committed are not simply religious convictions but also religious practices. The religiously committed, for example, regularly assemble to engage in religious rites, including corporate liturgical worship. Although the participation in liturgy is central to the religious lives of many, few philosophers have given it attention. In this collection of essays, Terence Cuneo turns his attention to liturgy, contending that the topic proves itself to be philosophically rich and rewarding. Taking the liturgical practices of Eastern Christianity as its focal point, *Ritualized Faith* examines issues such as what the ethical importance of ritualized religious activities might be, what it is to immerse oneself in such activities, and what the significance of liturgical singing and iconography are. In doing so, Cuneo makes sense of these liturgical practices and indicates why they deserve a place in the religiously committed life.

Terence Cuneo is Marsh Professor of Intellectual and Moral Philosophy at the University of Vermont.

Ritualized Faith

Essays on the Philosophy of Liturgy

TERENCE CUNEO

OXFORD
UNIVERSITY PRESS

OXFORD
UNIVERSITY PRESS

Great Clarendon Street, Oxford, OX2 6DP,
United Kingdom

Oxford University Press is a department of the University of Oxford.
It furthers the University's objective of excellence in research, scholarship,
and education by publishing worldwide. Oxford is a registered trade mark of
Oxford University Press in the UK and in certain other countries

First published 2016
First published in paperback 2018

Published in the United States of America by Oxford University Press
198 Madison Avenue, New York, NY 10016, United States of America

British Library Cataloguing in Publication Data
Data available

Library of Congress Cataloging in Publication Data
Data available

ISBN 978–0–19–875775–7 (Hbk.)
ISBN 978–0–19–882880–8 (Pbk.)

Preface

I can trace my interest in liturgy directly to Nick Wolterstorff's influence. When I read one of his papers on the topic twenty years ago, I had scarcely given liturgy a thought, at least as a subject that philosophers could dig their teeth into. I recall finding it both surprising that the subject was so philosophically interesting and that philosophers had given it so little attention. Twenty years later, the surprise has not worn off, although it's now surprise of a different sort. While I no longer find it remarkable that liturgy is of philosophical interest, I am frequently impressed by how philosophically rich a topic it is. There is a lot to think about! Because the topic is so underexplored by philosophers, even posing the right questions can be a challenge.

I say this while recognizing that, in the last fifty years or so, theologians have made important contributions to our understanding of liturgy.[1] Nevertheless, the questions that theologians raise, the ways that they address them, and the literature with which they engage tend to be different from the questions that interest philosophers, the ways in which philosophers pursue these questions, and the literature with which philosophers engage. An implication of this disciplinary difference has been that the essays that compose this book do not simply pick up the discussion of liturgy where the theologians have left off. In fact, with the notable exception of Alexander Schmemann's work, most of these essays explicitly engage with what theologians say about matters of liturgy rather less than I had anticipated when writing them. Our questions tend to be different.

I'm grateful to a cadre of philosophers and theologians who've helped to locate the right questions and fruitful ways to pursue them. In 2007, Jamie Smith, Reinhardt Hütter, Sarah Coakley, Peter Ochs, Nick Wolterstorff and I—a "seed group" funded by the Center for Worship at Calvin College—met at the University of Virginia to discuss our work in progress on liturgy. In 2008, Calvin College sponsored a conference on liturgy in which this work was presented, along with a host of other papers. In 2009, Nick Wolterstorff and I led a three-week summer seminar at Calvin College on liturgy that afforded the chance to reflect extensively and collectively on liturgy, read more widely on the subject, and locate important themes. I thank Calvin College—and, especially, John Witvliet—for making these events possible. I'd also like to thank those who participated in the 2008 conference and the 2009 seminar for helpful discussion. Specifically, I'd like to single out Andrew Chignell,

---

[1] Fagerberg (2004) provides an introduction to some of the main currents in liturgical theology, primarily within the Orthodox and Roman Catholic traditions.

Fr. Andrew Cuneo, David Manley, Mark Montague, David O'Hara, Mike Rea, Howie Wettstein, and Lori Wilson for answering questions and shining light on some puzzling topics. It goes without saying that I owe Nick Wolterstorff an enormous debt. He not only planted the seeds of interest in liturgy but also saw to it that they grew.

Finally, I owe special thanks to Janina Cuneo and Luke Reinsma for contributing their copy-editing skills to the preparation of the manuscript.

In 2012, I was awarded a grant by the Character Project at Wake Forest University (and funded by the John Templeton Foundation) to work on liturgy and character. The time this grant provided to reflect and write on liturgy has proved invaluable to me. Most of the essays in this volume were written under the auspices of this grant, and I thank Christian Miller, its director, for supporting this work. (Of course the views expressed in this book do not necessarily reflect those of the foundation itself.)

Academics are accustomed to thanking their home institutions when they provide research support. In this case, however, I'd like to thank a different type of "home" institution: a group of parishes that I've attended over the last couple of decades. Thanks to St. Vladimir's Seminary (Crestwood, NY), St. Paul Orthodox Church (Brier, WA), St. James Orthodox Church (Williamston, MI), and St. Jacob of Alaska Orthodox Church (Northfield Falls, VT), for the experience of being part of communal liturgical life.

Acknowledgments

The author and publisher would like to thank these publishers for permission to reproduce the essays in this volume.

Chapter 1, "Love and Liturgy," appeared in the *Journal of Religious Ethics* 43, 2015: 587–605.

Chapter 2, "Protesting Evil," appeared in *Theology Today* 70, 2014: 430–44.

Chapter 3 is a lightly amended version of "Another Look at Divine Hiddenness," which appeared in *Religious Studies* 49, 2013: 151–64.

Chapter 4, "Liturgical Immersion," appeared in the *Journal of Analytic Theology* 2, 2014: 117–39.

Chapter 5, "Liturgy and the Moral Life," appeared in Christian Miller, ed., *Character: New Directions from Philosophy, Psychology, and Theology*. Oxford: Oxford University Press, 2015: 572–89.

Chapter 6, "If These Walls Could Only Speak: Icons as Vehicles of Divine Speech," appeared in *Faith and Philosophy* 23, 2010: 123–41.

Chapter 7, "The Significance of Liturgical Singing," appeared in *Res Philosophica* 91, 2014: 411–29.

Chapter 8, "Ritual Knowledge," appeared in *Faith and Philosophy* 31, 2014: 365–85.

Chapter 9, "Transforming the Self: On the Baptismal Rite," appeared in *Religious Studies* 50, 2014: 279–96.

Chapter 10, "Rites of Remission," appeared in the *Journal of Analytic Theology* 3, 2014: 70–88.

Chapter 11, "Entering through Death, Living with Doubt," appeared in Rico Vitz., ed., *Turning East: Contemporary Philosophers and the Ancient Christian Faith*. St. Vladimir's Seminary Press, 2012: 157–76.

Table of Contents

Introduction

We philosophers are accustomed to having an audience in mind for whom we write. Those of us who work in metaphysics write for fellow metaphysicians. Those of us who work in ethics write for fellow moral philosophers. And so on. Of course we often hope that those outside our intended audience will listen and join in the conversation, seeing the relevance of our work for theirs or perhaps having their interest sparked by topics that they'd not considered before. But much of the time these hopes go unrealized; our intended audience more or less exhausts those who engage our work.

The essays that compose this book do not have an intended audience in anything like the sense just described. The simple explanation is that these essays are philosophical explorations of liturgy, and nearly no one in professional philosophy works on the topic of liturgy.[1] (In a moment, I will have more to say about how I am using the term "liturgy." For now, think of it as what many would call the *religious service*.) To state this explanation even more sharply, the chapters in this volume are mostly philosophical explorations of the liturgies of a specific Christian tradition, namely, the Christian East, and almost no one in professional philosophy works on the liturgies of the Christian East. At the risk of making an apparently esoteric topic seem even more so, if you were to identify those in fields such as theology, religious studies, and ritual studies who work on Christian liturgy, you would identify only a small number of scholars. And those who do work on the topic tend to approach it much differently than a philosopher would; their work is often purely historical, sociological, or philological, having little to do with the sorts

---

[1] A caveat: some contemporary philosophers and philosophically inclined theologians have written on the metaphysics of the eucharist. For example, see Adams (2006), Pruss (2009), Hütter (2010), Toner (2011), and Baber (2013). Generally speaking, however, this work on the metaphysics of the eucharist has treated it like any other puzzle in metaphysics, paying relatively little attention to the eucharistic celebration as a liturgical activity. In the broadly Anglo-American analytic tradition, Nicholas Wolterstorff is an exception to this trend, having worked on issues in the philosophy of liturgy for some years. See Wolterstorff (2011a) and (2015), especially. In the broadly Continental tradition, James K. A. Smith is also an exception; see Smith (2009).

of issues that would interest a philosopher, such as the ethical dimensions of ritualized activity.

Still, those familiar with the history of theology know that commentary and reflection on liturgy is nothing new. There is, for example, a venerable tradition in the Eastern Christian tradition in which figures such as Maximus the Confessor, in the seventh century, St. Germanos, in the eighth century, and Nicholas Cabasilas, in the fourteenth century, offered extensive commentaries on the Divine Liturgy. Might this collection of essays be viewed as an effort to rehabilitate this more or less forgotten and defunct tradition?

Not in any direct sense. While I locate myself within the religious tradition to which these figures belong—namely, Eastern Christianity—I find the neo-Platonic philosophical framework within which they operate alien in important respects. (In this, I doubt that I am unusual. Most contemporary philosophers would answer similarly.) For me, the experience of reading the commentaries just mentioned is that of entering into a philosophical world profoundly different from ours, animated by concerns and presuppositions that are often baffling. Connecting my own experience of the liturgy with what they have to say about it is challenging.

There is, perhaps, a deeper reason for not viewing this collection of essays as a natural extension of ancient liturgical commentary, articulated most sharply by the Orthodox liturgical scholar and theologian Alexander Schmemann. In his *Introduction to Liturgical Theology*, Schmemann notes that representatives of the so-called mysteriological school, such as Maximus, Germanos, and Cabasilas, take an approach to liturgical commentary that consists in offering elaborate symbolic and typological interpretations of the actions that compose the liturgy.[2] To give you a taste of their approach: if you were to attend a performance of the Orthodox Divine Liturgy, you would notice that early in the service the priest enters the altar holding a copy of the Gospel aloft. In their commentaries, advocates of the mysteriological school tell us that this action symbolically represents Christ's entrance into Jerusalem.

In Schmemann's view, this approach to liturgical interpretation is mistaken. The problem is not primarily that these figures offer forced, even artificial interpretations of liturgical action. It is rather that, in some important respects, they advance a deeply distorted understanding of the reality and significance of liturgical activity, according to which the liturgy is "a sanctifying mystery...a means of rising by way of initiation from the profane to the sacred, from the material to the spiritual, from the sensual to the *noumenal*."[3]

[2] Schmemann (1966). Central to Schmemann's work is the distinction between the liturgy itself and its reception. In Schmemann's view, while the reception of the liturgy has been heavily influenced by certain elements of neo-Platonism, the fundamentals of the liturgy itself have not.
[3] Schmemann (1966), 130. Elsewhere Schmemann writes: "The explanation of the Eucharistic liturgy as a symbolic depiction of the earthly life of Christ is an artificial explanation for anyone who is even slightly familiar with the history, prayers and structure of the liturgy. And yet not

Schmemann charges this approach with being deeply unfaithful to the Christian vision. I agree. When properly understood, the Christian vision does not operate with or presuppose the legitimacy of the categories to which Schmemann adverts, let alone advocate a view according to which worship consists in turning away from the profane to the sacred. Instead, liturgical worship presents the world as a manifestation of God and God's activity to which we, in worship, respond in thanks.

I have claimed that a collection of essays on the philosophy of liturgy is unlikely either to find a "ready-made" audience or to be a natural extension of a long-standing tradition of liturgical commentary that deserves rehabilitation. But if not, why write such essays? Why would anyone think it worthwhile to think philosophically about liturgy? Or to phrase the question somewhat more exactly: suppose that topics do not simply sort themselves into categories such as "amenable only to philosophical reflection" or "amenable only to theological reflection," since philosophers often legitimately reflect on topics of interest to theologians and vice-versa. If this is so, why think philosophically about liturgy? And if one were to do so, why focus on the liturgies of the Christian East?

Let me approach these questions indirectly. Those familiar with contemporary philosophy of religion know that, within the last forty years or so, the discipline has experienced a renaissance in the Anglo-American analytic tradition. As Nicholas Wolterstorff observes in his essay "Analytic Philosophy of Religion: Retrospect and Prospect," the renaissance is remarkable (in part) because it was unpredictable; during the heyday of logical positivism in the mid-twentieth century, it would have been impossible to have foreseen either the collapse of positivism or the resurgence of philosophy of religion, which occurred in the wake of positivism's collapse.[4]

While unpredictable, the renaissance in philosophy of religion has taken a definite shape. Most of those who have contributed to it are not neutral observers of religion but practitioners of one or another religious tradition, typically the Christian tradition. And to an overwhelming degree, within the philosophy of religion, their work has focused on issues of epistemology and metaphysics. In the epistemology of religious belief, the central issue has been to address the charge, leveled by many, that there is something deeply defective about religious belief: it is irrational, unreasonable, unjustified, in conflict with the findings of science, or the like. In this respect, work in the epistemology of religious belief has been outward looking, addressing a challenge that

---

only has it been since Byzantine times the most popular and widely accepted explanation, it may also be regarded as the occasion for a whole series of additions and accretions in the ritual of the liturgy which have tended to destroy its original structure" (98). Not all are as pessimistic, however. Meyendorff (1984) highlights what he takes to be of value in Germanos' commentary.

[4] Wolterstorff (2011b), ch. 1.

arises, in large measure, from outside the theistic traditions. In contrast, work in the metaphysics of theism has not been outward looking in the same way, as it has been primarily concerned to tackle issues that arise from the theistic traditions themselves, such as how to understand the divine attributes and to reconcile our freedom with God's foreknowledge or sovereignty. A third large-scale project of developing responses to the so-called problem of evil has cut across these two areas, drawing upon (among other areas) work in the metaphysics of modality and probability theory.[5]

Given its shape, the contemporary renaissance in philosophy of religion has had its limitations. The most obvious limitation, I believe, is that the contemporary discussion has tended to proceed at a very high level of abstraction, having relatively little to say about lived religious life "on the ground" and the sorts of questions and challenges that issue from and concern the religiously committed life. In this respect, contemporary work in philosophy of religion differs markedly from work done in other domains of philosophy, such as ethics. Within ethics, many dedicate themselves to addressing foundational and abstract questions, such as whether there are any moral truths, whether we can have moral knowledge, and what the nature of right action might be. But, in addition, many others primarily focus on the lived moral life and the questions and challenges it raises. Their discussions include fine-grained analyses of the virtues, explorations of whether we can legitimately hold corporations responsible for their actions, and assessments of the legitimacy of blame and praise—all of which are aimed at deepening our understanding of the lived ethical life.

In gesturing toward the limitations of contemporary work in the philosophy of religion, I need to emphasize that I have no interest in casting aspersions on it. On the contrary, I have a very high estimation of much of this work, largely because it has, in my view, considerably enriched the contemporary philosophical discussion. Unlike some philosophers and theologians, then, I do not believe that, when practiced in a way that is aware of its own tendencies and limitations, philosophical reflection on the nature of God or the problem of evil is morally or religiously illegitimate.[6] To gesture toward the limitations of a movement is not to disparage it.

And yet I harbor worries. My primary concern is not that contemporary philosophy of religion is entirely out of touch with religious life on the ground.

---

[5] Interestingly, although work on the problem of evil has made extensive assumptions about the nature of value and of the rights, responsibilities, and obligations we may have toward God and that God may have toward us, very little of this work has been done by those who work in value theory or the foundations of ethics. This, I believe, has heavily colored the discussion of the topic.

[6] I find myself ultimately disagreeing, then, with theologians such as Tilley (2000) and Surrin (2004) and philosophers such as Trakakis (2008), despite agreeing with some of what they say. Recent movements in so-called analytic theology might be a sign that changes are afoot in the discipline. See Crisp and Rea (2009).

What philosophers of religion talk about, after all, often springs from elements of the religious life. Anselm, for one, is famous for having formulated his ontological argument in the context of composing a prayer. Moreover, I am aware that the insights offered by contemporary philosophers of religion sometimes trickle down to communities of non-philosophers, helping them to appreciate the resources available for thinking through certain issues or addressing challenges. The issue that concerns me, then, is not that contemporary philosophy of religion and religious life fail to intersect. It is rather that, when they do intersect, they do so at only certain points, yielding a picture of the religious life that often looks to me oddly out of focus.

Let me present this concern in more detail. Begin by noting that while philosophical questions sometimes have their roots in the religious life, the lived religious life tends not to concern itself with the questions that animate philosophers, such as whether there are counterfactuals of creaturely freedom or whether God is metaphysically simple. Nor, for that matter, does the coherence, legitimacy, and attractiveness of this way of life ride on how philosophers answer these questions. In this regard, the religious life enjoys a certain degree of autonomy from higher-order reflections on it. What, then, does the lived religious life concern itself with? I would say that it primarily concerns itself with issues such as these: first, how to understand the teachings, ideals, practices, and responsibilities of the religious life as they are presented in one's religious tradition; second, how to conform one's life and the life of one's community to these teachings, ideals, practices, and responsibilities; and, third, when some teaching, ideal, practice, or putative responsibility with respect to some subject matter is deemed inadequate or unacceptable, how to identify—given one's religious commitments—other teachings, ideals, practices, and responsibilities with regard to that subject matter that are adequate or acceptable. As to the teachings, ideals, practices, or responsibilities that are the concern of the religiously committed life, these would include interpretation of scripture and other important texts, broadly ascetic practices such as fasting, prayer, and almsgiving, the education of children and converts in the ways of a tradition, the creation and engagement with works of the arts such as hymns and icons, being involved in or advocating certain social or political movements and, most relevantly for my purposes, corporate worship.

This last point is important for my purposes, since, for many of the religiously committed, corporate worship lies at the heart of their religious commitment. And yet I imagine that someone thoroughly familiar with contemporary philosophy of religion could, from having read this literature, only guess that an activity such as worship is important, let alone fundamental to the religious life. The topic is simply not addressed. In fact, if the amount of time and ink dedicated to an issue is any indication of the degree to which that issue matters, such a person might well have the impression that, when it comes to religion, what matters is the defensibility of Molinism or the rational credibility of religious belief.

The concern I am raising, then, is that much of the discussion in contemporary philosophy of religion is detached from the religious life in such a way that it threatens to offer a distorted picture of what is important to this way of life. A corollary is that contemporary philosophy of religion has largely failed to deepen our understanding of what it is to be a religiously committed agent and how one ought to be such an agent. A consequence, I believe, is that we do not understand crucial components of lived religious life as well as we should.

I can make the point I am pressing more vivid by returning to an analogue introduced earlier: imagine that philosophical work in ethics were more or less entirely consumed with metaethical questions about whether there are moral truths, answering skeptical challenges as to whether we ever have moral reasons to act, or what grounds our moral obligations. In this imagined scenario, moral philosophers touch only in passing upon lived ethical life and the sorts of issues that confront ethical agents. If this were the case, we would rightly be concerned that the field was not simply unbalanced but also disconnected from important elements of its subject matter. If someone were interested in better understanding various contours of the ethical life, this person would probably not be served by reading work in ethics, since the field fails to provide us with deeper understanding of what it is to be a moral agent and how we should understand the ethical life.

The concern I am voicing is that something similar is true of much of the contemporary discussion in philosophy of religion. This discussion is not simply incomplete but also, to a considerable extent, disconnected from what may be the very life-blood of religious ways of life. Arguably, though, we want discussions in philosophy of religion to proceed on multiple levels: we want to have not only high-level discussions of abstract topics about God, the epistemic status of religious belief, and the compatibility of freedom and foreknowledge but also philosophically astute reflection on the religious way of life that deepens our understanding of that way of life. The hope would be that, in these respects, philosophy of religion should more closely resemble contemporary work in ethics than it presently does.

Given the present orientation of philosophy of religion, it is natural to cast about for explanations as to why it's taken the direction it has. Specifically, it is natural to search for explanations as to why contemporary philosophy of religion has shown almost no interest in such a religiously fundamental activity as worship. As much as I would like to have some more or less comprehensive explanation, I have none. The best we can do, I believe, is to identify dynamics that might contribute to such an explanation.[7]

---

[7] Wolterstorff (2011b), ch. 1, also addresses some of these dynamics, drawing attention to the context in which contemporary philosophers of religion have worked.

To that end, consider the observation made by the late anthropologist of religion, Catherine Bell, that religious traditions divide into those that are more or less "orthopraxic" (from the Greek, meaning "straight, right practice") and those more or less "orthodoxic" (also from the Greek, meaning "straight, right belief"). Christianity is typically offered as the prime example of an orthodoxic tradition. Indeed, Bell writes that "being a Christian has meant, for a good part of Christian history, that one believes in the divinity of Jesus Christ . . . it is not sufficient simply to be born of Christian parents or raised in a Christian home."[8] As such, orthodoxic traditions such as Christianity, Bell writes, tend to cast rituals into a secondary role, "as *expressions* of things that should already be in the heart."[9] When reflecting on her own experience of teaching the subject of ritual to undergraduates, Bell continues:

> Students know they may be at a disadvantage when they step into one of my classes if their only previous coursework addressed Christianity, but I think the disadvantage is quite different from what they imagine. It is not of knowledge, but perspective. Christianity is the religious tradition least likely to be taught with reference to its key rituals. In most religious studies departments, undergraduate courses on Judaism or Islam naturally discuss some of the main ritual components of these traditions, often presented as more orthopraxic in orientation than Christianity. They also deal with the significance for a Jew or Muslim of the ideal of living a life defined by observing all of the ritual responsibilities laid out for a man and a woman. There are always classes celebrating a seder at Rosh Hashanah,[10] or making visits to mosque services . . . . Yet courses on Christian history or theology that refer to the liturgical expressions of key doctrinal ideas will do so without ever examining what these liturgical expressions mean to anyone but theologians.[11]

If Bell and other anthropologists of religion are right about how Christians have tended to understand their own tradition, then it might go some distance toward accounting for why, in contemporary philosophy of religion, some topics have received a great deal of attention and others have not.

Take, as an example, the epistemic status of religious belief. Suppose the belief that certain propositions are true were fundamental to the Christian way of life, since it is these beliefs that determine (at least in large measure) whether one belongs to the tradition. (The assumption must be that the attitude of faith, which any Christian would regard as central, includes something very belief-like.) And suppose that philosophers were primarily concerned to understand belief states and the various ways in which they can be meritorious or not. If we suppose these two things, then it would shed

---

[8] Bell (1997), 194.   [9] Ibid. Cf. also p. 215.
[10] I assume that this must be a slip of the pen on Bell's part. In the Jewish calendar, a seder is celebrated only once a year, at Passover.
[11] Bell (2007), 187.

light on why philosophers have paid so much attention to the epistemic credentials of religious belief. In doing so, they would be focusing on what, according to Christianity and to philosophy, matters. More importantly than this, however, Bell's observation would also help explain why other topics have been ignored by contemporary philosophers of religion, such as the role of ritualized activity. If ritualized activity belongs to the periphery of the Christian way of life, as Bell suggests many hold, then it would make some sense of why it is not a topic of philosophical conversation. Any importance it might have would be derivative, perhaps because it functions to express theological beliefs, strengthen our commitment to them, energize the faithful for doing good works, increase social cohesion, or the like.

If the proposal we're now considering were along the right lines, it would not only help to explain why liturgy has not been discussed by philosophers, but also deflect the charge that—to the extent that it engages with religion "on the ground" at all—contemporary philosophy of religion offers a distorted picture of the religious life. The reply is that while it would probably not be inappropriate for philosophers of religion to engage topics peripheral to the religious life, such as ritualized activity, they cannot be expected to do so. By not engaging secondary dimensions of the religious life, the contemporary discussion might be incomplete. But it would not, as I have suggested, thereby offer a misshapen portrayal of the religious life. To which it might be added that some philosophers will wonder what the fuss could be about, asking what *could* be said about liturgy that is of philosophical interest!

Were they correct, Bell's observations would represent only part of an explanation as to why contemporary philosophy of religion has taken the form it has. And as far as partial explanations go, it would be limited, for as Bell herself acknowledges, she paints with broad strokes in the passages I've quoted.[12] Christianity comes in many varieties, and not all are all belief-centered in the way that Bell describes. This is certainly true of various forms of the Roman Catholic, Anglican, and Mennonite traditions, for example—and might also be true of so-called non-liturgical traditions such as Quakerism. However that may be, it is especially true of the Christian tradition that occupies my attention in this book, namely, Eastern Christianity. While issues of correct belief have occupied its attention—this is, after all, the tradition that crafted the Nicean–Constantinopolitan creed—Eastern Christianity has much in common with Bell's description of Judaism and Islam: if one wished to introduce students to the tradition, there would be no adequate way to do so without taking into account the role that corporate ritualized activity, especially liturgical worship, plays in it. In fact, so far that I can see, the role that liturgy plays in Eastern Christianity has no parallel in

---

[12] See Bell (1997), 197.

other corners of Christendom. For Eastern Christians, the liturgy functions as the centerpiece of the Christian way of life. It is the paradigmatic expression of the tradition's *mind*—the sense of the term "mind" referring not simply or even primarily to various doctrines or claims but also to ways of conducting oneself and viewing the world, whose rich character and significance might be difficult and perhaps impossible to capture in wholly propositional terms.[13] In short, if one wanted to understand the religious and ethical vision of Eastern Christianity, one would have to attend carefully to its liturgies.

It may help to unpack these points, beginning with the claim about the liturgy's central role in the Eastern church. Why, in contrast to other branches of Christendom, would the liturgy play such a crucial role in the life of the Eastern church? In the memorable first chapter of his book *For the Life of the World*, Schmemann contends that the answer cannot be attributed to happenstance. Rather, the liturgy's central role is the expression of a deeply embedded anthropology in which the function of human beings is to play a mediating or "priestly" role. Commenting on this role, Schmemann writes:

> All rational, spiritual and other qualities of man, distinguishing him from other creatures, have their focus and ultimate fulfilment in this capacity to bless God, to know, so to speak, the meaning of the thirst and hunger that constitutes his life. "*Homo sapiens*," "*homo faber*" . . . yes, but, first of all, "*homo adorans*." The first, the basic definition of man is that he is *the priest*. He stands in the center of the world and unifies it in his act of blessing God, of both receiving the world from God and offering it to God—and by filling the world with this eucharist, he transforms his life, the one that he receives from the world, into life in God, into communion with Him.[14]

In this passage, Schmemann articulates a rationale for why liturgical action takes the form it does and why it would matter that human beings engage in it. His explanation is broadly teleological: by playing the mediating role of receiving the world from God and offering the world to God, we thereby transform both the world and ourselves, fulfilling our appointed role as human beings. If Schmemann is correct, this is why the liturgy deserves to occupy a central place in the religiously committed life, since it is an enactment of this role. The centrality of the liturgy to the Eastern Christian life, then, is simply the practical expression of the tradition's conviction that the liturgy deserves to occupy this role. While what Schmemann says seems to me broadly correct, I would prefer to state his insight somewhat differently, not in terms of identifying the implications of a particular "definition" of the human being but in terms of what we are called to do. Under this related approach, participating in liturgy with its rhythm of blessing and thanksgiving is not

---

[13] In speaking of the "mind" (φρόνημα) of the tradition, I follow Florovsky (1975), 18.
[14] Schmemann (1973), 13.

so much a fulfilment of our nature as a response to divine invitation. It is the recognition and fulfilment of a vocation.

The passage I have quoted from Schmemann makes it apparent why, for Eastern Christians, the liturgy could not be an addendum to the Christian life, something that one does when not performing good works or communicating the teachings of Jesus. Still, this passage conveys little of the richness of liturgical life, the multiple ways in which it expresses the mind of the tradition. Since conveying some of this richness will be useful, given my purpose of explaining why it is worthwhile to think philosophically about liturgy, let me turn to that task.

To do so, it will be helpful to have some distinctions before us. Begin with the distinction between a *liturgical script* and a *liturgy*. For present purposes, think of a liturgical script as a set of guidelines addressed to a group of people who might participate in the liturgy—what I'll call the assembly—that specifies which actions these people are to perform, who among them are to perform them, when, and how. A given script might, for example, direct someone in the role of deacon or priest to read a passage from the Gospels at a particular point in a certain way, say, by chanting it. While a script is a set of guidelines, it bears emphasizing that it needn't exist as a set of notations and can be more or less specific, leaving rather significant room for ways in which an assembly might conform to it.

Corresponding to each liturgical script is a liturgy, which is a sequence of act-types that its corresponding script instructs an assembly to perform. These act-types would, among others, typically include entering a space of worship, singing, bowing, listening, eating, and the like. When they form a sequence, these act-types are not stitched together by what Hume would call principles of association, but exhibit a certain type of unity—the sequence to which they belong having a proper beginning, middle, and end, which are specified by the guidelines of its corresponding liturgical script. Since such a sequence can be performed on multiple occasions by a variety of assemblies, it is naturally viewed as being a type of universal—an *action-sequence universal*. If this characterization of a liturgy is correct, it has the implication that an assembly could not perform a liturgy accidentally. Rather, for the performance of a sequence of act-types to count as a performance of a liturgy, it must conform to some sufficient degree to its corresponding script—where conforming to a script consists (at least in part) in an assembly having the intention to conform to that script by performing the actions it directs them to perform.[15]

As I've indicated, a liturgical script typically instructs an assembly to perform a wide variety of actions, such as singing, listening, eating, and the like. Prominent among these actions are those that engage with a *liturgical*

---

[15] Does this formulation imply that groups such as assemblies can have intentions? I am inclined to think so, but won't defend that claim here.

text, by which I have in mind a composition typically consisting in hymns, poetry, creedal declarations, and prayers, which a liturgical script directs the assembled to recite, follow, or listen to. (Like a liturgical script, a liturgical text needn't consist in a set of notations.) In fact, however, the scripts of the Eastern liturgies instruct assemblies to engage with a good deal more than texts. They also instruct them to engage with *liturgical props*, where these are non-linguistic items such as icons, chalices, vestments, candles, water, and oil. Those familiar with the liturgies of the Christian East know that these engagements take various forms: when performing the liturgy, the assembled do such things as decorate and kiss icons, bless food with water, vest bishops, light candles at particular times, and so forth. Those familiar with the Eastern liturgies also know that actions such as these are pervasive components of these liturgies.

What the distinctions we've drawn help us to see is at least these two things: first, while speaking in a loose and general way of liturgy is indispensable, speaking thus can mask a great deal of complexity, since it might concern any of the items distinguished above. Thinking philosophically about liturgy would require one to operate with these distinctions, paying attention to how the items they designate might relate, how we might relate to them, and what their significance might be. Second, and relatedly, by highlighting these distinctions, we are better placed to see why liturgy functions as a vehicle that can, in a wide variety of ways, express (and shape) the mind of the tradition, some of these ways being difficult to capture in wholly propositional terms. For by composing and authorizing a series of liturgical scripts and liturgical texts, the tradition expresses (and shapes) its mind not simply in the contents of the texts it selects for liturgical use, but also in the actions that it instructs an assembly to perform, the props with which it directs them to engage, and the understanding that they are to have of the assembly's actions.

Rather than simply issue these general claims, let me try to substantiate them to some degree by focusing for a moment on a particular dimension of liturgy, exploring some of its nuances. The topic that I address is one that, to my knowledge, philosophers have not discussed.

There is probably no theme more pervasive in the Gospels and the liturgy than that of repentance. In the Gospels, it is the very first injunction Jesus issues. Indeed, Jesus repeatedly enjoins his audiences to repent, even at the seemingly most inopportune moments, such as when they tell him of some horrifying actions taken by the Roman authorities (Luke 13: 3). In the Eastern Christian tradition, the activity of repenting is woven through all its liturgical activity, even at its most celebratory moments. At various points in the liturgical calendar, however, such as during the season of Great Lent, the activity of repenting assumes a central role in liturgical life.

At each weekday office during the services of Great Lent, the script of these liturgies instructs the assembly to recite the Prayer of St. Ephraim:

> O Lord and Master of my life, give me not a spirit of sloth, despair, lust for power, and idle talk.
> (prostration)
>
> But give to me your servant a spirit of sobriety, humility, patience, and love.
> (prostration)
>
> O Lord and King, grant me to see my own faults and not to condemn my brother: for blessed are you to the ages of ages. Amen.
> (prostration)[16]

This is the church's paradigmatic prayer of repentance. Interestingly, it is not a confession in any straightforward sense; were one to recite this prayer sincerely, one wouldn't thereby confess that one has wronged God or one's fellow human beings. That one has done so seems to be taken for granted. Instead, the prayer takes the form of a petition, asking God that one not have certain characteristics, such as lust for power and despair, but that one exhibit others, such as patience and humility. But if this is so, why think of this prayer as one of repentance?

The answer, I take it, lies in the bodily actions that one performs when reciting the prayer: after each verse, one fully *prostrates* oneself on the ground, touching the ground with one's forehead. Etymology is helpful here. The Greek term for repentance is the same as that used to refer to these prostrations, namely, *metanoia*. Once one sees the significance of the prostrations, it becomes evident that the prayer is a blend of petitioning and repenting. In the liturgical context, both the linguistic acts of uttering the text of the prayer and the bodily action of prostrating count as illocutionary (or speech) acts in which agents alter their normative position with regard to God and fellow members of the assembly with whom they perform these actions. If the tradition's understanding of repentance is correct, the alteration does not so much consist in expressing states of sorrow, guilt or regret—although it may include the expression of such states. (In fact, at some points the liturgical texts include petitions to acquire such states: "Give me tears, O God, as once you gave them to the woman that had sinned" [*LT*, 188]). Rather, the alteration primarily consists in taking on new commitments. Specifically, it consists in committing oneself to a commitment: that of transforming one's mind, turning away from a life that neglects one's mediating or priestly role—"transforming of mind" being the literal rendering of *metanoia*.

---

[16] I cite the prayer as it is found in Mother Mary and Ware (2002), 69. I'll insert page references to this work into the body of the text referring to it as *LT* (for *The Lenten Triodion*).

At this point, however, we need to mark a distinction. As I've said, what one does when one conforms to the liturgical script by saying the prayer of St. Ephraim is to perform the illocutionary act of repenting, committing oneself to a change of mind. But to perform the illocutionary act of repenting is not perforce to repent. One can, after all, perform the illocutionary act insincerely, as when one says "I'm sorry" when one is really not. Moreover, given the tradition's robust understanding of repentance, in which it is the enactment of a resolution to transform one's mind, one could perform the illocutionary act of repenting while falling short of enacting the resolution. Whether one enacts this commitment by genuinely turning away from what one is called to leave behind is something that happens over time to different degrees, taking place not simply in the performance of a speech act but also in one's day-to-day activities. When sincerely and competently performed, then, a liturgical action such as the speech act of repenting may have limited implications, since it wouldn't imply that the agent who performed it has actually repented. Although, it may be worth emphasizing that reciting a prayer such as that of St. Ephraim's may play the indispensable role of reminding one of that to which one has already committed oneself to. (Unless I indicate otherwise, when I speak of repenting, I will mean performing the *illocutionary act* of repenting.)

While often having limited implications, the character of repentance as it is performed in a liturgical context is striking. In the various prayers of repentance, there is never any attempt to identify the fault lines that separate that for which one is responsible from that for which one is not, or those aspects of oneself that are afflicted by disorder from those that are not. Instead, repentance is indiscriminate and unreserved. The indiscriminate character of repentance is evident in the norms that govern it, which instruct those who repent not to separate or disassociate themselves from their actions. The unreserved character of repentance is especially apparent in the sometimes hyperbolic language used in the liturgical text, such as when the assembly compare themselves to figures such as the Prodigal, the Publican, or the Prostitute who washes Jesus's feet with her hair.[17] In fact, the images used in the liturgical texts extend far beyond these. At points, the assembly speak of themselves as prisoners, wounded, barren, storm-tossed, distressed, and drunken.[18] Lying behind the indiscriminate and unreserved character of repentance, presumably, is the tradition's conviction that attempting to discriminate between that for which one is responsible and that for which one is not is generally unhelpful to the moral and spiritual life, and may lend itself

---

[17] "I fall down before You, and as tears I offer You my words. I have sinned as the Harlot never sinned, and I have transgressed as no person on earth. But take pity on Your creature, Master, and call me back" (*LT*, 160).

[18] Cf. *LT*, 178, 186, 191, 190, and 194, respectively.

too easily to offering justifications when there should be none. (This conviction also drives the practice of personal confession as it takes shape in the
tradition.) I would add that even if determining the extent to which one is
liable for who one is and what one has done were beneficial when repenting,
the character of liturgical repentance also expresses the tradition's conviction
that we couldn't make these distinctions accurately even if we tried.

Let me draw attention to a final point, which is the way in which
repentance—at least as it takes shape in the liturgy—stands in sharp contrast
with the correlative activity of forgiving. Unlike repenting—at least as it occurs
in the liturgical context—forgiving someone for having performed some
action, requires one to make fine-grained distinctions, distinguishing offenders from their acts in such a way that while one continues to be against
their acts, one is not against those who performed them; instead one enacts the
resolution not to hold those acts against the offenders.[19] When considered
together, a fundamental asymmetry between repentance and forgiveness
emerges: in the case of repentance, we are to forget about trying to distinguish
that for which we are liable and that for which are not; in the case of forgiveness,
we need to make fine-grained distinctions between the agents' actions and their
moral standing and apply them in certain ways. Interestingly, this asymmetry
between how we are to treat self and others in the activities of repentance and
forgiveness correlates with another, which is that while both repentance and
forgiveness receive liturgical expression, forgiveness plays a much less central
role in liturgical life than repentance.[20] Why is there this asymmetry? I am
not sure.

Obviously, there is more to say about the role of repentance in the liturgy
and what it presupposes about our relations to one another and God.[21] But
even this brief discussion should give you a sense of how the mind of the
tradition can manifest itself in the texts, actions, and presuppositions of the
liturgy. Having done this, let me now return to a question that I raised several
pages back, which is whether there is enough of theoretical interest in liturgy
to render it philosophically worthwhile to reflect on it. I hope to have made
some progress addressing this question, pointing out that by doing so, philosophers could tap into deep currents that run through the religiously committed life, bringing philosophical reflection to bear on topics that are
important but frequently overlooked, and deepening our understanding of
these topics. In principle, doing so would help to balance the contemporary
philosophical discussion, widening and enriching it in various ways. That, in

---

[19] Here I echo the account offered in Wolterstorff (2011b), ch. 15, which strikes me as
basically correct.
[20] I don't mean to suggest that forgiveness fails to play a role in liturgical life. For example, on
the Sunday immediately preceding Great Lent, the assembly performs the Rite of Forgiveness in
which each member individually asks other members for their forgiveness.
[21] I do so in Cuneo (forthcoming).

turn, might help to ameliorate the sense that the contemporary discussion in philosophy of religion is often disconnected from what matters in the religious life.[22] And, finally, I hope to have illustrated to some degree that thinking philosophically about liturgy requires one to focus on a variety of issues and how they relate: liturgical scripts, liturgical action, liturgical texts, liturgical actors, and so forth. As will be evident in the essays that follow, some of these topics come closest to those which philosophers of art address when they explore the nature of literary, music, and dance performance, the function of texts and the proper ways to interpret them, the social functions of works of the arts and the proper ways to engage them, and so forth. Indeed, of all the subfields within contemporary philosophy, work in philosophy of art has been especially helpful to me in thinking through various aspects of the liturgy.

Still, it might be asked why a discussion on liturgy should focus almost exclusively on the liturgies of one tradition, namely, the Christian East. The short answer is that I take this approach not simply because these liturgies are most familiar to me but also because I believe that the best way to make progress on the topic of liturgy is to speak not of liturgies in the abstract but particular liturgies, offering thick descriptions of them and drawing out their implications. For example, although Howie Wettstein writes on Jewish liturgy, I find his descriptions and interpretations of Jewish liturgical practice considerably more illuminating than general discussions of liturgy.[23] The same is true of Wolterstorff's descriptions and interpretations of the Reformed Christian liturgies.[24] Given the richness of their descriptions, it is easier to appreciate both points of contact with and genuine differences from them. That, in turn, often gives one a better sense of the questions to raise about ritualized activity as it takes shape in the Jewish and Reformed Christian traditions and, in my case, in the Eastern Christian tradition.

In addition to holding that a "particularist" approach is the best way to contribute to the philosophical conversation on liturgy, there is a personal dimension to this project that shapes its contents. As I've already indicated, I locate myself within the Eastern Orthodox Christian tradition and frequently find myself engaged in liturgical activity. I also frequently find myself puzzled by elements of this activity, wondering what certain actions and texts mean, why certain actions are performed, why liturgical texts say the things they do, why various things are not said, and so on. Many of the essays that follow are

---

[22] A theme that sometimes surfaces in theological discussions of liturgy is that liturgy is "first theology." See, for example, Florovsky (1972), Schmemann (1990), and Kavanaugh (1992). According to this view, our reflections on God and the religious life ought to be informed and shaped by liturgy in such a way that if particular theological views do not sit well with our liturgical practices, that is a prima facie reason to reject them. I have not advocated this view, focusing instead on understanding crucial aspects of the liturgy.

[23] See Wettstein (2012).   [24] In Wolterstorff (2011a) and (2015a).

attempts to work through questions that, as it were, the liturgy puts to its participants—at least those inclined to reflect on it. Since my own interests lie primarily in moral philosophy, some of the essays in this volume concern the ethical dimensions of corporate ritualized activity. The first two essays of this volume, "Love and Liturgy" and "Protesting Evil," reflect this interest, being attempts to explore the moral significance of liturgical activity—why it might matter morally for us to engage in liturgical rites of various sorts, especially in the face of vast evil against which we are often powerless. To be sure, these essays are not primarily addressed to those who lack religious sensibilities or are hostile to religion. Still, I hope that they help illustrate even to those who lack religious commitments why corporate liturgical activity might be of moral value, giving expression to sound moral conviction and shaping moral sensibilities in helpful ways.

Of the various chapters that compose this volume, the third chapter, "Another Look at Divine Hiddenness," comes closest to addressing a topic that receives attention in mainstream philosophy of religion. It also says the least about liturgy explicitly. Nonetheless, this chapter illustrates how one might approach the problem of divine hiddenness if one has first thought about what liturgical action—especially such action as it takes shape in those traditions committed to sacramental Christianity—presupposes about how human beings and God relate to one another. The contemporary discussion of divine hiddenness has assumed that, if God is anything like the theistic traditions claim, our awareness of God and God's activity would have to take the form of noticed awareness in which we take certain events of the world as being a manifestation of God or God's activity. Lying deep in the mind of the tradition, however, is the conviction that our awareness of God often does not take that form; often, we can be and are both aware of and rightly related to God via relating to the natural world, to each other, to art, and the like without have awareness of this type.

While it does not require extended effort to ascertain that the sacramental traditions assume that fellow human beings, the natural world, and art are and ought to be points of contact with God, the significance of other aspects of the liturgy are far less clear. For example, central to the Eastern Orthodox liturgies is the activity of reenacting elements of the core Christian narrative. To cite just one example, during Holy Week, the assembly reenact the burial of Jesus using props of various sorts. It is natural to wonder not only what it is to engage in such reenactment but also what the point of liturgical reenactment might be. In Chapter 4, "Liturgical Immersion," I explore the first issue, asking what it is to immerse oneself in liturgical performance—what sorts of attitudes and behaviors the liturgical script might call for from members of the assembly when it directs them to engage in liturgical reenactment. After canvassing several proposals, I defend a position that I call the *immersion model* of liturgical reenactment. If this model is correct, what the liturgical script calls for from the assembled is not that they pretend that they are figures such as Mary of Bethany, Joseph of Arimathea, or Jesus or that they are present in the circumstances that these biblical figures occupied. Rather, what the script calls for is that the assembled attend to the content of what I call the core narrative in such a way that they imaginatively situate themselves within it. The activity called for is imaginative engagement without pretense.

Chapter 5, "Liturgy and the Moral Life," takes up the second question regarding what the point of liturgical reenactment might be. While conceding that it could have multiple purposes, I focus on the way in which such reenactment contributes to the formation of what I call an agent's *narrative identity*—this being a story-like event that has an agent as a subject, to which that agent might refer were she to tell a story of her life. A close look at the liturgical texts and practices, I argue, reveals ways in which the liturgical script calls for its participants to construct and shape their narrative identities via liturgical reenactment. Some of this activity occurs by identifying with characters who are often, in important respects, deeply alien, such as Mary of Bethany, the Prodigal Son, or the Publican, and committing oneself in liturgical action to ideals that these characters represent.

Anyone who has attended one of the Eastern liturgies knows that they are multi-sensory in character, engaging all the sensory modalities—touching especially. The next two chapters concern some ways in which liturgical performance incorporates and engages some of the sensory modalities. In Chapter 6, "If These Walls Could Only Speak: Icons as Vehicles of Divine Speech," I consider what role icons might play in liturgical activity. Given its topic, one would expect the discussion to concern the ways in which sight is employed in liturgical performance. And, in a way, it does, but its primary focus is on not how we engage with the visual arts in a liturgical context but how icons can function as vehicles of divine action—the claim being that icons can fruitfully be viewed as vehicles by which God could perform various sorts of illocutionary acts. Chapter 7, "The Significance of Liturgical Singing," takes up a topic that, to my knowledge, philosophers of religion have not discussed, namely, singing. Its starting point is the observation that the liturgy is enveloped in song; there are hardly any actions performed in the liturgy that are not accompanied by singing. Why, however, would that be so? I present a position that develops the thought that, given its primary purposes, liturgical singing is particularly fitting and that its fittingness consists (at least in part) in a particular sort of form/content marriage in which singing the liturgical text thereby instantiates important elements of its content.

When engaging with Bell's observations, I noted that it is not uncommon to characterize (the core of) Christianity as a set of propositions and the status *being a Christian* as the property of being such as to accept or believe (some subset of) these propositions. In philosophy, this tendency has been mirrored in contemporary epistemology by an almost exclusive concern with propositional knowledge (and propositional belief). When these two tendencies combine in the contemporary discussion of the epistemology of religious belief, the result has been a discussion that focuses almost exclusively on the possibility and character of propositional religious knowledge and meritorious propositional religious belief.

Both these tendencies are, however, problematic. Christianity is not a set of propositions. To locate oneself in the tradition is not, moreover, primarily a matter of believing propositions of a certain range (although it might paradigmatically include that). Rather, Christianity is a way of life and one such that, in some of its paradigmatic forms, ritualized activity figures prominently. Furthermore, in addition to propositional knowledge, there is objectual knowledge in which we know not propositions but objects—some of these objects being subjects or persons. When we have knowledge of this last sort, we have personal knowledge in which the object that we know is a subject—often a subject distinct from ourselves.

But if Christianity is fundamentally a way of life and not all knowledge is propositional, then it is natural to ask about sort of knowledge is required to competently participate in this form of life—what kind of know-how its members would seek to acquire. In Chapter 8, "Ritual Knowledge," I engage this question, exploring the ways in which participating in liturgical activity might contribute to the ways in which we might know God by way of our gaining and exercising a certain kind of know-how.

As an initial approximation, the fundamental idea is that to know God would consist in knowing how to engage God. I then explore how knowing how to engage in rites of various sorts—liturgical rites in particular—might contribute in important ways to knowing how to engage God. As I've emphasized, these rites can be deeply perplexing even to those very familiar with them. To take one example, the text of the baptismal rite makes seemingly audacious claims about what it accomplishes, claiming that in virtue of being baptized, the one baptized enjoys states such as illumination, remission of sin, sanctification, cleansing of soul, and so on. In Chapter 9, "Transforming the Self: On the Baptismal Rite," I try to make sense of these claims, suggesting that there is a model that comes close to doing so—what I call the *process model*—according to which the performance of the rite is the initiation of processes of transformation in the one baptized. The chapter that follows, "Rites of Remission," continues in this vein, grappling with the question of how engaging in activities such as the eucharistic rite could effect remission of sin, as the liturgical text claims. I contend that making sense of this claim requires us to distinguish *forgiveness from sin* from *remission of sin*, the latter being interpreted to mean something like *being released from the grip of the sin-disorder*. While marking this distinction hardly dissolves the puzzles that face someone trying to understand how participation in a rite could effect remission of sin, I contend that it helps us to make progress on them, especially if we take account of the way in which rites can affect us on the sub-doxastic level.

This book closes with the autobiographical chapter "Entering by Death, Living with Doubt." This essay is my attempt to communicate what might draw one to Eastern Christianity and the liturgy, and the attitudes one might take up toward its claims by someone who is not a skeptic but who nonetheless harbors genuine doubt.[25]

[25] Jeroen deRidder, Rik Peels, Luke Reinsma, Russ Shafer-Landau, René van Woudenberg, Howie Wettstein, and Nick Wolterstorff all offered helpful feedback on an earlier version of this chapter.

1

Love and Liturgy

For two millennia Christians have assembled on the "day of the sun" to celebrate the liturgy together. But why do it? Why structure one's life in such a way that participation in ritualized religious activity is a fixed point in the weekly rhythm of one's comings and goings? There are standard answers to these questions, perhaps the most obvious of which is that by doing so Christians express devotion to God, who is supremely worthy of such devotion. Understood from this angle, the dominant purpose of assembling for the liturgy is to fulfill the first of the love commandments, namely, to love God with all one's heart, soul, and mind (Matt. 22: 37).

There are also, however, less obvious answers to these questions, ones that appeal to the ways in which participating in the liturgy fulfills not the first but the second love commandment.

But how could that be so? What does neighbor-love have to do with liturgy? In this chapter, I'll contend that the two have a great deal to do with one another and that authentically participating in the liturgy is an important way by which one can fulfill the injunction to love one's neighbor as oneself. My discussion will begin with the second love commandment itself and its role in the Christian tradition. Having offered an interpretation of the second love commandment, I then turn to the liturgy, exploring the ways in which participation in it is a way to fulfill the second love commandment, which enjoins love of neighbor.

Those who write on the ethical dimensions of liturgical action sometimes speak of liturgy in the abstract, as if there were some unified kind *the Christian liturgy* whose ethical dimensions we can investigate.[1] Given the great diversity of Christian liturgies, I believe that doing so threatens to impose unity where there is often none. So, in what follows, I will narrow my focus and limit myself to a discussion of the ancient liturgies of the Eastern Orthodox Church, exploring the ways in which participation in these liturgies is a way to fulfill the second love commandment. I take this approach not simply because these

---

[1] This is true, for example, of some early and important work on the topic by Ramsey (1979) and Saliers (1979) and (1998).

liturgies provide rich resources for reflection, but also because I believe that the best way to make progress on our topic is to offer thick descriptions of particular liturgies.[2] My own experience is that when engaging other religious traditions, thicker descriptions of their ritualized activities are often more helpful, mostly because it is easier to appreciate both points of contact and genuine difference. That, in turn, often gives one a better sense of the questions to raise about ritualized activity as it takes shape in these traditions and one's own, setting the stage for more informed and fruitful dialogue. That said, given the sometimes significant overlap between some Christian liturgical practices, I believe that much of what I say here will have direct relevance to those who locate themselves within other areas of the Christian tradition.

1.1. THE SECOND LOVE COMMANDMENT

In the Torah, the second love commandment makes its first appearance as the last of a long series of injunctions, which includes directives about how to harvest one's fields, how to allocate resources, and how to treat the poor:

> When you reap the harvest of your land, you shall not reap to the very edges of your field, or gather the gleanings of your harvest. You shall not strip your vineyard bare, or gather the fallen grapes of your vineyard; you shall leave them for the poor and the alien: I am the LORD your God.
>
> You shall not steal; you shall not deal falsely; and you shall not lie to one another. And you shall not swear falsely by my name, profaning the name of your God: I am the LORD.
>
> You shall not defraud your neighbor; you shall not steal; and you shall not keep for yourself the wages of a laborer until morning. You shall not revile the deaf or put a stumbling block before the blind; you shall fear your God: I am the LORD.
>
> You shall not render an unjust judgment; you shall not be partial to the poor or defer to the great; with justice you shall judge your neighbor. You shall not go around as a slanderer among your people, and you shall not profit by the blood of your neighbor: I am the LORD.

The passage closes by stating:

> You shall not hate in your heart anyone of your kin; you shall reprove your neighbor, or you will incur guilt yourself. You shall not take vengeance or bear a

---

[2] In this respect, the approach I take aligns more closely with that taken by Guroian (1985) and (1990) and Wettstein (2012a), who offer thick descriptions of liturgical practice of their religious traditions, than Saliers (1979) and Ramsey (1979), who tend to speak in more general ways about how liturgy contributes to the ethical life. That noted, my discussion is indebted to thinkers such as Saliers and Ramsey, since it is a response to their call to think more carefully about the ethical dimensions of ritualized religious activity.

grudge against any of your people, but you shall love your neighbor as yourself:
I am the LORD. (Lev. 9–18)[3]

Given the number and variety of commandments presented in this text, it would not be difficult to read right past the final commandment, viewing it as one more commandment among many. That, of course, would be a mistake. Both the Jewish and Christian traditions have viewed the final injunction as having special importance. But if it is best not to read this injunction as one injunction among many, the last of a long list, how should we understand it?

In his discussion of this matter, Nicholas Wolterstorff contends that it is the final commandment's generality that provides the clue for how to understand it.[4] Read the final commandment, Wolterstorff suggests, as a summary statement that captures both the letter and spirit of the injunctions that precede it. Specifically, read the last injunction as preceded by a tacit "in short": "*In short,* love your neighbor as yourself." This reading, Wolterstorff indicates, has the virtue of meshing with how Jesus and the Jewish tradition have typically understood the injunction to love one's neighbor as oneself.

Although this reading strikes me as being along the right lines, let me register a point of hesitation about it. The relationship between the love commandment and the injunctions that precede it, I believe, is probably best viewed not merely as one in which the former simply summarizes the latter. The relationship is better understood, I think, as one in which the specific injunctions present *paradigm cases* of what it is to love one's neighbor as oneself. Under this reading, the general love commandment does not merely summarize the specific injunctions that precede it. Rather, the injunctions that precede the love commandment help us to understand *what it is* to love another as oneself. In principle, different injunctions or cases could shed more light on what it is to love one's neighbor as one oneself.

In fact, Jesus is widely regarded as having done just that. That is, in the Gospel texts, Jesus is widely regarded as having not simply reiterated the second love commandment and its paradigm Mosaic cases, but also enriched it in various ways, giving us new and surprising focal cases of the commandment. These enrichments, arguably, take two primary forms. In the first place, there is an emphasis on caring for the distressed, even when they belong to out-groups, such as ethnic enemies or the ritually unclean. The story of the Good Samaritan vividly presents this dimension of Jesus's teaching.[5] The second related way in which Jesus enriches the various injunctions that compose the Mosaic law is by enjoining his followers to not enact vengeance

---

[3] Here and throughout I use the New Revised Standard Version (NRSV) translation.

[4] Wolterstorff 2011b, 82.

[5] As Waldron (2000), 1077 points out, Jesus's interlocutor in this story, a lawyer, knows and correctly states the answer to Jesus's question about who acts as a neighbor. Apparently, the point of the parable is not to introduce a wholly novel moral teaching. Cf. Deut. 10: 19.

on their enemies and, indeed, to bless those who curse them. In his discussion of this topic, Wolterstorff argues that when Jesus says these things in the Sermon on the Mount, we should hear them as not a mitigation of *lex talionis*, enjoining us to take no more than an eye for an eye, as some commentators have claimed. We should instead hear them as a wholesale rejection of what Wolterstorff calls the *reciprocity code*.

The reciprocity code is a dual directive, telling us, first, that if someone does you a favor, then you owe him a favor in return and, second, if someone visits an evil upon you, then you owe him an equal evil is return. Jesus's reply is that this code should be replaced by a different ethic:

> You have heard that it was said, "An eye for an eye and a tooth for a tooth." But I say to you, Do not resist an evildoer. But if anyone strikes you on the right cheek, turn the other also; and if anyone wants to sue you and take your coat, give your cloak as well . . .
>
> You have heard that it was said, "You shall love your neighbor and hate your enemy." But I say to you, Love your enemies and pray for those who persecute you, so that you may be children of your Father in heaven. . . . For if you love those who love you, what reward do you have? (Matt. 5: 38–48)

It is, to put it mildly, an issue of great controversy what exactly Jesus means when he uses these words. Is he advocating pacifism of the most radical sort, namely, that we are not to resist evildoers *at all*, in any respect? That would be the literal reading of the passage. The dominant interpretation in the Christian tradition, however, has been that this is not what Jesus means. Instead, by using vivid and often hyperbolic language, Jesus instructs his listeners, contrary to the reciprocity code, not to repay harm with harm and instead to seek the good of even those who do us evil by doing such things as praying for them.

As the Parable of the Good Samaritan makes clear, however, it is not enough simply to desire the good of others, to wish good for those who belong to out-groups or who are our enemies. We must also seek their good, sometimes to the point of giving of our own time, energy, and resources. When discussing this dimension of Jesus's teachings, Wolterstorff notes that the Parable of the Good Samaritan has often been interpreted as presenting an account of who is a neighbor that goes beyond the one that Moses employs in Leviticus. Rather than present an implicit definition of "neighbor" that includes simply one's kin (and resident aliens), Jesus is teaching us that all human beings are neighbors in the relevant sense. Wolterstorff contends that a close reading of the parable reveals that Jesus does not offer any such definition. When asked by his audience who counts as a neighbor, Jesus's reply is indirect; he does not explicitly say who is a neighbor. Rather, when commenting on his interlocutor's answer, Jesus says that the Samaritan who cares for the injured man on the side of the road—who is presumably a Jew and, thus, a member of an out-group—*acts* as a neighbor. In this way, the Samaritan is a neighbor *to* the injured man.[6]

What, then, is the lesson to be gleaned from the parable and Jesus's teaching regarding the reciprocity code? Wolterstorff suggests this:

> I take Jesus to be enjoining us to be alert to the obligations placed upon us by the needs of whomever we happen on, and to pay no attention to the fact, if it be a fact, that the needy person belongs to a group that is a disdained or disdaining out-group with respect to oneself. Every society has derogatory terms for members of one and another out-group: wop, dago, Hun, Jap, nigger, "Dutchman belly full o' straw." Whether we ourselves employ such terms or they are applied to us, they prevent us from recognizing our obligations to aid those in need. Discard them all, says Jesus. Do not let them deafen your ear to the cry for help or harden your heart.[7]

This reading of the Gospel passage strikes me as correct in one respect but incomplete in another. It seems right to conclude that, strictly speaking, Jesus does not offer an implicit definition of who counts as a neighbor—or, for that matter, a teaching according to which we are to surrender all (or nearly all) our time and goods to aid those in need. It also seems correct that a central message of the parable is to enjoin us to be open to recognizing the obligations that the needs of others place upon us, regardless of whether those others belong to some out-group.

Nonetheless, when the Parable of the Good Samaritan and the Sermon on the Mount are read side by side, it seems that Jesus intends to communicate more than this.

For note that one could be open to recognizing the obligations that are grounded in the needs of others—including those who belong to out-groups— but live one's life in such a way that one does nothing to put oneself in the path of those who belong to one or another out-group. Similarly, one could be open to recognizing these obligations but fail to exercise the sort of interest in others and discernment of their situation that would allow one actually to recognize them. Finally, one could be open to recognizing these obligations but downplay their significance, not allowing their import to shape the structure of one's day-to-day life. In the Sermon on the Mount, when Jesus says that we should pray for our enemies, part of what he seems to be driving at is that we are not only to be open to recognizing those obligations that come our way but also to take actions designed to re-orient ourselves to those who belong to various out-groups. We are not simply to be open to the needs of others. We are also to *open ourselves up* to the needs of others and the various sorts of obligations we may have toward them.

---

[6] Wolterstorff (2011b), 131–2.   [7] Wolterstorff (2011b), 132.

If this is correct, Jesus's teaching is that, in order to fulfill the second love commandment, we are not simply to react with an open heart to the needs and obligations we find but also to, some significant degree, direct our attention and energy to the needs of (and obligations to) those who belong to out-groups, making them the subject of our concern. In what follows, it will be helpful to have a way of speaking of this dimension of Jesus's teaching. Let me call it an *ethic of outwardness*. An ethic of outwardness is supposed to stand in contrast to an *ethic of proximity*, wherein we conform to various ethical directives and ideals—perhaps being open to meeting needs and obligations where we find them—but sparing little effort to expand our attention to the needs and obligations beyond those which we encounter in the various in-groups to which we belong, such as family, friends, church, synagogue, or country.

Understood as incorporating an ethic of outwardness, the second love commandment is, for most of us, an extraordinarily difficult injunction to fulfill. Among other things, most of us have many other things to focus on. Given the press of ordinary daily life, often we do not actively call to mind those who are distressed or remember those who hate us for the purpose of blessing or praying for them. We do not perform actions that expand our attention and our hearts. And even when we try to do so, these actions are often psychologically very difficult to perform. To love those who oppress us, to bless those who curse us often cuts against every fiber of our being. Some find themselves unable to do it. Others find themselves able to do these difficult things—or at least find themselves desiring to do them—but do so only sporadically.

For those who identify themselves as followers of Jesus, then, there is a question to face: How do we conduct our lives in such a way that we better conform to the second love commandment, where this is understood to enjoin an ethic of outwardness? In the next section, I explore the idea that an important way to do so is by participating in the liturgies of the church.

1.2. LITURGY

Even to those who are deeply familiar with them, the ancient liturgies of the Eastern church are remarkably complex and rich, full of imagery and beauty. In fact, these services are so complex and rich that it is easy for important themes to get buried, much in the way that a central melody of a musical work can be concealed by complex lines of harmony. Still, like many musical works, when one attends to the structure of the Divine Liturgy—the eucharistic service that is celebrated by Eastern Christians each Sunday—a pattern emerges. The pattern, which I will refer to as the *central pattern* of the liturgy, is that of an alternating rhythm of blessing, petitioning, and offering thanks to God.[8]

While the central pattern of the liturgy has a variety of features worth exploring, I wish to call attention here to the prominence within the pattern itself of petitioning. (I will have something to say about the liturgical activity of blessing later in this chapter.) In The Liturgy of St. John Chrysostom, for example, there are no less than seven petitionary litanies before the eucharistic celebration itself. To get a feel for how wide-ranging these litanies are, consider the text of the opening petitions or the Great Litany, which runs as follows:

> DEACON: In peace, let us pray to the Lord.
> PEOPLE: Lord have mercy [and so after each petition].
> DEACON: For the peace from above and for the salvation of our souls, let us pray to the Lord.
> For the peace of the whole world, for the welfare of the holy churches of God, and for the union of all, let us pray to the Lord.
> For this holy house and for those who enter with faith, reverence, and the awe of God, let us pray to the Lord.
> For our Metropolitan, for our Bishop, for the honorable Priesthood, the Diaconate in Christ; for all the clergy and people, let us pray to the Lord.
> For the President of our country, for all civil authorities, let us pray to the Lord.
> For this city, for every city and country, and for the faithful dwelling in them, let us pray to the Lord.
> For seasonable weather, for abundance of the fruits of the earth, and for peaceful times, let us pray to the Lord.
> For travelers by land, by sea, and by air; for the sick and the suffering; for captives and their safety and salvation, let us pray to the Lord.
> For our deliverance from all affliction, wrath, danger, and constraint, let us pray to the Lord.[9]

The text of the Great Litany expands and contracts, like lungs while breathing. It begins narrowly with petitions for those assembled, but then expands when the assembled offer prayers for the peace of the "whole world" and the "union

---

[8] I say that the central pattern of the liturgy is primarily constituted by these activities. One could, however, offer a description of this pattern that is considerably more fine-grained, one that distinguishes various types of blessing, petitioning, and thanking and includes actions that are not easily slotted into the pattern, such as listening to God. For present purposes, I will work with a fairly coarse-grained account of the central pattern, recognizing that in other contexts a fuller description of the pattern might be more illuminating.

[9] I am using the Thyateira (1995) translation of *The Divine Liturgy of Our Father Among the Saints John Chrysostom*; also available at <http://www.cappellaromana.org/DL_in_English_Booklet_Web.pdf> (accessed August 21, 2015).

of all." Contracting again, the text presents petitions for the church, but then steadily moves outward when the people petition God for the wellbeing of country, city, and the land. Continuing to move outward, the text presents petitions for the great many in need, "for the sick and the suffering, captives and their salvation." But then it seemingly contracts again, depending on how one interprets the referent of "our" and "us" in the last line, as these terms may designate either the assembled themselves or a much wider group, such as all those who have been the subject of the petitions. If the last option were the preferred interpretation, the Great Litany itself would be a vivid case of the people expressing union or solidarity with those for whom they pray. In the next section, I am going to return to this theme of solidarity, as I believe it lies at the heart of the actions that compose the liturgy.

In the Litany of Fervent Supplication, which follows the Gospel reading, this series of petitions is more or less repeated, although in some respects it is even more expansive, as it includes prayers not simply for the living but also for the dead. And again, the very same themes of these litanies are voiced by the celebrant before the Lord's Prayer when he asks:

> Remember, O Lord, the city in which we dwell, every city and country; those who in faith dwell in them. Remember, O Lord, travelers by land, by sea, and by air; the sick and the suffering; captives, and their safety and salvation. Remember, O Lord, those who bring offerings and care for the beauty of your holy churches; those who remember the poor; and send down upon us all your rich mercies.

And once again:

> Look down from heaven, O Master, upon those who have bowed their heads unto you, the awesome God. Do yourself, O Master, distribute these gifts here offered, unto all of us for good, according to the individual needs of each; sail with those who sail, travel with those who travel by land and by air; heal the sick, O you who are the physician of our souls and bodies.

It is worth, once again, calling attention to the universal scope of these petitions. The prayers are for *all* cities and countries, all their inhabitants, all travelers, all those who are sick and suffering.

A moment ago, I said that a striking feature of the central pattern of the liturgy is the prominence of petitioning. In saying this, I intended to highlight both its frequency in the liturgy and the extent to which it figures in the liturgical script.[10] In these respects, the Eastern liturgy has no analogue. Rather than being cyclical, taking up themes and frequently revisiting them in

---

[10] Kavanagh (1991), 135, draws attention not to the prominence but to the priority of petitioning in the liturgy when he writes: "In liturgical tradition, the very first thing a new member of Christ does after baptism is to join with the rest of the baptized in their *supplicatio* before God in Christ for the world, that is, in the great priestly Prayers of the Faithful. This must be done before the eucharist can begin."

modified forms, the liturgies of the Western church tend to be angular and succinct. The Anglican liturgies, for example, dedicate only one section to petitionary prayer of the sort found in the litanies of the Eastern church. This raises a question about the structure of the Eastern liturgies. Why the repetition? Why the insistence, on at least a weekly basis, of asking "again and again" for the peace of the world, of leaders, and of the sick and the suffering? Why do the Eastern liturgies take this form?

Let me propose a partial hypothesis: implicit in the liturgy is a recognition of our collective situation. Our collective situation is that we are naturally drawn to our own needs, the needs of our loved ones, and those who belong to the various communities of which we are a part. Many of us recognize (and are open to recognizing) the obligations that these needs generate—although it should be noted that even with regard to these needs and obligations we can be curiously insensitive. Competing with these needs for our attention are the many good things that fill our lives, including the good things that fill the lives of our loves ones and those who belong to the various communities of which we are a part. For these things we are often ready to give thanks—although, again, this is something that is often done only in fits and starts.

It is only with difficulty, however, that our attention is drawn from the cares, obligations, and goods that occupy our attention outward toward those who belong to out-groups, whether they be the ritually unclean, strangers, enemies, or oppressors. And, as I have emphasized, when our attention is drawn outward, it can be difficult to do what Jesus commands, such as blessing those who curse us and praying for those who persecute us. In this regard, we should not fail to see that the liturgy's prayers for those in authority have been, and often are, prayers for those who have oppressed the church. I want to suggest, then, that a central function of the cycle of petitions is to help break the grip that an ethic of proximity can have. It is to enable us to do, in part, what is so difficult for so many of us to do. The liturgy does this by making available to its participants, regularly and repeatedly, the very sorts of act-types that Jesus commands his followers to perform, such as praying for their enemies and blessing those who curse them.[11]

A pervasive theme in the work of the Orthodox theologian Alexander Schmemann is that to engage in the liturgy is not to leave secular space for sacred space. To the contrary, says Schmemann, there is only one world which is "*this world* (and not any 'other world')" and only one life, which is "*this life*

---

[11] Schmemann (1969), 100. The dynamic of what occurs in the liturgy is probably much more complex than I indicate. For, arguably, there is a sense in which the church performs actions on behalf of its members, even when those members do not perform those actions themselves. If that is so, there is a sense in which, when the church prays for those who hate us, it does so on behalf of its members, even when those members do not offer those prayers themselves. Still, if its members do not actively engage in the liturgical activity of petitioning, the petitioning may do nothing to break the grip that an ethic of proximity may have on them.

(and not some 'other life')," which is given to human beings "to be a sacrament of the divine presence."[12] If Schmemann is right, those who assemble for the liturgy do not abandon this world when they enter the church building to participate in the liturgy. If what I have suggested is correct, there is an additional thing to say, which is that in the liturgy, the world—in all its beauty, suffering, and need—is not simply present, but also *re-presented*. When I say this, I do not simply mean that the liturgical text refers to such evils or that they are the object of symbolic action in which the assembled stand against such evils. Rather, the claim is that, in the petitionary activity of the church, the world is re-presented to the assembled as something requiring focused attention, concern, and care. When the assembled pray for the sick, those in authority, strangers, and oppressors, they direct their attention outward toward those for whom they pray, lessening the "ethical distance" that may separate them from these people, treating these people not as somehow beyond concern but as their moral counterparts, as people whose good matters.

1.3. SOLIDARITY

In the ancient liturgical prayers of the church, such as the following sixth-century prayer, one can find "preparatory petitions" in which the people ask to be prepared to engage in acts of love:

> May he give us charity and brotherly love in the bond of peace.
> May he hear the requests of our hearts, he who alone holds power, the holy Master, resplendent with glory and honor, whose name is the Lord.[13]

The prayer of St. Ephrem, which figures prominently in the Lenten services of the Eastern church, is similar:

> Lord and Master of my life: take from me the spirit of sloth, despondency, lust for power, and idle talk. And give your servant instead a spirit of chastity, humility,

---

[12] See also ibid., p. 27. Schmemann (1966) writes elsewhere: "In the eschatological consciousness of the early Church the central categories were not 'sacred' and 'profane' but 'old' and 'new'; the fallen and the saved; the regenerated. . . . Their life was not divided up into 'profane working days' and 'sacred feast days.' The old had passed, now all things were new. So then their calendar could not be merely a rhythmic alteration of 'profane' and 'sacred' days. It expressed the antithetical conjunction of the Church and the world, in which 'this world' and its time . . . is [*sic*] transformed into a 'new creation' . . ." (183; cf. pp. 114–20, 126–7, 130).

[13] As found in Deiss (1967), 244. In addition to such preparatory petitions, there is also exhortatory hymnody that exhorts us to follow the examples of figures such as the Publican and the Prodigal Son. See, for example, the liturgical scripts for the Sundays of the Publican and the Pharisee and the Prodigal Son in Mother Mary and Ware (2002).

forbearing, and love. O Lord my King, grant that I might see my own shortcomings and not judge my fellows. For blessed are you to the ages of ages.[14]

The petitions of the liturgy tend not to be, however, of the preparatory variety, requests that God grant the assembled the strength to act well. Rather, these prayers, or so I have been suggesting, are themselves *enactments* of love, the fulfillment of Jesus's injunction to cultivate an ethic of outwardness. This dimension of the petitions is especially evident in the *Apostolic Constitutions*, when the assembled pray:

> And we entreat you for those that hate and persecute us for the sake of your name, for those who are outside and have gone astray, that you would turn them back to good and soften their hearts.[15]

It is also evident in The Liturgy of St. Basil, which echoes similar themes:

> Be mindful, O God, of those who face trial, those in the mines, in exile, in bitter slavery, in all tribulation, necessity, and affliction; of all who need your great compassion; those who love us, those who hate us, and those who commended us, though unworthy, to pray for them.[16]

Similar themes are present in the Liturgy of St. Mark:

> Bless, Lord, the crown of the year of your goodness, for the poor of your people, for the widow and the orphan, for the stranger and the proselyte, for all of us who trust in you and call upon your holy name: "for the eyes of all hope for you."[17]

The point I have been stressing is that, by offering these petitions, those assembled for the liturgy fulfill Jesus's command to cultivate and enact an ethic not of proximity but of outwardness. It is a striking feature of the biblical narrative, however, that when Jesus issues the commands to bless those who curse you and to be a neighbor to those who belong to out-groups, he does not also specify what is accomplished ethically by doing these things. Rather, Jesus emphasizes that the "reward will be great" for those who fulfill these commands; their status will be "children of the Most High" (Luke 6: 35).

Yet, beyond being united to God in such a way that one can properly be called a child of the Most High, there must be an ethical rationale for performing those actions that Jesus commands. That rationale, presumably,

---

[14] As quoted in McGuckin (2011), 178. Of chastity Schmemann (1969), 36, writes: "If one does not reduce this term, as is so often and erroneously done, only to its sexual connotations, it is understood as the positive counterpart to sloth. The exact and full translation of the Greek *sofrosini* and the Russian *tselomudryie* ought to be *whole-mindedness*."

[15] As found in Jasper and Cuming (1987), 112.

[16] I am using the translation contained in the *Service Book of the Holy Eastern Orthodox Catholic and Apostolic Church according to the use of the Antiochian Orthodox Christian Archdiocese of North America*, 11th edition (2002).

[17] As found in Jasper and Cuming (1987), 61.

does not lie in the fact that by blessing those who curse you or praying for the aliens, it is likely that their lives go better. For, by all appearances, as often as not, the lives of those who are the objects of our petitions do not go better. As often as not, the sick do not recover. As often as not, the prisoners are not delivered. And as often as not, oppressors do not turn from their ways. But if the ethical import of enacting an ethic of outwardness does not lie in enhancing the wellbeing of the objects of our blessings and petitions, where might it lie?

It lies in at least this: by doing such things as praying for the sick, the oppressed, the stranger, or the ritually unclean, one stands in solidarity with them, saying in effect that, regardless of your circumstance or station, we will not abandon you if we can possibly avoid it.[18] Indeed, this activity of standing in solidarity is not limited to the activity of petitioning. When, for example, in the liturgy the assembled sing the beatitudes, this is probably best understood not simply as a case in which they, for the sake of being edified, call to mind Jesus's words about the mourners, the meek, the poor in spirit, the peacemakers, and the persecuted. It is also *to bless* the members of these groups by saying these words. In saying to the members of these groups "May you be blessed," the people also bless them, taking Jesus's words as their own. And in blessing them, the assembled express solidarity with the mourners, the meek, the poor in spirit, the peacemakers, and the persecuted, saying in effect that we stand with you even when the rest of the world does not. In fact, in the context of the liturgy, there is really a double solidarity at work when the assembled engage in the litanies and sing the beatitudes. For the assembled stand in solidarity not only with those for whom they pray or bless but also with each other. In the very first petition of the liturgy, for example, the deacon emphasizes that it is in concord or peace that the assembled pray together. And in some striking language, the Liturgy of St. Basil similarly speaks of the assembled as having one common life: "let us commit ourselves, one another, and our whole life to Christ our God."[19]

Throughout our discussion, I have assumed that it is illuminating to understand liturgical action against the backdrop of the ethical vision that animates the scriptural narrative. When we do so, we can see that engaging in the petitions and blessings are ways by which those engaging in liturgical action fulfill the second love commandment. This strategy of understanding liturgical activity against important elements of the scriptural narrative, I believe,

---

[18] What about prayers for one's oppressors? Does one stand in solidarity with them when one prays for or blesses them? No, not in the sense of "solidarity" with which I have been working. Something different, then, needs to be said about what is accomplished when one prays for or blesses the oppressors. I touch upon what is accomplished in the last section of this chapter.

[19] I discuss the import of this language in Cuneo (2014d). This essay is included as Chapter 7 of the present volume.

can be extended, as it also helps us to understand the ethical significance of the activity of standing in solidarity with others.

Think for a moment about the New Testament narrative and the extent to which its stories are filled with cases of abandonment by others. The cases that immediately spring to mind are those of Peter's abandonment of Jesus before Jesus's death, and Jesus's own cry of dereliction from the cross. Given our topic, which concerns the importance of prayer, a particularly interesting case is described in the 26th chapter of Matthew. In an emotional state that the writer of Matthew describes as being "deeply distressed," Jesus asks his favored disciples Peter, James, and John to keep vigil with him in the Garden of Gethsemane, where he will pray that he might not undergo an excruciating death as a result of being abandoned and betrayed by another of his followers, Judas. But rather than finding them holding vigil, Jesus finds his followers asleep—on three separate occasions. "What?" he asks incredulously, "Could you not watch with me one hour?" (Matt. 26: 40) Abandoning Jesus in his hour of greatest need is, apparently, something that comes easily to those who know him best and are most devoted to him. Admittedly, given the circumstances, there is little the disciples can do to alleviate Jesus's suffering or otherwise alter what is going to happen to him; the wheels of his betrayal and death are already in motion. And yet it is extremely important to Jesus that they hold vigil with him. What matters, apparently, is not their ability to alter Jesus's condition or somehow enhance Jesus's well-being by way of their prayers. Rather, what matters, the text indicates, is that they stand in solidarity with him in this, his darkest of hours.

Taking full account of the theme of abandonment in the biblical text would require considering cases not just of dereliction and betrayal but also those in which men and women stand steadfast in the most difficult of circumstances, such as Joseph's refusal to abandon Mary upon learning that she is pregnant with another's child; Mary's own refusal to abandon Jesus when Jesus is being crucified; and the myrrh-bearing women's refusal to abandon the body of Jesus after his death. Even without exploring this theme in greater detail, however, the ethical significance to the Christian life of standing in solidarity with others should be apparent.

When we stand in solidarity with others, whether they belong to some supposed out-group or not, we express the conviction that their cares and concerns are not beneath us or too far removed from our ordinary lives to be the subject of our attention and concern. Rather, we express the stance that it does not matter how far removed the other might be in physical or social distance. Their plight matters. It is our responsibility to not abandon but to stand with them. It should also be more evident how the liturgy can function as a powerful bulwark against the strong tendency to not stand with the marginalized—the mourners, the meek, and the distressed. For by inserting ourselves in the liturgical activities of petitioning and blessing, those who identify themselves as the followers of Jesus are provided with the means by which to fulfill Jesus's command not simply to open themselves to their needs but also to stand with them when they most need it.

Up to this point, I have not emphasized the ways in which fulfilling the second love commandment is also a way to fulfill the first. But it is worth taking note—if only in passing—of the fact that by standing in solidarity with the marginalized we ally ourselves with what are, according to the scriptural narrative, God's purposes. Given traditional Christian theology, the beatitudes are divine blessings: it is God, in the person of Jesus, who blesses the mourners, the meek, the poor in spirit, the peacemakers, and the persecuted. When in the liturgy the assembled bless what God blesses, want what God wants, stand with those whom God stands with, they enact what are surely some of the most important ways by which one can love God.[20]

1.4. REPENTANCE

My topic has been how participating in the liturgy is an important way in which one might both develop and enact an ethic of outwardness, where this is understood to include not only the activity of opening ourselves up to the needs of others but also standing in solidarity with them. These activities, I have suggested, are important ways in which one can fulfill the second love commandment. Let me close this discussion with an observation regarding how the liturgical activities of petitioning and blessing are to be performed.

The liturgical text offers no instruction regarding the motives from which those assembled are to engage in the activities of petitioning and blessing. It does not instruct those assembled—not even tacitly—to offer their petitions for the sick from motives of empathy. Likewise, it does not instruct those assembled—not even tacitly—to offer prayers for their enemies from motives of sympathy or compassion. Nothing at all is said (or assumed) about the mental states that one must be in when one offers these prayers or blesses the mourners, the meek, or the persecuted. The fact that the liturgical script is not directive in this way naturally feeds a concern that one might harbor about what occurs in the liturgy. For one might naturally worry that the liturgical activity of petitioning and blessing often is, even for the most devoted, a matter of merely going through the motions. After all, often those who pray for the sick and bless the mourners are not at all moved by their plight. And, if that is right, it is difficult to see how the liturgical activity of petitioning and blessing could reliably be considered ways of fulfilling Jesus's command to love one's

---

[20] This theme is developed in Adams (1986).

neighbor as oneself. In the Parable of the Good Samaritan, it is worth remembering, the Samaritan is said to have been moved by "pity" for the wounded man on the side of the road.

A pair of observations about this concern: the first is that it is commonly thought that the Christian ethic does require particular types of motivations to achieve its ideal. Richard Rorty, for example, writes:

> From a Christian standpoint this tendency to feel closer to those with whom imaginative identification is easier is deplorable, a temptation to be avoided. It is part of the Christian idea of moral perfection to treat everyone, even the guards at Auschwitz or in the Gulag, as a fellow sinner. For Christians, sanctity is not achieved as long as obligation is felt more strongly to one child of God than to another; invidious contrasts are to be avoided in principle. Secular universalism has taken over this attitude from Christianity.[21]

Whatever one might think of Rorty's description of the "Christian standpoint," when one considers the scriptural texts, one finds that Jesus himself does not enjoin those who conform to the second love commandment to do so from some particular range of motives. That is not to say that Jesus does not have a great deal to say about our interior mental lives. He does. But the second great commandment is not accompanied by a directive concerning how one should conform to it. In his discussion of this matter, Wolterstorff writes:

> what strikes one immediately is that Jesus says nothing at all about reasons or motives for loving the neighbor; all he says is that one should love one's neighbor as oneself. He nowhere rejects caring about some people because one is attached to them, caring about others because one feels compassion for them, caring about yet others because one finds oneself attracted to them, and so forth. In all such cases one is doing what Jesus commanded, caring about the other, seeking to promote her good and to secure her rights as ends in themselves.[22]

Wolterstorff continues:

> Rather than dismissing care about the other grounded in compassion as not measuring up to what he is calling for, Jesus offers such care as an example of what he is calling for. The natural dynamics that lead us to care about the other are often malformed in their workings. But when they are not malformed, it makes no difference whether we care about the other because we are attached to her, because we are attracted to her, because we feel solidarity with her, because we are moved by compassion, or because we see it as our duty to care about her. Just see to it that you care not only about yourself but also about your neighbor.[23]

---

[21] Rorty (1989), 191.   [22] Wolterstorff (2011b), 116.
[23] Wolterstorff (2011b), 118.

If this is right, provided that our motives are not malformed, it does not matter what the motives are from which the assembled offer the liturgical petitionary prayers or blessings.[24] They can be properly offered from compassion, attachment, or duty. What matters is that they are offered. What matters is that the assembled open themselves up to the plight of those who are the subject of these prayers, bless those who curse them, and stand in solidarity with those who are under duress.

The second observation I would like to make is that while the eucharist liturgy is celebratory—its central event, the eucharistic meal, is fundamentally an act of thanksgiving—it is also deeply penitential. After each petition in the litanies, after all, the people sing "kyrie eleison" or "Lord have mercy." This phrase is colored with different shades of meaning: on the one hand, it is a cry for healing and deliverance; on the other, it is an expression of repentance. When, then, the deacon prays for "travelers by land, by sea, and by air; for the sick and the suffering; for captives and their safety and salvation" and the assembled respond with "kyrie eleison," we should hear this in two ways. We should hear it, first, as a corporate affirmation of the deacon's words, something to the effect of: "Lord have mercy *on them*: save, deliver, heal those for whom we pray." But we should also hear the use of this same phrase as an expression of repentance, something to the effect of: "Lord have mercy *on us*: forgive us, who offer these petitions, of our failings."

If this is so, the liturgical script (and the community's understanding of it) might be more or less non-committal with regard to the motives from which the petitions and blessings should be offered. But it is not neutral with regard to the *stance* from which those assembled offer their petitions and blessings. They are to issue from a stance in which those who offer these petitions actively repent of their own shortcomings and, insofar as these petitions are offered as a community, for the failures of their community. The pattern of petition, repentance, and blessing of the liturgy is, apparently, not accidental. Each of these activities complements the other.

It is a good question why this should be so, why in the liturgy the activity of petitioning is not only accompanied by the activity of repenting but also issues from a stance of repentance.[25] The obvious answer is that doing so is a way of fulfilling one of Jesus's most consistent injunctions. In the Gospels, Jesus repeatedly instructs his audience to repent, even in the face of atrocities, such as Pilate's murder of Galilean worshippers: "Unless you repent, you

---

[24] In this regard, I take myself to disagree with Saliers (1979), 178, who seems to assume that the affections play a central role in the liturgical activity of intercession. But see Anderson and Morrill (1998) for nuances regarding Saliers's views.

[25] I have only touched upon the degree to which repentance figures in the eucharistic service. A closer look reveals that it is interspersed throughout the liturgical script, especially in the Lenten services.

will all likewise perish" (Luke 13: 3). That noted, let me offer two further observations on this score.

In a passage I have just quoted, Wolterstorff notes that the "natural dynamics that lead us to care about the other are often malformed in their workings. But when they are not malformed, it makes no difference whether we care about the other because we are attached to her, because we are attracted to her, because we feel solidarity with her, because we are moved by compassion, or because we see it as our duty to care about her."[26] This observation generalizes, as the dynamics that move us to express concern for the other in the form of petitionary prayer are often malformed: we care too little, we go through the motions, our minds are elsewhere. Often, moreover, we are unaware of the degree to which our motives are deficient. Indeed, rather deep in the Christian tradition is the conviction that, given how opaque we are to ourselves, we are often unable to genuinely appreciate the extent to which our motives are deficient. To repent while offering these prayers is in effect to acknowledge, to help one see, and to distance oneself from these deficiencies; it is to strive for something better while we pray.

The purpose of offering the petitions from a stance of repentance, however, comes to more than this. In his reflections on repentance in *Great Lent*, Schmemann writes that repentance "is, above all else, a desperate call for . . . divine help."[27] If that is so, those who call on God to help those for whom they pray simultaneously acknowledge that they, too, are in need of help; in the mouths of those who offer these prayers, the phrase "kyrie eleison" is to a plea that God have mercy *on us* who pray. The activity of repenting while petitioning is, then, to acknowledge that there is little difference between the plight of those for whom we pray and those who pray for them. To return to the theme that I developed earlier, the activity of repenting is another way by which the people express solidarity with those for whom they pray. It is another way to acknowledge our common condition.[28]

---

[26] Wolterstorff (2011b), 118.

[27] Schmemann (1969), 29. Elsewhere, Schmemann writes: "Repentance is all this: man *seeing* his sinfulness and weakness, realizing his state of separation from God, experiencing sorrow and pain because of that state, desiring forgiveness and reconciliation, rejecting the evil and opting for a return to God, and finally desiring Communion for the 'healing of soul and body'" (124).

[28] My thanks to Arthur Kuflik, Luke Reinsma, Nick Wolterstorff, and two anonymous referees for their feedback on an earlier version of this chapter.

2

Protesting Evil

Though I walk through the valley of the shadow of death
... You prepare a table before me in the presence of my enemies.

John the Baptizer has been rotting in a Roman prison cell. His crime was that of having accused the local ruler, Herod Antipas, of having unlawfully wedded his brother's wife, Herodias. Although John must have known that his behavior would provoke some such response, the Gospel narrative intimates that John assumed that he wouldn't linger in prison, for John believed that the messiah was in their midst. But as John's days in prison grew longer, the doubts in his mind loomed larger. Wishing to address these growing doubts, John sends two of his disciples to Jesus to ask whether Jesus is in fact the Chosen One. Jesus's reply is enigmatic: "Go and tell John the things you have seen and heard: that the blind see, the lame walk, the lepers are cleansed, the deaf hear, the dead are raised, the poor have the gospel preached to them" (Luke 7: 22). While hardly a direct reply to John's query, it must nonetheless have given John hope. Jesus was exercising power—power of a sort sufficient to deliver John from prison. Those familiar with the Gospel narrative know, however, that these hopes are dashed, for there is no deliverance. Rather than be emancipated, John is beheaded soon after his inquiry.

The news of John's murder quickly makes its way to Jesus. It is clear to anyone following the Gospel narrative that John's death is not simply one death among others. On the contrary, it is a major blow to the kingdom that Jesus claimed to be inaugurating. According to the scriptural narrative, that kingdom had been announced by John himself. Not only had John announced the coming of this kingdom, he had also baptized Jesus—this baptismal event being, if orthodox Christian theology is to be believed, the occasion of the great Theophany or revelation of the Trinity. It is also what seals John's reputation as one genuinely set apart. "Among those born of women," says Jesus, "there is not a greater prophet than John the Baptizer" (Luke 7: 28). Wild, uncompromising, overflowing with charisma, John had much more life in him. Even at two thousand years' distance, his death seems like a tragic waste. Political positioning, sexual intrigue, and ultimately the abuse of political power cut his life far too short.

Jesus responds to the news of John's death not by ranting against the powers, but by attempting to withdraw from the public eye with his disciples. The attempt proves futile, however. Jesus's popularity is so great that the crowds anticipate where he intends to go; when Jesus arrives at his destination, they are there waiting for him. Rather than disperse the crowds or attempt to withdraw even farther, the Gospels tell us that Jesus was moved with compassion. Aware that the crowds had grown hungry while waiting for him, he engages in a series of unusual actions. Jesus orders the disciples to gather whatever food they can find and bring it to him. This they do, presenting him with five loaves of bread and two fish. Jesus then blesses and divides this food, distributing it to his disciples. According to the Gospel narrative, they then distribute enough food to feed five thousand people. Jesus, the disciples, and the people eat together in what the scriptures describe as a "deserted place" (Luke 9: 12; see also Matt. 14: 13–21; Mark 6: 30–44).

It is tempting to view these two episodes recorded in the Gospels, the murder and the meal, as more or less disconnected, having little to do with each other—the subjects of two pericopes stitched together by an anonymous editor. But this would, I believe, be a mistake. The feeding of the five thousand takes place in the shadow of John's death. Given John's stature and importance to Jesus, it could not be otherwise. Might there, however, be an even more intimate relation between these two events, one according to which the feeding of the multitudes does not simply take place in the shadow of John's murder but is also supposed to be a response to it?

There are textual considerations that favor such a reading. Look, for example, at the ways in which the two episodes are isomorphic, using parallel imagery. There are two feasts, the first taking place in a Roman palace to celebrate Herod's birthday; the second taking place in a deserted place. Food is, moreover, central to both episodes. In the first episode, there is plenty to eat; the feast is sumptuous. Yet the feast takes a bizarre turn when Herod augments the feast by ordering that which is inedible—namely, John's head—to be presented on a platter as if it were food. In the second episode, by contrast, initially there is almost nothing to eat; the people are going hungry. This feast, however, also takes a very strange turn when Jesus produces an abundance of food for the multitude from several loaves and fish. The contrast couldn't be more striking: on the one hand, appalling waste, excess, and desecration of the dead and, on the other, uncanny resourcefulness, abundance, and nourishment for the living.

There is, in addition, a curious interplay between power and voluntary powerlessness during both feasts. In the first feast, Herod is so enchanted by the erotic dancing of his step daughter that he promises her anything that she might want. After consulting with her mother, who has put her up to this seduction, Herod's step daughter tells him that she wants John's head on a platter. The text reports Herod as being sorry for having made such a rash promise. But, in an odd episode of saving face and moral rigorism, Herod takes his hands to be tied; a promise is a promise and he intends to keep his. So he issues the command to have John beheaded. In so doing, he commands what no man has authority to command: the murder of an innocent. In the second feast, Jesus also exercises remarkable power, although of a fundamentally different sort from Herod's. Jesus's power lies not in his having the authority to order the slaughter of an innocent. Rather, according to the scriptural narrative, it consists in his having authority over that which no other man has authority, namely, the very elements of nature itself ("even the wind and the waves obey his command"). Still, the exercise of Jesus's power is muted. Given his mission, Jesus is in a situation of relative powerlessness: a tragedy has occurred and there is nothing at present that he can do about it. He cannot level the books, avenge, or rectify it. His mission requires that he will soon suffer a death much like John's; that is, perhaps a reason for thinking that Jesus found the news regarding John to be not only tragic but also ominous.

The feeding of the five thousand, then, is not a redemption or rectification of John's death. But it does take place in its shadow. And, given the parallels between the two episodes, one has the sense—or at least I have the sense—that Jesus's actions *address* what has happened to John. But if so, his is a curious way of addressing John's death. Why would Jesus respond to John's murder by doing things with food, providing a meal to feed the people? Is there something especially fitting about his doing so?

In what follows, I want to pursue these questions. My aim in doing so, however, is not primarily to dwell on the significance of the feeding of the five thousand. Rather, it is to reflect on this event in order to understand better certain elements of the Christian liturgy. For nearly all the early Christians commentators took the feeding of the five thousand to have liturgical import, as they believed it to be a proto-eucharistic event. I propose to follow the lead of these early commentators, albeit at a certain distance. These commentators were primarily interested in the typological similarities between the feeding of the five thousand and the eucharistic celebration. I, by contrast, want to probe the significance of the context in which both the feeding of the five thousand and the eucharistic celebration takes place. That context is one in which the assembled eat in the shadow and recognition of vast evil. Taking into account the significance of this context, I claim, helps us to understand not simply a fundamental dynamic of the eucharistic liturgy but also its significance.

2.1. SYMBOLIC VALUE

Tucked away in Robert Adams's magisterial book *Finite and Infinite Goods* is a fascinating chapter on symbolic value. Adams notes that most modern and contemporary moral philosophers have had virtually nothing to say about the topic. The diagnosis of this silence that Adams offers is that, while most philosophers would agree that the ethical life consists in being for the good and being against evil, they have understood these phenomena almost exclusively in terms of the consequences of our actions; we are for the good and against evil, these philosophers claim, to the extent that we promote the good and prevent evils in various ways by our actions. In this respect, there is a relentlessly pragmatic cast to modern and contemporary ethical theorizing.

But consider, Adams suggests, situations of relative helplessness, such as those circumstances in which we or those whom we care about are in great need but whose need we are more or less helpless to meet. Imagine, for example, a case in which you are terminally ill, lying in a hospital bed. In circumstances such as these, Adams writes, it is important to have ways of being for the good, even though there is very little I or anyone else can do about the situation. Ethics, after all, says Adams:

> is not only about how to act well, but more broadly about how to *live* well. And whether we like it or not, helplessness is a large part of life. Human life both begins and ends in helplessness. Between infancy and death, moreover, we may find ourselves in the grip of a disease or a dictatorship to which we may be able to adapt but which we cannot conquer. Even if our individual situation is more fortunate, we will find ourselves relatively helpless spectators of most of the events in the world about which we should care somewhat, and many of those about which we should care most, if we are good people. Dealing well with our helplessness is therefore an important part of living well. An ethical theory that has nothing to say about this abandons us in what is literally the hour of our greatest need.[1]

What, then, ought we to do in circumstances of relative helplessness? Adams's answer is that one "of the most obvious answers is that we can give more reality to our being for the goods and against the evils by expressing our loyalties symbolically in action." When our friends are ill,

> most of us are not able to do much about their health. But we can still be for them, and that is important to all of us. Sending cards and flowers are ways of being for a sick person symbolically. They may also have the good consequence of cheering up the patient, but that will be because he is glad that his friends are for him. The symbolic value of the deed is primary in such a case.[2]

Our lives are lived in the shadow of evil. Often, our only recourse when living in the shadow is to be for the good and against evil symbolically. Composing music, making sculpture, planting trees, lighting candles, holding vigil: these are some of the ways in which a person might symbolically be for the good in the face of evil, such as a friend's illness or death.

---

[1] Adams (1999), 224.   [2] Ibid.

At no point in his discussion does Adams offer anything like an account or analysis of what it is symbolically to be for the good or against evil. One can understand why. Offering an account of symbolic action proves to be extraordinarily challenging; it is extremely difficult to identify a set of necessary and sufficient conditions which specify how intentions, conventions, the employment of symbol systems, and fittingness relations conspire to generate symbolic actions which express that an agent is for the good or against evil. As will become evident in a moment, the category of symbolically being for the good and against evil is central to the topic that I wish to explore. Like Adams, however, I have no account to offer of the phenomenon. I will have to assume that we can recognize central cases of symbolic action, even if there are other cases that are much more difficult to assess.

While I have no account to offer of the phenomenon of symbolic action, there is at least one observation about it that deserves mention. Rather often, symbolic action has a dual directionality. By this I mean that often a person's symbolically being for the good at one and the same time counts as his symbolically being against evil and vice versa. The point I am making is not the trivial one that to be for the good is ipso facto to be against evil and vice versa. It is, rather, that symbolically being for the good is often the way in which we address, stand up against, protest, or pronounce a No to evil.

I say it is often that; but it is not always. In her book *For the End of Time: The Story of the Messiaen Quartet*, Rebecca Rischin tells the story of the French composer Olivier Messiaen.[3] In the early 1940s, Messiaen had been taken into a Nazi death camp, where he and his fellow prisoners suffered considerably. During this time, Messiaen composed and, with a group of fellow prisoners, performed for the first time, what is probably his best-known work, *Quartet for the End of Time*. Messiaen engaged in these activities for multiple reasons. But what emerges from Rischin's telling of the story is that the composition and the performance were largely motivated by Messiaen's attempt to cope with his surroundings. Messiaen's actions were primarily ways of addressing evil not so much by standing against it but by coping with it. The dual directionality of symbolic action in which I am interested is different from this. It is not that of symbolically being for the good by performing actions that allow us to cope with evil, although this is an extraordinarily important way in which we can be for the good. Nor is it symbolically being against evil by simply doing a little bit of good in the world, whatever that might be. Rather, the phenomenon in which I am interested is a matter of purposively pronouncing a No to evil *by* symbolically being for the good in the performance of one or another action. The type of symbolic action in which I am interested, we might say, has vocative import; it addresses a situation, expressing recognition of it as being an evil that calls for a response in which we express our allegiance to the good.

---

[3] Rischin (2003).

2.2. IN THE FACE OF EVIL

Earlier I mentioned that when the early Christians read the scriptural texts, they were struck by the obvious parallels between the feeding of the five thousand and the celebration of the eucharist. The parallels between the Gospels' presentation of the feeding and what they took to be the original eucharistic event, the Last Supper, were so evident that they found it irresistible to read the former as anything other than a proto-eucharistic event. The most obvious commonality between the two episodes is the fourfold action sequence in which Jesus engages. In both episodes, the Gospels describe Jesus as taking bread, blessing it, breaking it, and then distributing it. This action sequence, as theologians such as Dom Gregory Dix have emphasized, is incorporated into all the ancient eucharistic liturgies of the church.[4] What rendered this sort of proto-eucharistic reading of the feeding of the five thousand irresistible, however, is not so much the structural parallels that they found between the action sequence described in the feeding of the five thousand and the Last Supper, but rather the narrative presented in the sixth chapter of John's Gospel. For it is in this chapter that, immediately after the feeding of the five thousand, Jesus himself draws a connection between the feeding and the eucharist. In this chapter, Jesus declares that he is the true bread of life, saying—much to the puzzlement and dismay of his audience— that this bread is also his flesh and that it must be eaten.

I have no interest, on this occasion, in trying to diagnose what Jesus might have meant by this saying. However, the parallels that the early Christian commentators noted between the feeding of the five thousand and the eucharist interest me. This interest, as I mentioned earlier, concerns not the typological features that the feeding and the celebration of the eucharist might share with one another—these being what primarily commanded the attention of the ancient commentators. Rather, it lies in uncovering the significance of the context in which these events take place. Specifically, I am interested in discovering whether what we have said about the context of the feeding of the five thousand helps us to understand the context of the eucharistic liturgy and, ultimately, whether this helps us to understand what it is that we are doing when we participate in that liturgy. Lying in the background is the assumption—which I won't try to defend—that which actions we perform on a given occasion are determined in part by contextual features of that occasion.

Let me remind you of what we said about the feeding of the five thousand. The feeding takes place in a charged context, one in which Jesus has just received the news of John's beheading. This context, I suggested, is important for understanding what is happening during the feeding of the five thousand,

---

[4] Dix (1945).

as this event takes place in the face of a great evil that mattered deeply to Jesus. The feeding, however, is itself not a lashing out against this evil. Nor is it redemption of the evil. Nor is it merely an attempt to cope with this evil. Nor, finally, is it plausibly viewed as a case in which someone is trying to do a little good, whatever that might be, when things have gotten really bad. Instead, I suggested that the feeding *addresses* the evil—is a response to it. Specifically, to use Adams' conceptuality, it is a response in which, by feeding the multitudes, Jesus thereby symbolically protests or stands against the evil by symbolically being for the good. Of course protests come in different forms. The sort of protest at issue is not a collective shaking of the fist, a symbolic declaration that evil of these sorts will not happen again if we can help it. Rather, to say it again, it is a case in which Jesus stands against evil by taking food, blessing, and then multiplying it. Why do these actions count as a case of standing against evil? And why, more generally, would blessing food and eating together count as a fitting protest to evil? To this point, I have left these questions unanswered. But we can now, I think, make headway on them by reflecting on the Christian liturgy.

At the heart of all the ancient liturgies of the church—I have in mind particularly the ancient liturgies of the Christian East, those of St. Mark, St. James, St. Basil, and St. John Chrysostom—is a meal, the celebration of the eucharist. The texts of each of these liturgies clearly communicate the context in which this meal takes place: it occurs in the face and recognition of vast evil. Here is how, for example, the liturgy of St. Basil begins. Immediately after the priest declares the kingdom of the Father, Son, and Holy Spirit to be blessed and after the assembled respond with their Amen or "let it be so," there is the Great Litany, which is a dialogue between the deacon and the people. The deacon begins with the exhortation:

> In peace let us pray to the Lord.

He continues:

> For travelers by land and sea, for the sick, the suffering, the captives, and for their deliverance, let us pray to the Lord.
> For our deliverance from all affliction, wrath, danger, and distress, let us pray to the Lord.[5]

To each petition, the people respond with "kyrie eleison" or "Lord, have mercy." The connotations of this phrase are lost in its English translation— the root of "eleison" being the Greek term for olive oil: that which is used to

---

[5] I am quoting from Jasper and Cuming (1987). There are different translations offered of this last sentence. Some translate "distress" as "tribulation," others as "necessity," still others as "constraint."

soothe and heal. The cry is not a request for God to stay God's hand or desist from condemning, but for God to comfort, heal, and deliver.[6]

After the antiphons are chanted, the scriptures read, the creed and Lord's Prayer sung, the assembly prepares itself to celebrate the eucharist. Interestingly, during the sequence of events just mentioned, those assembled are, during the singing of the cherubic hymn, directed not to dwell on evil but to "set aside all earthly cares." But this injunction to set aside earthly cares is only a moment in the script. The theme of the shadow of evil is introduced once again, as the text of the anaphora recapitulates in greater detail themes voiced at the outset of the liturgy in the Great Litany. After having commemorated the living and the dead, for example, the celebrant says this:

> Remember, Lord, the people who stand here ... nourish the infants, instruct the youth, strengthen the old, comfort the fainthearted, gather the scattered, bring back the wanderers ... sail with those that sail, journey with those that journey; defend the widows, protect the orphans, rescue the captives, heal the sick. Be mindful, O God, of those who face trial, those in the mines, in exile, in bitter slavery, in all tribulation, necessity, and affliction; of all who need your great compassion.[7]

The anaphora of the liturgy of St. Mark, used by the Alexandrian church, is similar:

> Visit, Lord, the sick among your people and in mercy and compassion heal them. Drive away from them and from us every disease and illness; expel the spirit of weakness [from them]. Raise up those who have lain in lengthy illnesses.... Have mercy on all those who are held in prison, or in the mines, in exile or bitter slavery.[8]

The anaphora of the liturgy of St. James, used by the church of Jerusalem, echoes the same themes:

> Remember, Lord, [Christians at sea, on the road, abroad], our fathers and brothers in chains and prisons, in [captivity and] exile, [in mines and tortures and bitter slavery ...
>   Remember, Lord, those in old age and infirmity,] those who are sick, ill, or troubled by unclean spirits.[9]

---

[6] Paul Meyendorff cites the following prayer used in the Eastern churches for the consecration of oil: "O Lord, in your mercy (*eleei*) and compassion you heal the afflictions of our souls and bodies; sanctify now this oil (*elaion*), O Master, that it may bring healing to those who are anointed with it.... For you are our mercy (*eleein*) and salvation, O our God" (Meyendorff (2009), 42). Lost in translation is the Greek play on words between oil (*elaion*) and mercy (*eleos*).

[7] Jasper and Cuming (1987), 121.   [8] Ibid., 60.   [9] Ibid., 95.

For the most part, these liturgical texts refer not to particular historic evils but to types of evils, ranging from illness to appalling injustice.[10] These evils, the text reminds us, are all around us. We might easily forget—or even try to forget—that they are all around us. The text pronounces that we are not to do that. We are to be mindful of them and, in particular, mindful of them at this point in the service. Moreover, the text addresses these evils in full recognition that most of them are such that we can do nothing to prevent, correct, or redeem them. They are too many in number; many are too far removed in space and time. Even those that occur in our midst are such that we are often powerless to prevent or alter them.

The text, then, calls us to bring these evils to mind in full recognition that we are relatively powerless before them. These evils are, after all, the subject matter of *petitions*, calls for help. It may be worth adding that this powerlessness is to some degree self-imposed. The types of evils to which the text refers touch us at various points. Many of the assembled know those who are or who have been held unjustly in prison, subjected to slavery or human trafficking, widowed or orphaned because of injustice, and so on. Human nature being what it is, many of us are naturally inclined to try to rectify these evils by avenging them. In his teaching, however, Jesus forbids us to do that; we are not to return these evils in kind:

> You have heard that it was said, "An eye for an eye and a tooth for a tooth." But I say to you, Do not resist an evildoer. But if anyone strikes you on the right cheek, turn the other also; and if anyone wants to sue you and take your coat, give your cloak as well. . . .
>
> You have heard that it was said, "You shall love your neighbor and hate your enemy." But I say to you, Love your enemies and pray for those who persecute you, so that you may be children of your Father in heaven. . . . For if you love those who love you, what reward do you have? (Matt. 5: 38–47)

While puzzling in certain respects, this passage arguably expresses the very heart of the Gospel's ethical teaching: we are to reject the ancient reciprocity code. We are, that is, to reject that code of conduct that instructs us to return favors for favors and evils for evils; it is to be for us a dead letter.[11] It is this ethical stance that forms the backdrop against which the assembled pray the anaphora. The people call to mind the evils that we suffer in the recognition that not only is there often little we can do about them, but also that we are forbidden to prevent or respond to them in certain ways. We are not, for example, to try to rectify them by avenging them.

---

[10] The anaphora of the liturgy of St. Mark is an interesting exception. In addition to citing types of evils, it includes references to particular historic evils: "Remember, Lord, our holy fathers who were put to death by the barbarians in the holy mountain of Sinai and in Raitho" (p. 98).

[11] On this, see Wolterstorff (2011b), 121–9.

After having recited the anaphora, the celebrant, on behalf of the people, then engages in the very sequence of actions that Jesus himself engaged in, according to the scriptural presentation of both the feeding of the five thousand and the Last Supper. The celebrant takes the bread, which has been provided by the assembly itself, blesses it, breaks it, and then distributes it. The people respond by eating together the food that is blessed. The blessing of the bread, the breaking of it, and the sharing and eating of it are what constitute the eucharistic meal.

At this point, the parallels between the feeding of the five thousand and the eucharistic celebration that I have been pursuing should be plain enough. The feeding of the multitudes and the eucharistic celebration share a common context, both meals taking place in the shadow and recognition of vast evil against which the assembled recognize themselves as being largely powerless. But I have not yet said why either the feeding of the five thousand or the eucharistic celebration are plausibly viewed as cases of events in which the assembled also symbolically address evil by pronouncing a No to it. After all, the mere fact that both these meals take place in the face and recognition of evil needn't also suggest that they in any interesting sense address it. More-over, the scripts of the ancient liturgies themselves do not demand any such interpretation. The eucharistic liturgy might best be understood as having two distinct moments: one in which we call evil to mind, the other in which we eat—the two events being such that they would appear to have relatively little to do with one another.

I want to suggest, however, that fundamental to the eucharistic liturgy is the dynamic between these two moments in the script—the dynamic between the petitions, on the one hand, and the blessings that constitute the eucharistic meal, on the other. Let me try to lay out a case for this understanding by returning to a theme voiced earlier. A few paragraphs back, I suggested that the petitions of the anaphora are best understood against the backdrop of Jesus's teaching that we are to reject the reciprocity code. We call to mind various types of evils during the anaphora in the recognition that not only is there often little we can do about their occurrences, but also that we are not permitted to try to rectify them by avenging them.

This rejection of the reciprocity code represents, however, only half of Jesus's teaching on the Sermon on the Mount. The other, positive side of Jesus's teaching is the injunction to bless those who hate and curse you and to pray for those who abuse you (Luke 6: 27). This is not an isolated theme in the writings of the early Christians. The same theme is taken up in the epistolary literature in the New Testament. "Do not," writes the author 1 Peter, "repay evil for evil or abuse for abuse; but, on the contrary, repay with a blessing" (1 Pet. 3: 9; see also 1 Thess. 5: 15; Rom. 1: 17–19). And again in the early extra-biblical literature: the *Didache*, for example, tells us that the first maxim of "the way of life" is "to bless those who curse you."[12] The *Letter to Diognetus* maintains that what, in part, distinguishes Christians from their neighbors is that they "are reviled, and yet they bless."[13] In the ancient liturgies, this ethical stance is also voiced in the *Apostolic Constitutions*, when the people pray:

> And we entreat you for those that hate and persecute us for the sake of your name, for those who are outside and have gone astray, that you would turn them back to good and soften their hearts.[14]

It is also voiced in the liturgy of St. Basil, when immediately before partaking of the eucharist, the assembled pray for "all those who love us and all those who hate us."

In the face of evil, then, Christians are called to do a very difficult thing. They are called to bless. They are not called to bless evil. The early Christians did not understand Jesus to propound the idea, which Nietzsche once defended, that we are to accept or smile upon whatever evil comes our way. To the contrary, they understood Jesus to teach that blessing those who curse you requires the one who blesses to see the cursing as an evil. And that requires the one who blesses to be against that evil. Nonetheless, they understood Jesus to teach that blessing also requires not being against the person who has performed the evil in the sense of wishing evil upon her. Rather, it requires expressing the thought or desire that the person who perpetrates the evil be treated in a way that befits her worth, which is considerable. Hence the extraordinarily demanding nature of the act of blessing—demanding not simply because it is not easy to bless in the face of evil, but also because it requires the one who blesses to take up that finely balanced ethical stance of at once pronouncing a No to evil and yet blessing the evildoer, treating him or her as one's moral counterpart.

The activity of blessing, I realize, comes in a variety of forms. In the preceding paragraph, I have spoken of only one such form that figures prominently in Jesus's teaching in the Gospels. Still, we are looking for patterns, and if our discussion is along the right lines, we have at hand an important clue about how to understand the link between two moments in the liturgical text: the petitions, in which the people call various types of evils to mind, and the eucharistic blessings, in which the celebrant, on behalf of the people, blesses in response to these evils. The blessing—if the pattern we have uncovered is illuminating—is a response to the evils; the recognition of evil and the response of blessing go hand in hand. What we have in the eucharistic liturgy, I suggest, is the liturgical appropriation and enactment of Jesus's teaching on the Sermon on the Mount.

---

[12] I am quoting from the translation found in Richardson (1996), 171.
[13] Ibid., 217.   [14] Jasper and Cuming (1987), 112.

If this is right, lying at the heart of the eucharistic liturgy is the dynamic between petitioning and blessing, the blessings being a response to the evils that the petitions call to our attention. These evils, I have said, touch us at various points in our lives. To say that they touch us at various points in our lives is, however, to understate the reality. The reality is that these evils often jolt us, triggering in us a variety of instinctive responses. Among the most pronounced are to disengage from, to despair over, or to curse the natural world that has produced the tornados, the cancer, the earthquakes; the inclination to disengage from, to despair over, or to curse our fellow human beings, who have imprisoned the innocent, orphaned the children, or enslaved the free; to disengage from, to despair over, or to curse a God, who for reasons that remain almost completely opaque to us, has permitted the cancer, the widowing, and the enslavement to occur. In the face and recognition of evil, our worlds often turn dark; we lose the ability to discriminate. And when we do, we often view or treat as evil the yield of the natural world, each other, and God. Many speak, for example, of the world as a fundamentally hostile place or losing their faith in God or humanity.

It is in the face and recognition of these evils that affect us in these ways that the celebrant takes in hand the products of the natural world, the bread and the wine—themselves joint products of nature and human hands—and, on behalf of the people, blesses them. The celebrant then gives thanks to God, on behalf of the people, for these things, blessing God for them. Finally, the celebrant distributes what has been blessed to the people themselves, thereby blessing them with these good things. At the core of the eucharistic meal is a threefold blessing. In the face and recognition of vast evil, the celebrant, on behalf of the people, blesses the yield of the natural world, God, and the people.

The threefold blessing pronounces good that which we are often inclined in our lives to call or treat as evil. In this respect, it is a discriminatory response to evil. To the sufferings and the wrongings, the petitions pronounce a No. We are not, for example, to accept passively the suffering inflicted upon those in the mines and in slavery but to be against it, even if we can be so only symbolically. To the natural world, one another, and God, in contrast, the blessings pronounce a Yes, affirming their goodness. The blessings, for example, affirm and treat the natural world, as symbolized in the bread and wine, as being a means of communion, a point of contact with God. If I understand it aright, however, the threefold blessing does not simply respond to the evils brought to mind in the petitions by symbolically affirming the goodness of the natural world, God, and each other. It does so in the face of the *power* that evil tends to wield over us. For evil can hold us under its sway, exerting pressure on us to live lives in which we, sometimes unwittingly, stand opposed to the good—lives, for example, in which things go dark and in which we disengage from the goodness of the natural world, each other, and God, treating the former not as points of contact with but as barriers to God and one another.

To this power, this pressure that evil exerts on us, the threefold blessing also pronounces a No. In so doing, the assembled thereby pronounces that evil will not worm its way into our lives, separating us from the goodness of the natural world, each other, and God. That is also how we symbolically stand against it.

In the Gospels, Jesus admonishes his listeners, telling them that unless they become like little children, they will not inherit the kingdom of God (Matt. 18: 3). This passage is often interpreted as one in which Jesus calls for innocent and childlike faith, the sort of faith that does not fully reckon with evil. But our discussion suggests another reading of this passage. According to this reading, we are to reckon with evil; this, we have seen, is one important function of the petitions in the eucharistic liturgy. But in doing so, we are not to allow our worlds to turn dark. In reckoning with evil, we are not to become cynical, jaded, or disengaged. Rather, we are to be like children who, for all their shortcomings, are remarkably resistant to the darkness and power of evil. Jesus, it should be noted, makes no claims about this being an easy task. It may be that the exhortation to become like little children belongs to the hard sayings of Jesus, one whose fulfillment requires the difficult activity of blessing in the face and recognition of evil.

When viewed against the liturgical petitions, the eucharistic blessings are, I have said, helpfully viewed as a symbolic protest against evil. When describing these blessings, I have spoken of the celebrant, on behalf of the people, engaging in a scripted sequence of act-types, which are themselves presented in the Gospels as having been performed by Jesus. It might, however, be helpful to speak somewhat more precisely. For the self-understanding of the church is that the actions that the celebrant and the people perform are actions performed *by* the church. If this is right, in the celebration of the eucharist, it is the church that blesses the natural order, each other, and God by way of the actions of the celebrant and the people. What we have here, then, is a case of collective action. Not only is it a case of collective action, if the picture I have presented fits the reality, it is also a case in which the church symbolically expresses its allegiance to the good by symbolically standing against evil—both evils of the sort to which it has called our attention in the script of the liturgy and to the power it tends to wield over us. When assembled, the church addresses evil, protesting its presence in the world by symbolically being for the good in the taking, blessing, breaking, and sharing of the bread, just as Jesus did in the feeding of the five thousand.

2.3. ON THE NEED TO BE FOR THE GOOD

My aim in this discussion has been to arrive at self-understanding of a certain kind. Specifically, it has been to gain a better understanding of what actions the church performs when celebrating the eucharistic liturgy. In so doing, I have, however, no reductive aspirations. It is not my purpose to claim that the eucharistic celebration is nothing more than a way by which the church, in a situation of relative powerlessness, symbolically stands against evil by symbolically being for the good. I mean only to point to one, albeit one important, dimension of that complex sequence of actions that constitutes the eucharistic celebration. One matter that would be ripe for further exploration, given the parallels that hold between the eucharistic celebration and the feeding of the five thousand, is the interplay between the exercise of power and powerlessness in both cases. I have emphasized the sense in which, as the assembly stands before evil, it acknowledges that it is largely powerless to prevent or rectify it. It calls for help. But as the church has traditionally understood the eucharistic celebration, it is, like the feeding of the five thousand, an occasion for the exercise of divine power. In the celebration of the eucharist—so the church has affirmed—God also exercises authority over the elements of nature. According to the Eastern church's understanding, God exercises authority over the elements of nature in such a way that they become a means of communion, points of contact with God. They are swept up into the divine life, rendering it apt to call both them and the assembled people the body of Christ.

The church's understanding and celebration of the eucharist has undergone significant alteration in the last five hundred years. Large stretches of the Christian community rarely celebrate the eucharist. And the liturgical scripts they employ to celebrate it tend to be very different from those which we find in the ancient liturgies; they are considerably starker, raising no awareness that the eucharistic meal occurs in the shadow of evil. Nor, for that matter, do they prescribe the performance of actions that allow us symbolically to stand against evil in the celebration of the eucharist. The dynamic of petition and blessing is absent. This alteration in the Christian community's understanding and celebration of the eucharist seems to me a turn for the worse. I say this not primarily out of the conviction that the liturgical practices of the contemporary Christian community should more nearly articulate with those of the ancient church. I say it because, to live well, we need ways of symbolically being against evil by symbolically being for the good. About this Adams seems to be absolutely right. Here is how Adams himself makes the point, this time in a passage in which he addresses the issue of worship:

> Something of ethical importance can be done in worship that we cannot accomplish except symbolically. . . . [W]e can hardly deny that our ability to do good, and even to conceive of good and care about it, is limited. Our nonsymbolic activity, perforce, is a little of this and a little of that. Getting ourselves dressed in the morning, driving or riding or walking to work, and then home again to dinner, we try, on the way and in between, to do some good, to love people and be kind to them, to enjoy and perhaps create some beauty. But none of this is very

perfect, even when we succeed; and all of it is very fragmentary. One who loves the good should be for the good wherever it occurs or is at stake. But we don't even know about most of the good and opportunities for good in the world, and we cannot do very much about most of what we do not. We can care effectively only about fragments that are accessible to us.... I have an inkling of goodness too wonderful for us to comprehend, but concretely I must devote myself to getting the text I am writing a little clearer and more cogently argued than the last draft.

Symbolically we can do better. Symbolically I can be *for* the Good as such, and not just for the bits and pieces of it that I can concretely promote or embody.[15]

I would add only that, to live well, we need ways in which we can *regularly* and *corporately* symbolically stand against evil by symbolically being for the good. On these matters, we are better left not to our own individual whims. There are multiple reasons for this, some of which are closely connected with the psychological difficulty of pronouncing a No to evil by blessing the natural world, each other, or God in the face and recognition of this evil. For sometimes we find ourselves psychologically unable to bless in these ways. The pain is too raw, the resentment too hot, the light of hope too dim. When this is the case, sometimes we can, by engaging in the corporate actions of the church, perform those actions that, simply by our own power, we would otherwise find impossible to perform.[16]

---

[15] Adams (1999), 227.

[16] I delivered a version of this chapter at Georgetown University and thank members of the audience there, especially my commentator, Karen Stohr, for their feedback. Thanks, also, to Nick Wolterstorff, Rico Vitz, and two anonymous referees for their helpful comments.

3

Another Look at Divine Hiddenness

In a passage appealed to frequently by homilists but rarely by philosophers, the author of the Gospel of Matthew attributes the following words to Jesus:

> Then the King will say to those on His right hand,
> "Come you blessed of My Father, inherit the kingdom prepared for you from the foundation of the world: for I was hungry and you gave Me food; I was thirsty and you gave Me drink; I was a stranger and you took Me in; I was naked and you clothed Me; I was sick and you visited Me; I was in prison and you came to Me."
> "Then the just will answer Him, saying, 'Lord, when did we see You hungry and feed You, or thirsty and give You drink? When did we see You a stranger and take You in, or naked and clothe You? Or when did we see You sick, or in prison, and come to You?"
> "And the King will answer and say to them, 'Assuredly, I say to you, inasmuch as you did it to one of the least of these My brethren, you did it to Me.'" (Matt. 25: 34–40)

Those familiar with this text know that its context is one in which Jesus is presenting his teaching regarding the Great Day of Judgment. Among other things, Jesus is informing his listeners that they will be judged on the basis not of such things as their degree of conformance to cultic requirements, but rather how they have treated "the least of these." Indeed, under a natural reading, this passage tells us that the Great Judgment will be rendered primarily on the basis of how we have treated the hungry, the alienated, and the sick.

Like so many passages from the Gospels, this passage from Matthew is at once gripping and puzzling. It is also, I want to suggest, important to take into account when thinking through the phenomenon of divine hiddenness, at least from the perspective of traditional Christian theism. My task in this chapter is to explain why.

3.1. WHAT JESUS IS SAYING

What exactly is Jesus saying in the passage just quoted? Jesus is presumably saying something more than that he approves of feeding the hungry, housing the stranger, and visiting the sick. After all, who wouldn't? The pivotal sentence is the one in which Jesus says that inasmuch as we do such things as visit the sick, we do these things to him. The performance of such actions, Jesus claims, *counts as* actions taken toward him. Those of us who are reading this passage as philosophers, however, want to know which actions Jesus is claiming we are performing towards him by doing such things as visiting the sick. A flat-footed reading might have it that Jesus is claiming that, by visiting a sick person, we thereby visit Jesus, who is also sick. But this cannot be what Jesus means. If Jesus is among the persons with whom we can visit, then presumably he is not also sick.

We needn't cast about much, however, to see what Jesus is getting at, for analogies are close at hand. When I was a child, my grandmother would tell us the story of how her family fled from their Russian homeland to Estonia to escape the October Revolution. As family lore has it, while in Estonia, on a cold winter's night, the family took in a total stranger in a park who had nowhere to go. Out of gratitude, this woman pledged to be their sponsor in America if the family wished to immigrate; she told them that she had the right connections to provide work for my great-grandfather. When the family eventually decided to immigrate, this virtual stranger did as she promised, sponsoring my great-grandfather. By doing this, she had thereby performed an act of great kindness toward the entire family. Things, of course, could've gone very differently. Had this stranger repaid the hospitality shown her by breaking her promise upon my great-grandfather's arrival in America, she would've thereby wronged the entire family.

When understood in light of such analogies, Jesus's pronouncement comes into focus: by doing such things as feeding the hungry and visiting the sick, Jesus claims, we thereby bless and honor him. Conversely, by doing such things as ignoring or harming the least of these, we thereby wrong and dishonor him. In this respect, Jesus highlights a striking difference between the relationship that he bears to the least of these and the ones that we typically do. I cannot bring it about that providing food for a Haitian refugee counts as my having performed an act of kindness toward John Schellenberg (whose work I'll engage with in a moment). Nor can I bring it about that my having failed to visit a stranger in prison counts as my having wronged Schellenberg. Neither I nor Schellenberg bear the right sort of relationship to these people for this to be the case. Under a natural reading, Jesus claims that he does, however. If the passage from Matthew is to be believed, a person's having fed the hungry counts as her having blessed or honored Jesus. Her failing to do so, by contrast, counts as her having wronged or dishonored him (see Matt. 25: 41–6). Suppose one now adds to the mix the traditional Christian claims regarding the divinity of Christ. If so, then Jesus's claim is that a person's having fed the hungry counts as her having blessed God, while her failing to do so counts as her having wronged God.[1]

---

[1] Recall, also, St. Paul's account of his experience on the road to Damascus in which, after having violently persecuted the early Christian church, he reports having been blinded and

On this occasion, I won't pause to reflect on what it is about Jesus's relationship with the least of these that brings it about that a person's performing actions of one sort toward them counts as performing actions of another sort toward God. Suffice it to say that in the passage quoted above, Jesus himself indicates that it is because he bears something akin to an intimate familial relation to the least of these. Most important for my purposes is to highlight the following implication of Jesus's words, at least when they are understood against the backdrop of traditional Christian theology: it is in virtue of an agent's having behaved or failed to behave in certain ways toward the least of these that she bears morally freighted relations with God, including, if the text is to be believed, being a friend of God. According to the biblical text, then, these actions and omissions are such that they bring her into a meaningful relationship with God in a perfectly ordinary English sense of the phrase "meaningful relationship." Because of her actions or omissions with respect to the least of these, she can, for example, be the object of divine approbation or disapprobation, as the case may be.

To this point, I have drawn attention to the claim, made by the author of the Gospel of Matthew, that certain actions of ours taken toward the least of these count as actions taken toward God. Because of this, we find ourselves in relationships of various kinds with God, ones for which we can be held accountable. There is, however, another point that bears emphasis, which is this: according to the biblical text, we can be entirely ignorant of the fact that we stand in these relationships in virtue of our actions and omissions. "When did we see You sick, or in prison?" ask the characters in Jesus's story. Remarkably, the biblical text suggests, whether we have correct beliefs regarding God or God's relationship to the least of these does not matter much when it comes to the Great Day. The divine judgment is, at least in large measure, determined by the ways in which we have actually conducted ourselves toward the least of these and, thus, toward God.

We also have analogies to which we can appeal to understand this. Suppose, in the story I told earlier, the stranger in the park had met, on that cold winter's night, not my grandmother's entire family, but only my great-grandfather. Suppose, for illustration's sake, that she had no idea whether my great-grandfather had a family. If the stranger had done my great-grandfather a favor or harm, she would've thereby brought herself into a meaningful relationship with my grandmother's family. A favor would've formed the basis for gratitude; violence would've been the occasion for rightful resentment. For these things to be true, it wouldn't matter what beliefs the stranger had about my great-grandfather. If the stranger had returned my great-grandfather's kindness with harm, for example, her ignorance or false beliefs about my

---

hearing an audible question posed to him by the risen Christ: "Saul, Saul, why do you persecute me?" (Acts 9: 4).

great-grandfather's identity would be irrelevant to the issue of whether she had wronged him. Jesus indicates that our relationship to God is similar. To pinch a phrase from Hilary Putnam, Jesus appears to suggest that vitally important components of the divine-human relationship just ain't in the head.

3.2. DIVINE HIDDENNESS

For nearly twenty years, John Schellenberg has pressed a type of argument against traditional theism that he calls the Hiddenness Argument. In his fine book *The Wisdom to Doubt*, Schellenberg redeploys the argument to advance a version of religious skepticism, this being the view (roughly) that we should withhold judgment regarding whether there is some ultimate and salvific reality whose properties we could apprehend.[2] In the context of Schellenberg's discussion, the Hiddenness Argument is not supposed to function as an isolated justification for religious skepticism. It is but a single strand of argument that Schellenberg offers for the view. Still, it is an interesting strand, well-deserving of attention. In what follows, I wish to explore it.

Schellenberg formulates the Hiddenness Argument as follows:

(1) Necessarily, if God exists, anyone who is (i) not resisting God and (ii) capable of a meaningful conscious relationship with God is also (iii) in a position to participate in such a relationship (able to do so just by trying).

(2) Necessarily, one is at a time in a position to participate in a meaningful conscious relationship with God only if at that time one believes that God exists.

(3) Necessarily, if God exists, anyone who is (i) not resisting God and (ii) capable of a meaningful conscious relationship with God also (iii) believes that God exists.

(4) There are (and often have been) people who are (i) not resisting God and (ii) capable of a meaningful conscious relationship with God *without* also (iii) believing that God exists.

(5) So, God does not exist (204–6).

There is a great deal to say about this argument. In the interest of brevity, I will assume that we should accept premises (2) and (4). I propose to focus on the argument's first premise, which Schellenberg tells us is the critical one. I shall argue, first, that this premise deserves a different gloss from the one that

---

[2] Schellenberg (2007). I will insert references to this book parenthetically in the text.

Schellenberg gives it. I shall then contend that, even when glossed differently, the theist has insufficient reason to accept it.

Let me begin with the first task. Consider a case of a person who, in no interesting sense, willfully resists the divine. Suppose, furthermore, that this nonresistance is stable; it doesn't wax and wane. Call such a person a *nonresister*. If God exists, a nonresister, Schellenberg states, is at all times "in a position to" engage in a meaningful, conscious relationship with God. She can do so just by trying and, apparently, with little effort. Schellenberg takes this to be a very plausible, albeit "radically democratized" account of the conditions under which we can experience God. For if God were perfectly loving, Schellenberg argues, then some form of conscious awareness of God is "not the preserve of the spiritually elite." It should be readily available to any nonresister (201).

I am dubious. It is one thing to say that awareness of God is not the preserve of the spiritually elite. It is another to suggest that it is easy to achieve for the nonresister, as Schellenberg suggests. After all, through no fault of her own, a person might inhabit social conditions that are fairly hostile to theistic belief. Imagine, for example, her society's attitude toward religion has been power-fully shaped by the resisters, even though she herself is not among them. As a result, those with whom she regularly interacts tend to fall into two camps: they are either resisters or those who tend not to think about God at all.

In this case, an agent who is a nonresister and curious about God might find herself puzzled by what she has been taught about God and the attitudes about God that are "in the air." In such conditions, it might take some hard work on her part to cut through the prevailing attitudes and teachings to get to such a point where it makes sense from her point of view to think seriously about and be open to a meaningful relationship to the divine.

If this is right, however, then we should understand premise (1) of the Hiddenness Argument differently from the way that Schellenberg does. To be in a position to participate in a meaningful, conscious relationship with God might take an honest and extended effort. And because it may require such an effort, I find it implausible to say, as Schellenberg does, that "all capable creatures would at all times have available to them some form of conscious awareness of God, if there were a God" (201). In what follows, then, I shall understand premise (1) of the Hiddenness Argument to incorporate this quali-fication. I shall understand it to say that, if God exists, then a nonresister, having made an honest effort to engage in a meaningful, conscious relationship with God, is in a position to do so. I will assume correlatively that the nonresisters of which Schellenberg speaks in premise (4) are also of this variety.

So much for the issue of how to understand premise (1) of the argument.[3] Let me now indicate why I believe a traditional Christian theist will have insufficient reason to accept this premise. The first premise, recall, says:

---

[3] Does the gloss of premise (1) I have offered beg the question against the proponent of the Hiddenness Argument? It is difficult to see how. This gloss is, after all, consistent with our being

(1) Necessarily, if God exists, anyone who is (i) not resisting God and (ii) capable of a meaningful conscious relationship with God is also (iii) in a position to participate in such a relationship (able to do so just by trying).

Focus for the moment on the phrase "meaningful conscious relationship with God" and, in particular, the qualifier "conscious." The Christian theist who has Matthew 25 in mind will wonder: Why suppose that, if God exists, then at all times, a nonresister can participate in a meaningful *conscious* relationship with God just by trying? Why not instead affirm something weaker, namely, if God exists, then at all times, a nonresister can participate in a meaningful relationship with God just by trying, even though she may not be aware of God *as* God?

We can, then, distinguish two versions of the first premise of the Hiddenness Argument. The first is that accepted by Schellenberg, which I have just stated. The second, I am suggesting, is that accepted by a certain range of traditional theists. It says:

(1') Necessarily, if God exists, anyone who is (i) not resisting God and (ii) capable of a meaningful relationship with God is also (iii) in a position to participate in such a relationship (able to do so just by trying).

While many traditional theists will be wary of (1), they will not be similarly wary of (1'). In fact, they will embrace not only it, but also two further claims. In the first place, they will affirm that:

Necessarily, if God exists, anyone who is not resisting God and capable of a meaningful relationship with God is in a position not only to participate in such a relationship but also to apprehend God's presence and activity.

The idea behind this last claim is that a nonresister needn't remain at a distance from God in this sense: she can apprehend the presence and activity of God inasmuch as she apprehends and positively interacts with the goodness

---

able to come into a conscious relationship with God just by trying, which is what (1) says; it simply specifies what the trying might involve. Moreover, the Hiddenness Argument allows that there can be resisters whose actions can have all sorts of deleterious effects on the world. If so, it is difficult to see how the argument could rule out the possibility that among these effects is the creation of inhospitable conditions (for nonresisters and resisters alike) for apprehending God. In fact, I am tempted to say that if the proponent of the Hiddenness Argument were to claim that such a thing is impossible, he has stacked the deck against the theist. For, if I understand the argument correctly, its strategy is to claim that, given what we know about the nature of love and what theists say about God and God's relationship to human beings, God would not actualize a world that included nonresisting nonbelievers. But if this is so, the proponent of the argument must be prepared to concede, for argument's sake, certain things that theists say about God and God's relation to human beings. Among the things that theists say is this: no one is brought into proper relationship with God, others, and the natural world alone. Your actions may abet or impede my ability to rightly relate to God, you, and the natural world. This is the theme, prominent in the Christian East, of the *solidarity of salvation*.

and beauty she finds in the natural world, in her activities, and in her relations with other human beings. For these qualities, the Christian will maintain, bear particularly intimate relationships with God, such as being manifestations of divine activity or ways in which some aspect of the divine nature discloses itself. The Eastern Christian tradition, for example, speaks of these manifestations and disclosures as the *divine energies*. Fundamental to the spiritual life, according to this tradition, is the aim of learning to see the natural world, our activities, and our relationships with others as manifestations of these energies. To be sure, the nonbelieving nonresister will not think of the goodness and beauty she apprehends as manifestations of divine activity or energies. Still, the important point to see is that traditional Christian theists will grant that, at all times, a nonresister is in a position both to enter into a meaningful relationship with God and to apprehend God's presence and activity.

But, traditional Christian theists will continue, we will not always see through a glass darkly. For it is also true, they will claim, that:

> There will be some time in which every nonbelieving nonresister will be in a position to have a meaningful conscious relationship with God.

Perhaps that time will be at the Great Day of Judgment, as Matthew 25 suggests.

I have distinguished two ways of understanding the first premise of the Hiddenness Argument—a strong and a weak version. From this point forward, I shall understand the weak version to incorporate the claim that every nonresister is in a position not only to have a meaningful relationship with God but also to apprehend God's presence and activity, albeit in some cases only in a veiled manner. Schellenberg needs the strong version of the first premise for his argument to go through. So, why does he think we should accept it?

We should accept it, says Schellenberg, because embracing the alternative is incoherent. What I shall call the *Case from Love* helps us to see why. Both theists and their rivals, Schellenberg claims, should accept:

> (i) If God expresses the most perfect love toward each human being at all times, then there is no time at which nonresisters are not in a position to apprehend God's presence as God's presence.

If, however, premise (1) of the Hiddenness Argument were false, then it would be true that:

> (ii) There are times at which nonresisters are not in a position to apprehend God's presence as God's presence.

But theists are also committed to:

> (iii) God expresses the most perfect love toward each human being at all times.

If this last claim were true, however, then theists would be committed to the inconsistent position that God both does and does not express the most perfect love to each human being at all times (201–3).

The Case from Love turns on the truth of (i). Yet (i), Schellenberg tells us, is extremely plausible. It is, he says, implied by the following conceptual truth: every case in which a person A loves a person B in an admirable way is such that "A does whatever she can to ensure that B is always able just by trying to engage in a meaningful conscious relationship with A." This, Schellenberg maintains, "is just *part* of love for any admirably loving mother or husband or brother or friend" (202–3). Since God's love would have to be admirable, it follows that God would have to do whatever God could to ensure that humans are always able, just by trying, to engage in a meaningful conscious relationship with God wherein they apprehend God as God. For ease of reference, let's call this claim regarding what must be true of any admirable love relationship, whether human or divine, the *consciousness constraint*.

We have been exploring the question why we should accept premise (1) of the Hiddenness Argument. The pattern of argument that we've uncovered so far is this. Premise (1) of the Hiddenness Argument is implied by the Case from Love. The Case from Love, in turn, rests on premise (i). (i), however, is not a stand-alone assumption. It is, says Schellenberg, implied (when combined with some auxiliary premises) by the consciousness constraint, which is itself a conceptual truth. If this is right, the argument before us has the following distinguishing characteristic: officially, it appeals to claims about what would have to be true of perfect love. But closer inspection reveals that these claims about perfect love are not doing any real work in the argument. For one could replace all instances of the phrase "most perfect love" with "admirable love," and the argument would go through. Properly understood, Schellenberg's charge is that, if God were hidden, then God's love would not be admirable, let alone perfect.

Is this right? Is it true that anything worth calling admirable love between persons is subject to the consciousness constraint? I believe not. Let me illustrate why by offering a modified version of the stranger-in-the-park story I introduced earlier.

Imagine that, on a wintry evening, you have taken in a person who, to the best of your knowledge, is a complete stranger. Imagine, however, that in reality this person is no stranger at all. She is your benefactor. Because she is your benefactor, she has been and is keenly interested in your long-term flourishing. Unbeknownst to you, it was she who had orchestrated your family's escape from Russia some years ago. Your benefactor, however, does not wish to retain perpetual anonymity. She also wishes to pursue a close friendship with you, partly because you are kin. While the benefactor could easily reveal her identity to you on this wintry evening, she conceals it instead, choosing to remain anonymous for present purposes.

This is for two reasons. First, she knows that because there is time for a friendship to develop, there is no special urgency attached to revealing her identity here and now. And, second, she knows that entering into a close friendship with you will, in some respects, be difficult. For the benefactor is dedicated to numerous and demanding benevolent purposes, including working in dangerous conditions to emancipate others from political oppression. Close friendship will require that you work together closely on these projects. In fact, if you do form a close friendship, the benefactor will have to depend on you in significant ways, giving you weighty responsibilities. This, she knows, will not be easy for you, as you are rather attached to your own projects, as trivial as they may be. Given the situation, the benefactor knows that the better tactic at this point is patience. Being patient does not, however, imply remaining idle. In the meanwhile, the benefactor intends to forge bonds of various sorts with you. She will give you numerous opportunities to dedicate yourself to causes that are important to her, although you will be ignorant of their provenance. If you react well and wisely to these opportunities, you are likely to develop the sorts of characteristics and commitments that will promise, in the long run, a close and stable friendship.

Is the benefactor in this story exercising love of an admirable sort? I would think so. She has your best interests in mind. She is, moreover, pursuing, in a patient and resourceful way, a more intimate relationship with you. Finally, by remaining anonymous she does not wrong you, nor has she demeaned you in any fashion. Yet her care for you fails the consciousness constraint. She is not doing whatever she can to ensure that, just by trying, you can have constant conscious awareness of her true identity. That, however, is not a reason for believing that the benefactor fails to love you in an admirable and resourceful way. It is, rather, an excellent reason to believe that the consciousness constraint is, far from being a conceptual truth, not even true. But if it is not, then the case Schellenberg offers for premise (1) of the Hiddenness Argument is defective. The consciousness constraint does not specify a minimum threshold that anything worth calling admirable love must satisfy. It is possible for one's love of another to be altogether admirable and resourceful, while simultaneously failing the consciousness constraint.

3.3. ANOTHER LINE OF THOUGHT

I have presented the official line of argument that Schellenberg offers for the first premise of the Hiddenness Argument, arguing that it rests on a false claim. I suspect, however, that the official line of argument that Schellenberg presents may not be what lies deepest in Schellenberg's thought. In what remains, I would like to offer an alternate interpretation of the consciousness constraint that could be employed to justify the Hiddenness Argument's first premise. I do this with some hesitation, as Schellenberg nowhere explicitly endorses this further line of argument. Still, I think it is a line of argument worth presenting. This is not because I think this argument is better than Schellenberg's official argument. It isn't. Rather, it is because having this line of argument before us should allow us better to see why there is reason to believe that the constraint, even when modified, fails to apply to God.

It did not require a great feat of imagination to produce counterexamples to the consciousness constraint. Given more space, we could easily present others. Nonetheless, Schellenberg is clearly impressed by the constraint. He presents it as if it were an obvious conceptual truth. Why is that? A clue might lie in a passage that I quoted earlier in which Schellenberg claims that the constraint is true of "any admirably loving mother or husband or brother or friend" (202–3; cf. also p. 235). This phrase suggests that Schellenberg thinks of the consciousness constraint as being true not of all admirable love relationships but only of admirable love relationships of a certain range, such as that between a parent and a child under ordinary conditions. And that seems plausible. Under ordinary conditions, admirable intimate relationships of these types are subject to the consciousness constraint.

To appreciate this last point, consider another variant of the stranger-in-the-park story. According to this version of the story, you have an anonymous benefactor. While she could easily reveal her true identity to you, she conceals it instead. However, according to this version of the story, you bear the following special relation to your benefactor: you are her *child*. This version of the story, it might be said, strains the imagination. Unless she had very powerful countervailing reasons to remain anonymous, how could she non-defectively love you and fail to reveal her true identity? It might be claimed, however, that it is this version of the story that more nearly approximates what God's relationship to human beings would have to be like, were God to exist. God's love, it might be said, would have to be akin to that which a parent has toward her child in which there is the constant intended availability of some form of conscious relationship, at least under ordinary conditions. If so, advocates of the Hiddenness Argument needn't defend an unqualified version of the consciousness constraint. They need only defend a qualified version of the consciousness constraint, arguing that it would have to apply to God.[4]

In various places, Schellenberg chastises theists for trimming their conception of God to fit the actual world rather than honestly stating what God would have to be like were God to exist (197–8). There is, however, an equally dangerous tendency to which religious skeptics may fall prey. And that is to

[4] In his response to an earlier version of this chapter, Schellenberg pressed something similar to this line of argument.

engage in overly simple analogical thinking when characterizing divine love, insisting that God's love would, on the whole, have to resemble that of a human parent (or some other form of familial love) under ordinary conditions. This tendency, arguably, is at work in the argument we are considering. But it is a tendency that should be resisted. True enough, in its dogged and unconditional pursuit of our wellbeing, God's love may be like a parent's love for a child under favorable conditions. And certainly scripture presents God's love in this light (think of the story of the prodigal son in this regard). Still, insofar as genuine intimacy with God is contingent upon our aligning our will and purposes with God's, divine love may be rather unlike a parent's love for a child. In some respects, it may be more akin to the sort of care which a visionary philanthropist has for those to whom he has entrusted the day-to-day operations of his foundation, as scripture also suggests (cf. Matt. 18, 20). At any rate, the point is that we cannot assume that features that are typically true of ordinary parent-child relationships (or familial love in general) would also be true of divine-human relationships, as the argument we are considering does.

This last point, in fact, may understate just how radical the gulf is between divine and human love. Let me try to highlight this difference by reflecting on the consciousness constraint for a moment longer. The consciousness constraint, I have suggested, is probably best understood to apply to a certain range of intimate relationships under ordinary conditions. The reason it applies is this: absent the availability of conscious awareness, we typically cannot form or sustain the bonds of union and intimacy in which love between persons consists, as there typically are no other available means by which to form and sustain these bonds. Think, for example, of friendship under ordinary conditions. Imagine that two people have been fast friends for years but that their relationship has recently deteriorated. While the one friend does all she can to keep in contact, the other does not. Perhaps this is because she is no longer invested in the friendship. Or perhaps this is because she is too busy with other matters and will be so for many years. Typically, when something like this happens, the friendship withers and dies; what remains are memories. Given our human condition, this is how things must be.

Contrast this with God's relationship to the world. Christian theists maintain that God bears a relationship to the world of such a kind that the world's beauty and goodness are manifestations of the divine life, and certain actions we perform toward each other count as actions performed toward God. If this were so, then God's relationship to the world is utterly different from ours. The world is not and could not be permeated in the same way by whatever goodness and beauty we might have. Earlier I pointed out that this has the implication that nonresisters could, in principle, be aware of God at all times. The point I wish to make now is that, if Christian theism were true, then there would be ways of being aware of God and God's activities that, in general, are not and could not be ways of being aware of each other and each other's activities.

Take a case in which I am aware of beauty, such as when I listen to a fine performance of Mahler's *Third Symphony*. Upon doing so, I could be reminded of the goodness and beauty of your character. But I would not thereby be presented with your goodness and beauty; the beauty of the symphony is not (and ordinarily could not be) a way in which you disclose your goodness and beauty to me. You do not bear the right sort of relationship to the symphony's beauty for this to be so. Theists claim, by contrast, that the beauty of a performance of Mahler's *Third* is in fact a manifestation of God's goodness and beauty; it is a way in which God discloses God's goodness and beauty to us. It is a commitment to this understanding of God's presence in the world, I take it, that lies at the heart of the sacramental traditions of Christianity. For these traditions maintain that the created order is the primary locus of divine presence and activity—the primary means by which we are presented with the divine energies.

Let me elaborate on this last point. A striking feature of the liturgies of the sacramental traditions, such as those of Eastern Orthodox Christianity, is their emphasis on beauty—beauty in the art displayed, the vestments worn, the movements made, the music sung. One way to think of this emphasis is that it represents an effort on the assembly's part to offer their best to God. (As a child, this is the reason I was given for why we dress up for church.) In fact, however, the emphasis in these traditions falls on not the assembly's efforts but the ways in which God acts via the assembly's actions. The beauty of the visual art produced or the music sung is not something that *accompanies* God's presence and activity in the liturgy, whatever that might be. Rather, it is itself a *manifestation* of God's presence and activity, whether one is aware of it or not. Those with no religious commitments are often drawn to this beauty. (The Irish novelist James Joyce, who was not religious, made it a point to attend the services of Holy Week in the Orthodox Church annually because of their beauty.) The tradition would say that in being so drawn, these people are being drawn to God in such a way that their connection with this beauty can and sometimes does form the basis of a meaningful relationship with God.

With these points in mind, suppose God were not to do everything possible for us to be in a conscious relationship with God at all times. Even if this were so, there would, nonetheless, be untold ways in which God could manifest Godself to us and for us to be aware of God. These manifestations, moreover, could be expressions of divine love, as they could be the means by which God forges and builds bonds of union and intimacy with us, even when we do not recognize them as such. Not only could they be the means by which God forges and builds bonds of union and intimacy, these manifestations could also be *constitutive* of such union and intimacy, even when we do not recognize them as such. Whether they are constitutive of such bonds will depend on how we respond to the goodness, beauty, and need we find in the world.[5] It follows that, even if God were not to do everything possible for us to be in a conscious relationship with God at all times, there could be ample, intimate, and lovely ways of being in relationship with God at those times. In this way, the divine-human relationship would enjoy a multidimensionality and resilience that, in general, is not present in relationships between human persons. It may even be that, as Matthew 25 suggests, what matters most to God is forging and building union and intimacy of this sort. And it may be that the importance of our consciously recognizing the true nature of this union and intimacy is, for God, secondary. However that may be, the upshot is this: the main reason we have to think that the consciousness constraint is true of any case of admirable and intimate human love in ordinary conditions— viz., that typically we have no other available means by which to form and sustain the bonds of union and intimacy—is not a reason to think that the constraint is also true of any admirable and intimate case of divine love for human beings.

Let me summarize. The first premise of the Hiddenness Argument, I have claimed, admits of two readings. The strong reading has it that every non-resister would be in a position to be aware of God as God, while a weak reading implies only that every nonresister would be in a position to be aware of God, although not necessarily as God. Schellenberg maintains that we should accept the strong reading. We have seen that his case for this version of the premise turns on the truth of the consciousness constraint. We have also seen that there are excellent reasons to believe that this constraint is false. There are, however, weaker versions of this constraint that could be used to support a strong reading of premise (1) of the Hiddenness Argument. But a weakened version of the constraint could support such a premise only if God's love were, in the relevant respects, like a human parent's love for his children under normal conditions. This last claim, I have said, should also be rejected, as divine-human love may be subject to demands fundamentally different from ordinary cases of parental love (or familial love in general). Finally, we saw that there is reason to believe that there is an even deeper divide between human and divine love. While there are reasons to believe that the conscious-ness constraint applies to admirable and intimate love relations under ordin-ary conditions, these reasons are absent when it comes to divine love. For, unlike human beings, God has resources available both to express and com-municate God's love and to draw us into and build intimate relationships even when God does not at all times do everything God could for us to recognize God as God. Were a modified understanding of the consciousness constraint

---

[5] A consequence of this way of thinking is that it becomes increasingly difficult to specify what a nonresister is. To the extent that we fail to respond well and wisely to the goodness, beauty, and need we encounter, we are all resisters.

true of divine love, then it would not be for the same reason that it is true of the love we have for each other. There would have to be some other reason.

Let me close by picking up a loose strand of argument. Earlier I pointed out that Schellenberg's official argument for the first premise of the Hiddenness Argument—the Case from Love—does not essentially hinge on the claim that God's love is perfect. Rather, it turns on the consciousness constraint, which identifies a minimum threshold that anything worth calling admirable love must satisfy. The charge that Schellenberg levels is that God's love fails to satisfy this minimum threshold. Suppose, however, an advocate of the Hiddenness Argument were to concede that God's love meets the minimum threshold of admirability. This person could still insist that, if theism were true, God's love would have to be not only admirable but also perfect. And the phenomenon of divine hiddenness, this person might claim, is evidence that God's love is not perfect. For wouldn't it be better—a more fitting expression of love—this person might ask, if God ensured that all nonresisters are in a position vividly to apprehend God's presence as God's presence?

This is a fair question. Let me make one observation in response. Throughout his discussion, Schellenberg repeatedly claims that God could do better than God does (200–3). Given God's power and resourcefulness, God could easily bring it about that there are no (or few) nonbelieving nonresisters. Furthermore, Schellenberg maintains, it is difficult to see how a world in which there are no (or few) nonbelieving nonresisters could fail to be better than the actual world, in which there are lots of them. After all, the constant availability of conscious awareness of God would arguably be the greatest gift that God could grant us. Why, then, the stinginess?

We should, I think, be deeply wary of this style of argument. For there is no straightforward inference from the claim that:

actualizing a state of affairs would be better than actualizing its available alternatives,

to the further claim that:

a failure to actualize this state of affairs would count as a defect in the goodness or the love of a person who could actualize it.

If this were so, we cannot infer from the fact that it would be better that there are no nonresisting nonbelievers the further claim that God's love is somehow deficient—somehow less than perfect. Whether such a failure would count as a defect hangs on the correct answer to deeply contested issues in normative ethics, ones which divide consequentialists from their rivals. It is to these matters, I believe, that further discussion concerning divine love must turn.[6]

[6] Thanks to Dan Howard-Snyder, Steve Layman, and John Schellenberg for their comments on an earlier version of this chapter.

4

Liturgical Immersion

Call that story, central to the Christian tradition, which presents the history of both the ways in which human beings have engaged God and the ways in which God has engaged human beings the *core narrative*.[1] The ancient Christian liturgies engage the core narrative in a striking variety of ways: they retell it, interpret it to explore its meaning, reenact elements of it, celebrate it, and creatively extend it in some surprising ways. It is as if, despite their highly scripted character, these liturgies are restless, determined to explore the core narrative from as many angles as they feasibly can.

An intriguing feature of the Eastern Orthodox liturgies is that the activity of reenacting central elements of the core narrative figures so prominently. When I say that these liturgies reenact elements of the core narrative, I have something fairly specific in mind. I mean that there is a sequence of act-types that is prescribed by the liturgical script—what I call the *liturgical sequence*—and a sequence of event-types that belong to the core narrative—which I call the *narrative sequence*—that bear the following relations to one another: the performance of some segment of the liturgical sequence represents some segment of the narrative sequence because either (i) the former imitates and repeats the latter or (ii) the former, via the use of non-linguistic symbols or props, imitates the latter but does not repeat it. An example of the first type of reenactment would be the actions that compose the eucharistic rite. During this rite, the celebrant performs actions that imitate and repeat a sequence of act-types that the Gospels attribute to Jesus at the Last Supper, which includes

---

[1] There are at least two different ways to understand the ontological status of the core narrative. According to what we can call the *object theory*, the narrative consists in those events reported in scripture and the oral tradition and their properties and relations to one another. According to the *content theory*, the narrative consists in a representation of these events and their properties and relations to one another (where "representation" is not taken to be a success term). The latter view has the advantage of allowing for there being elements of the narrative that do not refer to any actual events or their properties and relations. Given its flexibility, I will think of the core narrative along the lines of the content theory, although I will often speak loosely of the actions and events that compose the core narrative. (I use the term "event" broadly enough so that it can refer to either events that are acts or those that are not.)

taking bread, breaking it, blessing it, distributing it to his followers, and then eating it with them. An example of the second type of reenactment would be the actions that compose the Orthodox service of Holy Friday. In this service, the assembled use props—such as an icon of the entombed Christ and a "tomb" that is constructed, adorned with flowers, and placed in the nave— to perform actions that signify the act-sequence of burying the body of Jesus but without repeating that act-sequence.[2]

Two main questions face anyone wishing to understand liturgical reenact- ment: First, how should we understand its character, what it is that occurs when one competently engages in liturgical reenactment? And, second, what are its purposes, its dominant functions in the context of liturgical action? As should be apparent, these questions are closely related, for there is no neat separation of the descriptive from the normative in liturgical action: to explain what it is, you need to understand what it is for. While these two questions are closely related, it is nonetheless possible to devote the bulk of one's attention to one question rather than the other. In this discussion, I focus on the first question, exploring the second question at more length elsewhere.[3]

Those who have theorized about the ancient Christian liturgies have offered some deeply puzzling accounts of the character of liturgical reenactment. In what follows, I will spend some time engaging with some of these theories, explaining why I find them unsatisfactory. The primary purpose of doing so is to introduce an alternative model, what I call the *immersion model* of liturgical reenactment. This model, I believe, puts us in a much better position to tackle the larger question of what the dominant functions of liturgical reenactment might be.

4.1. LITURGICAL REENACTMENT

The fact that the Orthodox liturgies incorporate liturgical reenactment does not distinguish them from many other Christian liturgies. Nearly all the Christian liturgies that bear any sort of affinity to the ancient liturgies incorp- orate elements of liturgical reenactment to some degree or other. Rather, what sets the Orthodox liturgies apart from so many of these other liturgies is—as I indicated earlier in this chapter—the prominence that they give to the activity of liturgical reenactment. It will be helpful, I think, to begin by giving you a taste of the place of reenactment in the Orthodox liturgies. In doing so,

---

[2] Here I use the term "icon" loosely. Typically, what is used in this service is the epitaphion, which is an oblong piece of cloth on which is painted or embroidered the figure of the dead Christ laid out for burial.

[3] In Cuneo (2015a), included as Chapter 5 of the present volume.

I should note that there is a venerable history of liturgical commentary, and many who have contributed to this project—such as those who operate within the "mystagogical" tradition, including Theodore of Mopsusestia, Maximus the Confessor, and Germanus—work with an extremely permissive account of liturgical reenactment.[4] These thinkers find liturgical reenactment at nearly every turn in the liturgy, interpreting actions of all sorts as signifying actions depicted in the core narrative. I will not be working with anywhere near such a permissive approach.

Let us begin with the obvious cases of reenactment. These would include the services of Holy Week, such as the rite of foot washing, which is celebrated by many Orthodox on Holy Thursday, and the burial of Christ, which is celebrated the day thereafter, on Holy Friday. In the first rite, by washing the feet of the parishioners or the deacons, the celebrant reenacts the biblical story in which Jesus washes the feet of his disciples. The hymnody leaves no question about the rite's significance: "Humbling yourself in your compassion, you have washed the feet of your disciples, teaching them to take the path that you have followed."[5] In the second rite, by the employment of a series of props, the assembled reenact the burial of Christ. The reenactment typically involves a deacon or priest reading the Gospel account of Jesus's burial ("and taking the body, Joseph wrapped it in a white cloth") while the Priest removes a wooden corpus of Christ from a replica of the cross, wrapping it in a white cloth. The priest then chants a mourning hymn: "Down from the tree Joseph of Arimathea took you dead, who is the life of all, and wrapped you . . . in a linen cloth with spices."[6] Once again, in this case, there is no ambiguity concerning the significance of the liturgical acts performed. It is interesting to note, though, that the cases of reenactment just mentioned incorporate elements not found in the biblical narrative, creatively extending it in certain directions. At various points, for example, the people sing hymns from the perspective of Joseph: "How shall I bury you, O my God? How can I wrap you in a shroud? . . . What songs can I sing for your exodus, O Compassionate One?"[7] At other points, the people sing hymns from the perspective of Mary Theotokos, who is present at the burial, lamenting: "In my arms I hold you as a corpse. . . . I long to die with you . . . for I cannot bear to look upon you lifeless and without breath. . . . Where are you going now, my son? Have you left me here alone?"[8] In these passages, the liturgical script invites the participants to take up something like Joseph of Arimathea's and Mary's first-person perspectives on Jesus's death and burial.

---

[4] These commentaries date from the fifth, seventh, and eighth centuries, respectively.

[5] And: "let us remain at the Master's side, that we may see how he washes the feet of the disciples and wipes them with a towel; and let us do as we have seen, subjecting ourselves to each other and washing one another's feet" (Mary and Ware [2002]), 550, 552. I have modernized the English used in the translation. In what follows, I will refer to this work as *LT*.

[6] *LT*, 614.   [7] *LT*, 615.   [8] *LT*, 619, 620.

Other liturgical actions lack the overtly dramatic elements of the rite of foot washing and the burial of Jesus but are plausibly viewed as cases of liturgical reenactment nonetheless. These would include the eucharistic rite in which the celebrant performs the act-sequence that the Gospels attribute to Jesus at the Last Supper of taking bread, breaking it, blessing it, distributing it to his disciples, and eating it together. They would also include—somewhat more controversially—the baptismal rite, which is said to be "after the pattern" of Christ's burial and resurrection.[9] Arguably, however, some of the more interesting cases of reenactment are more subtle and interspersed throughout the liturgy. Some of these are actions performed by the celebrant. At various points during the liturgy, for example, the priest turns from facing the altar, moves toward the assembled, and blesses them with Jesus's words to the disciples gathered together in the upper room: "Peace be with you" (Luke 24: 36; John 20: 19). The Gospels report that, immediately after uttering this blessing, Jesus "breathed on them and said, 'Receive the Holy Spirit.'" Anyone who has witnessed the Orthodox baptismal rite and knows of its pneumatological dimensions will recognize that this is exactly the act-type that the priest performs with regard to the one to be baptized: he breathes on him or her three times, making the sign of the cross with his actions.

Other examples of reenactment—also not decisively clear cases but suggestive nonetheless—are actions performed not by the priest but by the assembled. During the procession of the eucharistic gifts, for example, the assembled will often reach out to touch the hem of the priest's vestments, just as the woman with a hemorrhage is said to have touched Jesus's garments (Matt. 9: 20–2; Mark 5: 25–35; Luke 8: 43–8).[10] Moreover, it is customary for those entering the nave to venerate the icon of Jesus by kissing it, imitating the action, which the tradition attributes to Mary of Bethany, of kissing Jesus's body (Luke 7: 38; John 12: 1–8).[11] Interestingly, on Wednesday of Holy Week, the hymnody explicitly identifies the actions of the assembled with Mary's, taking poetic liberties with the biblical text: "I will kiss your most pure feet and wipe them with the hairs of my head, those feet whose sound Eve heard at

---

[9] *Service Book of the Holy Eastern Orthodox Catholic and Apostolic Church according to the use of the Antiochian Orthodox Christian Archdiocese of North America* (2002), 156. See also, Gregory of Nazianzus's comments on baptism in his *Festal Orations* (2008), 125. There is an interesting question of the role that intentions play in liturgical reenactment. If some act-sequence counts as a liturgical reenactment, must it be inserted in the liturgy with the intention that it function as a reenactment? Although I won't defend the point, I am assuming that it needn't.

[10] Interestingly, the Lenten prayers also refer to the event: "O wretched soul, do as the woman with an issue of blood: run quickly, grasp the hem of the garment of Christ; so shall you be healed of your afflictions and hear Him say, 'Your faith has saved you'" (*LT*, 396).

[11] For a discussion of the matter, see Stump (2010), ch. 12. Although the liturgical script simply refers to this woman as "the woman who had sinned," I'll refer to her as Mary of Bethany for ease of reference.

dusk in Paradise."[12] Finally, the phrase of repentance issued by the Publican in Jesus's story of the Publican and the Pharisee (Luke 18: 9–14) is repeated over and over in the liturgy when the assembled respond to the petitions with their "kyrie eleison." On the Sunday of the Pharisee and the Publican, the church's hymnody draws the connection between this phrase and the biblical story: "In days of old, humility exalted the Publican who cried aloud lamenting 'Be merciful,' and he was justified. Let us follow his example, for we have fallen down into the depths of evil. Let us cry to the Saviour from the depths of our hearts: We have sinned, be merciful, O you alone who loves humankind."[13]

4.2. HOW SHOULD WE UNDERSTAND REENACTMENT?

If our primary project were the descriptive one of illustrating the extent to which the Orthodox liturgies incorporate reenactment, there are a good many other examples to which we could appeal. Let us, however, move from the level of description to the level of interpretation in which we address the question of how to understand the character of these reenactments. To do so, unfortunately, is immediately to leave *terra firma* and step into a philosophical void, for philosophers have had next to nothing to say about the issue of ritual reenactment. Indeed, I am aware of only one essay that addresses the topic: Nicholas Wolterstorff's "Remembrance of Things (Not) Past." As it happens, this is an excellent place to start, so let's begin our exploration with Wolterstorff's discussion.[14]

Wolterstorff frames his wide-ranging essay by presenting and rejecting two accounts of the character of liturgical reenactment.[15] The first account, which I'll call the *anamnetic theory*, takes several forms, but its guiding idea is that by reenacting in the liturgy event-types that belong to the core narrative, the events belonging to the core narrative are made present to those assembled at the liturgy.[16] In the hands of the influential anthropologist of religion Mircea Eliade, the view tells us that by engaging in ritual events, those who perform them take themselves to enter into a different time frame—so-called sacred time—in which these events originally occurred. Moreover, when they so enter, they understand their performance of these ritual events to actualize

---

[12] *LT*, 540.   [13] *LT*, 103.   [14] Wolterstorff (1990).

[15] These are not the only two views that Wolterstorff considers, but they are the ones on which he focuses.

[16] Literally rendered, the Greek term "anamnesis" (ἀνάμνησις) means *memorial*. But as numerous liturgical commentators point out, the term expresses the idea of a memorial—a remembering—that makes what is remembered present. It is this last idea of making present that I am picking up in my use of the term "anamnesis."

the events they appear to be reenacting.[17] By contrast, in the hands of Church Fathers such as Cyril of Jerusalem, Gregory of Nazianzus, and Theodore of Mopsuestia—at least under a certain reading—the performance of some segment of the liturgical sequence somehow makes mystically present to those assembled at the liturgy the corresponding events that belong to the narrative sequence. It is as if, under this view, event-tokens are the sorts of things that can be conjured from the past (or, in the case of Theodore, the future) by repeating the types under which they fall.[18]

The second view that Wolterstorff considers, what he labels the *dramatic representation theory*, is much less exotic. At the heart of this view is the claim that by performing some segment of the liturgical sequence, the assembled reenact a corresponding segment of the narrative sequence. They do so, moreover, by *playing the roles* of those agents who act in the core narrative. No entrance into sacred time, no mystically making present what is past; rather, liturgical reenactment consists in the dramatic performance of event-types of the same sort that compose the core narrative.

Neither of these views, Wolterstorff maintains, is satisfactory. Begin with the anamnetic theory and, in particular, Eliade's version of it. This position, Wolterstorff charges, is oddly imperceptive. When Eliade develops his theory, he does so with the aim of providing an account of the character not of liturgical reenactment in particular but of religious ritual reenactment in general. And, at a certain point, he indicates that his theory applies to the Christian liturgy, since the liturgy retains elements of the mentality characteristic of "archaic" ritual.[19] But even a moment's reflection reveals that Eliade's account of ritual reenactment does not apply to the Christian liturgy. For, according to the Christian tradition, the sequence of event-types that compose the core narrative occurs not in some other temporal dimension—so-called sacred time—but in the same temporal dimension that you and I presently occupy. Hence the oddly imperceptive character of Eliade's interpretation; it fails to take into account the historically embedded character of the core Christian narrative.

In principle, Eliade's account could be modified to allow for the fact that, according to the Christian tradition, the core narrative occurs not in sacred time but in the same time frame that you and I occupy. However, if Eliade's account were so modified, Wolterstorff charges, the view would be fantastic. For Eliade's theory implies that the performance of the liturgical sequence actualizes the corresponding segments of the narrative sequence; strictly

---

[17] Wolterstorff (1990), 125, 129. In his discussion, Wolterstorff distinguishes two readings of Eliade. I am working with the second interpretation that Wolterstorff identifies, the "actualization" interpretation.

[18] See, for example, Finn (1976) and Harrison (2008). The figure who seems to be chiefly responsible for propagating this reading of the Church Fathers is Odo Casel; see Casel (1962).

[19] Wolterstorff (1990), 127.

speaking, then, in Eliade's view, there is no liturgical reenactment, as the performance of those act-tokens that compose the liturgical sequence is numerically identical with the occurrence of those act-tokens that compose the narrative sequence. If it were correct, Eliade's theory would imply (among other things) that the Christian tradition takes those who participate in liturgical reenactment to engage in time travel, transporting themselves to those times at which events of the core narrative occurred, such as that time at which the Last Supper took place. By all appearances, however, this is not so. The tradition does not hold that when engaging in liturgical reenactment, the assembled engage in time travel.[20]

Wolterstorff has little to say about the second version of the anemnetic theory, despite its presence within the Christian tradition itself. Since the view may be even less familiar than Eliade's, let me quote a recent elaboration of it, in which the view is attributed to Gregory of Nazianzus:

> Anamnesis means re-presentation of God's saving works so that the worshipers can participate in these events as present realities and thereby receive the eschatological salvation, new life and sanctification divinely accomplished through them. Anamnesis thus unites past, present and future in a single present event of worship.

If this is so,

> Anamnesis is historical but is not primarily looking back to the past. Festal celebration is not nostalgia, it is not a commemoration of what once took place but is now present only as a memory, a mere mental phenomenon that the worshipers work to reinforce in order to preserve it from oblivion. Rather, anamnesis is an encounter in the present with the Lord who transfigures and transcends history...it is important to note that the saving *events* are made present in their liturgical celebration, not only the persons who once participated in those events.... Since God's saving actions transcend the limitations of temporal sequence, the historical events in which God has acted can be present now and in the future.... In festal celebration the boundaries of sequential time are transcended as the original saving events and the present experience of the congregation join together. The past events of Christ's incarnate life and the Spirit's descent, the present experience of the Christian community, and the future participation in God's kingdom are made one.[21]

Under a natural reading, the view is not that liturgical reenactment renders past events present in the way that, say, film footage of the Normandy Invasion makes that historical event present to viewers here and now. Rather, the position seems to be that, in liturgical reenactment, something extraordinarily unusual takes place: the ordinary temporal divisions between past,

---

[20] Wolterstorff (1990), 129.   [21] Harrison (2008), 24–5.

present, and future no longer hold; liturgical reenactment somehow binds together all three temporal dimensions in one time frame.

Given what Wolterstorff says about Eliade's position, it is not difficult to discern what he would say about this second version of the anamnetic theory. For one thing, rather than feel like an explication of the tradition's understanding of what occurs in liturgical reenactment—and what various figures such as Nazianzus have said about such reenactment—it feels more like interpolation. When N. V. Harrison, for example, attributes the anamnetic theory to Nazianzus, she cites passages in which Nazianzus writes such things as:

> Christ is born, give glory; Christ is from the heavens, go to meet him.

And:

> Today salvation has come to the world, to things visible and to things invisible. Christ is risen from the dead; rise with him.[22]

But liturgical data of this sort radically underdetermine the anamnetic interpretation of liturgical reenactment. There is just no way to squeeze the theory's understanding of liturgical reenactment out of pronouncements such as these, evocative as they may be.

The deeper worry about the view, however, is this: there might be models of time and our relation to it that render the anamnetic theory coherent. For example, it might be coherent to claim that, in liturgical reenactment, we enter some other temporal dimension, "liturgical hyper-time," in which we can simultaneously experience past, present, and future events of ordinary time. But it is one thing to say that such models are coherent; it is another thing altogether to maintain that, when engaging in liturgical reenactment, participants in the liturgy regularly enter into such a temporal dimension.[23] This proposal, like Eliade's position, is extravagant.

When compared to the anamnetic theory, the dramatic representation theory looks pedestrian. Even so, Wolterstorff finds the view no more compelling than the anamnetic theory, albeit for different reasons. One concern, says Wolterstorff, is that when one actually looks at the liturgical scripts of the ancient liturgies, they do not conform to the theory's account of their character. Consider, for example, the eucharistic rite. Proponents of the dramatic representation theory would be correct in their observation that, in the ancient

---

[22] Harrison (2008), 25. See also Mantzaridis (1996).

[23] This is not to deny that the Christian tradition has advocated claims regarding the eucharistic rite, such as the doctrine of transubstantiation, that also appear fantastic. Regardless of what one thinks of such doctrines, they seem to belong to a different category, as they are the attempt to work out a deep commitment of the church, namely, that the bread and wine used in the eucharist rite become the body and blood of Christ. That liturgical reenactment makes event-tokens of the core narrative present, by contrast, does not have this sort of pedigree; it can hardly be considered part of the tradition's self-understanding.

Christian traditions, the priest not only represents Christ but also quotes Christ's words in this rite, saying such things as "This is my body which is broken for you" and "Do this in remembrance of me." But, Wolterstorff maintains, this would not imply that the priest *plays the role* of Christ in the eucharist rite. To represent a figure and to quote what he has said needn't be to play the role of his saying it.

To this first point, Wolterstorff adds a second, which is worth quoting. The theory, Wolterstorff writes, "feels all wrong":

> [the] celebrant actually blesses; he does not play the role of Christ blessing. We actually give thanks; we do not play the role of the disciples giving thanks. What matters is that the celebrant actually gives bread and wine, not that he plays the role of Christ long ago giving bread and wine to his disciples. What matters is that we actually eat the bread and drink the wine, not that we play the role of the disciples long ago eating the bread and drinking the wine distributed to them by Christ. The dramatic representation theory displaces the focus from the actuality of what is presently taking place.[24]

While I find the objections that Wolterstorff presses against the anamnetic theory decisive, I find neither of the reasons offered against the dramatic representation theory persuasive, at least in their present form. Let me explain why, since doing so will help to throw into sharper relief the model I wish to defend.

Begin with the first objection. When one takes account of the full range of rites performed in the Orthodox liturgies, which includes not simply the eucharistic rite but also the rites of foot washing and the burial of Christ, it is, I submit, difficult *not* to be struck by the fact that they bear the marks of being dramatic reenactments of events that compose the core narrative, segments of the narrative sequence. Interestingly, many of the early liturgical commentators agree. Earlier I mentioned that Theodore of Mopsuestia is sometimes presented as an advocate of the anamnetic theory. But the case for his being a proponent of the dramatic representation theory is, arguably, more impressive. Commenting on the eucharistic rite, Theodore writes:

> The duty of the High Priest of the New Covenant (i.e., Jesus) is to offer this sacrifice which revealed the nature of the New Covenant. We ought to believe that the bishop who is now at the altar is playing the part of this High Priest.[25]

Concerning the Great Entrance in which the Gospel is brought to the altar, Theodore says: "By means of the signs we must see Christ now being led away to His passion . . . you must imagine that Christ our Lord is being led out to His passion."[26] And regarding the baptismal rite, Cyril of Jerusalem maintains:

---

[24] Wolterstorff (1990), 146.   [25] Quoted in Meyendorff (1984), 29.
[26] Quoted in Meyendorff (1984), 31.

"You . . . submerged yourselves three times in the water and emerged: by this gesture you were secretly re-enacting the burial of Christ's three days in the tomb."[27] By quoting these passages, I am not suggesting that their interpretations of liturgical reenactment are correct or normative. I wish only to advance the point that these thinkers found something like the dramatic representation theory, with its emphasis on role-playing, to be the natural interpretation of important elements of the liturgy.

Why would one disagree? Here is a diagnosis: when Wolterstorff offers his reasons for holding that the eucharistic rite is not a dramatic reenactment, he focuses almost exclusively on the acts of speech performed in this rite. In the context of the liturgy, to perform the same speech act-types as Jesus, Wolterstorff points out, is not perforce to play the role of Jesus performing those speech act-types. Suppose, though, we were to focus our attention not on the verbal actions performed in the rite but on the non-verbal ones. Were we to do so, I submit, the dramatic representation theory would begin to look considerably more attractive. For, as we noted earlier, the rite consists in the celebrant performing the same act-type sequence that the Gospels report Jesus as having performed, namely: taking bread, blessing it, breaking it, distributing it, and eating it with his followers.[28] This last observation, admittedly, hardly vindicates the dramatic representation theory, but it should give its opponents pause; any case against the view has to consider carefully the character of the non-verbal actions performed in the liturgy.

Let's now turn to the second objection that Wolterstorff offers against the dramatic representation theory, which is contained in the longer passage I quoted a few paragraphs back. As I read it, this objection contains two sub-arguments. Let me postpone engaging with the first sub-argument and consider the second, which is that if role-playing were central to participating in the liturgy, it would displace "the focus from the actuality of what is presently taking place." The idea seems to be that by directing our attention to role-playing, the theory offers us a distorted depiction of what is going on in the performance of the liturgical rite. What is fundamental to the performance of the rite is not playing the role of blessing but actually blessing, not playing the role of thanking but actually thanking, and so on.

I doubt, however, that the dramatic representation theory displaces, obstructs, or overshadows what actually takes place in the performance of liturgical action. At least it needn't. By drawing our attention to the fact that the celebrant plays the role of Jesus in the rite of foot washing, the theory needn't obstruct or distort the significance of what is happening in the rite, namely, that the celebrant is expressing Christ-like humility in washing others'

---

[27] Quoted in Meyendorff (1984), 34.
[28] Wolterstorff is aware of the point; see Wolterstorff (1990), 151. But I am not sure why he does not bring the point to bear upon his treatment of the dramatic representation theory.

feet and setting an example for the rest of us. In fact, in this case, I suspect that the opposite is true. If a model of liturgical reenactment were to disassociate the celebrant's actions from those that Jesus performed when he washed the disciples' feet, then it would genuinely displace or obstruct appreciation of the actuality of what takes place. It is precisely because the dramatic representation theory draws our attention to the fact that the celebrant, by imitating Jesus's actions, plays the role of Jesus that we can better appreciate the rite's significance, and what it is to express humility.

The dramatic representation theory, then, seems to me not vulnerable to the objections that we've been considering. Nonetheless, I do not think that we should accept it, for I share Wolterstorff's underlying suspicion about its adequacy. The problem with the dramatic representation theory, I believe, is not that it somehow displaces, obstructs, or overshadows what actually takes place in the performance of liturgical action. Rather, it is that the theory is insufficiently illuminating. For what we ultimately want from a model of liturgical reenactment is an account of its dominant functions—what it is for. The dramatic representation theory, however, does not give us any sense of why role-playing is especially important or apt in the liturgical context. If, for example, the point of liturgical activity is to do such things as bless and give thanks, the dramatic representation theory owes us an explanation of what it is about role-playing that helps us do these things.[29] It provides no such explanation.

4.3. THE IMMERSION MODEL

In the last section, we considered two theories of liturgical reenactment: the anamnetic theory and the dramatic representation theory. By engaging with Wolterstorff's treatment of these views, we found that there is ample reason to reject the first view: it is, among other things, extravagant. We also saw that the second position is not so much clearly wrongheaded as incomplete; we need more from an adequate model of liturgical reenactment. One of the lessons that emerged from our discussion, I believe, is that given the diversity of types

---

[29] In his essay, Wolterstorff focuses on the liturgical activity of commemorating, recommending what he calls *the imitation/repetition interpretation,* according to which commemorative liturgical reenactment is a matter of not playing roles but imitating the behavior represented in the core narrative by repeating the act-types performed in that narrative (Wolterstorff [1990], 150–2). If the imitation/repetition interpretation were offered as a general model for understanding liturgical reenactment, I think it would be vulnerable to the same type of worries just raised regarding the dramatic representation theory. Imitation can, after all, be used to many different ends. To be satisfactory, the model would have to give us insight into why, in the context of liturgical action, imitation is so important.

of liturgical reenactment, we should probably be wary of trying to identify a single model that covers all cases of the phenomenon. Some models might be suited to explain some cases; other models others. Still, we're looking for models that smoothly accommodate a wide range of liturgical data and are supple enough to incorporate the best insights and commitments of rival models. At this point, we're in search of such a model.

It might be worth stepping back for a moment to identify what we want from a satisfactory model of liturgical reenactment. I think any such model will have at least three characteristics. In the first place, it will be both sensitive to the diversity of liturgical actions and fit the liturgical data, not distorting what the model is trying to accommodate and explain. Unlike Eliade's theory, then, it won't impose an interpretation on the liturgical data that is incompatible with core commitments of the Christian tradition, such as the claim that important elements of the narrative sequence occur not in sacred time but in ordinary history.

Second, any such model will not simply describe what participants are doing—or what they think they are doing—when engaging in liturgical reenactment. Much of what we actually do—and think we are doing—when participating in the liturgy is, after all, defective, the expression of false or inapt views about the significance, value, or role of liturgical action.[30] Nor will such a model simply reiterate what the liturgical script says about the character of such reenactment, since the liturgical script is typically silent on this matter. Rather, an adequate model will identify those ways of engaging in liturgical reenactment that the liturgical script *calls for*. Admittedly, it is not easy to specify precisely what this "calls for" relation is, but actors and musicians are familiar with it. Scripts and scores prescribe actions. But there are more or less fitting ways to perform these actions, ways of acting about which scripts and scores say little or nothing. Given a script or score, good actors and good musicians will not simply identify the actions prescribed by that script or score but also interpret that script or score in such a way as to identify fitting or apt ways of performing those actions. A good model of liturgical reenactment, then, will be one that identifies the sorts of attitudes and behaviors called for by the liturgical script—with this qualification: the attitudes and behaviors called for are those of competent participants in the liturgy, these being those who are sufficiently familiar with the performance-plan of the liturgy and the character of the core narrative. In what follows, I'll assume this qualification to be understood.

Finally, a good model will identify what the purposes might be of engaging in liturgical reenactment. That is, it will identify why it is that imaginative engagement of the sort that the liturgical script calls for is important for the

---

[30] On this matter, see Schmemann's comments on liturgical piety in Schmemann (1966).

ethically and religiously committed life—what it is supposed to accomplish. Unlike the dramatic representation theory, then, a satisfactory model will illuminate why liturgical reenactment takes the form it does.

In this section, I introduce what I believe is a promising model of liturgical reenactment. As will be apparent, this model, which I referred to earlier as the *immersion model*, has affinities with but is not simply a variant of the dramatic representation theory. Let me introduce the immersion model somewhat indirectly by returning to Wolterstorff's discussion of role-playing in the liturgy. My point in doing so is to identify an important element of the liturgical data that a good model of liturgical reenactment should accommodate. Once we have identified this element, we will be in a better position to appreciate the attractions of the immersion model.

Recall that Wolterstorff raises the concern that, given its emphasis on role-playing, the dramatic representation theory misrepresents the character of liturgical action. In liturgical reenactment, the priest does not play the role of someone who blesses; he actually blesses; the people do not play the role of those who thank; they actually thank. And so forth.[31] While there is something to this worry, it is important to recognize that roles come in different varieties.

One sort of role—the type on which Wolterstorff seems to have his eye—is a *pretense role*. In occupying a pretense role, one pretends to act or be some way; one "plays the part" in the sense of pretending to act or be some way. Another sort of role, of a rather different sort, is what I shall call a *target role*. When one assumes a target role, one acts the part of being some way for the purpose of *being that way*, becoming like or identifying with that which one imitates. One doesn't pretend to be that way; rather, in acting in that way, one thereby aspires to be that way.[32] My own view is that pretense roles have almost no place in the liturgy (despite what commentators such as Theodore of Mopsuestia seem to suggest in places). The scripts of the eucharistic rite and the rite of foot washing, for example, do not call for the activity of pretending to be a disciple at the Last Supper. Nor, for that matter, does the performance-plan of the liturgy call for the activity, when venerating the icons of Christ, of pretending to be Mary of Bethany. Any such interpretation of the liturgical performance-plan strikes me as forced, requiring of those assembled at the

---

[31] Under a natural reading, Wolterstorff seems to rely on the principle that if one plays the role of one who Xs, in playing that role one does not thereby X. Applied to the case at hand, the claim seems to be that if, in the liturgy, the priest plays the role of being one who blesses, he does not actually bless. The principle just enunciated, however, is false—and it is false no matter how one thinks of roles. Suppose, in a dramatic reenactment, I pretend to be someone who amuses others, playing the role of a comedian. That's compatible with my being such that, in virtue of playing that role, I actually amuse others.

[32] As I am thinking of them, target roles come cheaply. I assume that when one identifies with a character by imitating her in one's own actions for the purpose of being like her—"playing the part"—one thereby assumes a target role. Nothing more is needed.

liturgy to engage in rather extraordinary feats of imagination, the success of which threatens to distract from the actuality of what is taking place. Participation in the liturgy shouldn't require the skills of an expert Shakespearean actor![33]

By contrast, that the liturgical script invites those participating in the liturgy to assume target roles is, I believe, apparent in the script itself. Consider, for example, just a sample of texts from the services in Holy Week. The script from the Monday of Holy Week has the assembled sing:

> When the Lord was going to his voluntary passion, he said to the Apostles on the way, "Behold, we go up to Jerusalem, and the Son of Man shall be delivered up, as it is written of him." Come, then, let us also go with him, purified in mind. Let us be crucified with him and die for his sake to the pleasures of this life.[34]

On the Sunday of the Publican and the Pharisee, the people sing:

> In our prayer let us fall down before God, with tears and fervent cries of sorrow, emulating the Publican in the humility which lifted him on high.... Let us make haste to follow the Pharisee in his virtues and to emulate the Publican in his humility.[35]

In some places, the script does not so much exhort the assembled to assume a target role as direct the people then and there to assume such a role, such as that of the Prodigal Son:

> As the Prodigal Son I come to you, merciful Lord. I have wasted my whole life in a foreign land.... With the words of the Prodigal I cry aloud: I have sinned, O Father; like him, receive me now in your embrace.[36]

Or the righteous thief:

> But we, imitating the righteous thief, cry out in faith: Remember us also, O Savior, in your kingdom.[37]

And, as we saw earlier with the cases of Joseph of Arimathea and Mary Theotokos, sometimes the script has the assembled take up something like the first-person perspective of one or another character in the core narrative, such as that of Adam:

> In my wretchedness I have cast off the robe woven by God, disobeying your divine command, O Lord, at the counsel of the enemy; and I am clothed now in fig leaves and in garments of skin.[38]

---

[33] There are other reasons to resist the suggestion that the liturgical script calls for the activity of assuming pretense roles, which I canvass in Cuneo (2015a). This essay is included as Chapter 5 in the present volume.

[34] *LT*, 514.   [35] *LT*, 107, 105.   [36] *LT*, 113, 116.

[37] *LT*, 589.   [38] *LT*, 168.

And Jesus:

> I who am rich in Godhead have come to minister to Adam who is grown poor.
> I who fashioned him have of my own will put on his form. I . . . have come to lay
> down my life as a ransom for him.[39]

A good model of liturgical reenactment, I believe, needs to take these texts into
account. It needs, moreover, to recognize that the liturgical script appears to
call for from those assembled a type of imaginative engagement with the core
narrative in which, when engaging in liturgical reenactment, they assume
target roles of various sorts. But—to say it again—it seems to me that the
model ought not to interpret the liturgical script so that it calls for behavior of
such a kind that, when the assembled engage in activities such as the rite of
foot washing, the burial of Jesus, the eucharistic rite, or the uttering of the
words of the Righteous Thief, they thereby pretend to be characters such as
Joseph of Arimathea or pretend to be present as their ordinary selves at the
events that these rites reenact. But if this is so, what other options are
available? What sort of imaginative engagement with the core narrative
could the script be calling for?

Let us look for analogues. A helpful analogue, I believe, is the activity of
reading. More exactly, a helpful analogue is the activity of reading works that
present narratives—what I'll call "narrative-works." The reason this makes for
a good analogue is that often narrative-works call for the activity of immersing
oneself in the narrative presented in a work. Or to look at the same phenomenon from the opposite angle, they often call for the activity of allowing
oneself to be *absorbed by* the narrative of a work.[40] But the activity called for
needn't involve anything like pretending to be a character in the work or
pretending to be present in one's own person at the events described in the
work. The territory we are exploring is imaginative engagement without
pretense.

Let's call immersion of this sort *non-fictive immersion*. (I use the modifier
"non-fictive" to distinguish it from fictive immersion, which would be immersing oneself in a work by pretending to be a character of the work or to be
present in one's own person at the events represented in that work.) And let's
specify more exactly what is it to engage in non-fictive immersion, at least
when reading narrative-works. In the first place, it means attending to the
content of the narrative of the work—what it is communicating—and properties of that content—such as how its various elements hang together—while

---

[39] *LT*, 513.

[40] In what follows, I've been helped by Liao (n.d.) and Harris (2000), but the view I sketch
differs from theirs in some important ways. Stephen Grimm has pointed out to me that the
philosopher of science Peter Lipton also works with the concept of immersion to explain his own
engagement with the Jewish liturgies. See Lipton (2007).

not attending to features of the presentation of the narrative, such as the author's word choice or use of certain grammatical constructions. Or to put this point about attending somewhat more guardedly: we all have the capacity to rapidly direct our attention to rather different aspects of any given situation that we may occupy, first attending to this and then attending to that. The sort of attention required in non-fictive immersion is that of prioritizing the content of a narrative in such a way that, when one directs one's attention to features of its presentation, it is for the purpose of better attending to the content of the narrative itself. So, when reading, for example, one can momentarily marvel at the use of an unusual metaphor, asking oneself why the author would use it in this context. But the point in doing so is to better engage with the content of the work in which the metaphor is being used. If this is right, non-fictive immersion is compatible with one's attention floating between the content of a narrative and features of its presentation, provided that attention to the former assumes a certain kind of priority. Or so I say initially; in a moment, I will add an important qualification.

If this is so, non-fictive immersion involves "screening off" certain features of the presentation of a work. The screening-off might, however, involve more than simply not attending to these features. Depending on the character of the narrative, it might also require bracketing or suspending doubts, questions, or incredulity regarding one or another feature of the narrative itself, these all being the sorts of considerations that can divert one's attention from the content of the narrative presented by the work. Still, non-fictive immersion is more than just attending to the content of a work in such a way that one screens off certain features of its presentation and properties of the narrative itself. It is also to take up a certain kind of vantage point with regard to the narrative presented by the work.

It is difficult to capture this phenomenon of taking up a vantage point, but the idea is that when non-fictively immersing oneself in the narrative of a work, one imaginatively enters the narrative of the work by situating oneself within it.[41] In taking up such a vantage point, one does not take oneself to be a character in the work or to be present in one's own person at the events described in the work; nonetheless there is a sense in which one is "inside" it. Its characters and events loom large in one's consciousness, and one becomes emotionally engaged to some significant degree with these characters and events. In a wide range of cases, taking up the vantage point of not a spectator or a critic but of one inside a work who is emotionally engaged with it is called for by the work itself. For, as Noël Carroll points out, in the typical case, the characters and events in narratives are not merely described. Rather, the narratives themselves are typically emotionally colored, as an evaluative stance

---

[41] Harris (2000) offers some interesting empirical data that supports this way of thinking about immersion.

toward their characters and events is built into how they are described.[42]
When, for example, the Gospels present the event of Mary of Bethany's
washing Jesus's feet with her tears, her actions are presented admiringly, in a
way intended to call forth admiration from the audience. To be immersed in
this narrative is to allow one's emotional response to be shaped by these
features of its presentation. Indeed, it might be that to understand the story
properly, to genuinely grasp its import, more is required than that one allow
one's emotional response to be shaped by the narrative. For, arguably, understanding a narrative such as this one requires that one's emotions already be
mobilized while immersing oneself in that narrative; it requires that one
positively construe Mary's action as at once bold, beautiful, and bracing. If
this is right, experiencing the emotions that a narrative calls for would be
constitutive of understanding that narrative itself.

Participating in liturgical reenactment, I realize, is not to engage in the
activity of reading a narrative-work. It is, rather, to insert oneself into a
complex sequence of scripted action performance. In its use of various sensory
modalities and bodily movement, it is more similar to both dramatic performance and the observation of such performance. (Perhaps it is most similar to
audience-participation dramatic performance.) Still, I trust that the analogy
with reading that I have presented helps us to see the structure of what I am
calling the immersion model of liturgical reenactment.

According to the immersion model, liturgical reenactment involves non-
fictive immersion. When one participates in the rite of washing feet, for
example, the script calls for a great deal of imaginative activity. One does
not approach the rite as an observer or a cultural critic but as a participant.
But—to say it again—the activity called for is not that of pretending to be a
disciple present at the rite or pretending to be present at the rite in one's own
person. Rather, what the script calls for is that those assembled attend to and
take up a vantage point within the core narrative, screening-off various
features of the presentation of this narrative and sometimes certain features
of the narrative itself. Or, to state the phenomenon from the opposite angle,
what the script calls for is that those assembled allow themselves to be
absorbed by those elements of the core narrative presented by the performance
of liturgical action, taking up a vantage point within them.[43] Needless to say,
imaginative engagement of this sort does not come intuitively for many.

---

[42] See Carroll (2001a), 281–4 and (2011a), 376.

[43] The view I am presenting, then, differs significantly from "simulationist" proposals in the
aesthetics literature that attempt to understand immersion in terms of taking up the perspective
of the characters in a narrative. In my view, while simulation of this sort might have a limited role
to play—such as when the liturgical script invites us to see things from the perspective of a
character such as Joseph of Arimathea or Mary Theotokos—we ought not to understand the
phenomenon of immersion in terms of it. For a development of the simulationist view, see Currie
(1994).

Participating in liturgical reenactment is as much about training and conditioning as it is about competent engagement.

As I noted a moment ago, the disanalogies between immersing oneself in liturgical reenactment and immersing oneself in reading narrative-works are important. Perhaps the most obvious disanalogy is that immersing oneself in liturgical reenactment typically involves using one's body in certain ways, responding to the bodily movements of others, and engaging with symbols and props of various sorts. One sings, kisses, eats, touches, and bows, and does so not only when responding to the actions of others but also when engaging with icons, replicas of the cross, water, candles, and the like. Because of this, the sort of attention that is required in liturgical reenactment is, I would say, of a different character than that required in reading narrative-works. Let me elaborate.

Some cases of liturgical engagement are such that, by the performance of actions of various sorts, elements of the core narrative are presented to those assembled. For example, in the eucharistic rite, the celebrant's actions present that segment of the core narrative that consists in Jesus's eating with his disciples. And, in the rite of foot washing, the celebrant's actions present that segment of the core narrative that consists in Jesus's washing the feet of his disciples. In other cases, elements of the core narrative are not presented to those assembled. Rather, the reenactment is simply a matter of engaging in actions whereby one immerses oneself in the core narrative. So, for example, when someone kisses the icon of Christ, she does not respond to an element of the core narrative that is presented to her by the icon or the actions of the priest. Rather, she simply enacts part of the performance-plan of the liturgy, which is to engage in act-types that signify elements of the core narrative—in this case, the actions of Mary of Bethany. The sorts of attention that are required in the two types of cases are different: in the first case, one has to attend to a presentation of elements of the core narrative, while in the second case, one does not. That noted, when engaging in reenactment of the first type, a certain type of suppleness of attention is required. To perform the actions called for by the script, one has to be able to negotiate between attending to features of the presentation of elements of the core narrative—such as the celebrant's actions—and the content of what is being presented. It is not as if one "reads past" the actions of the celebrant. Rather, one *responds* to them. In this sense, the actions of the celebrant call attention to themselves in a way that words often do not.

This last observation requires that we now enter an important qualification to what I said earlier about what it is to attend to the content of a narrative. A moment ago, I said that one immerses oneself in a narrative-work by bracketing certain features of the presentation of the narrative in order to attend to the content of the narrative itself. But if what we just said is correct, it would be better to say that sometimes immersion requires attending to certain features of the presentation of the core narrative *for the purpose of* immersing oneself in the narrative. Indeed, it shouldn't escape our attention that, in the Orthodox liturgies, the vast majority of the content of the liturgical script is sung. When the script instructs the assembled to repeat the words of the Publican, the Righteous Thief, or the Prodigal Son, the repetition it calls for is typically performed in song. In these cases, then, the response that the liturgical script calls for is not one that ignores or brackets the musical dimensions of these reenactments. Rather, the response called for is that one enter into the narrative by way of its musical presentation; one simultaneously immerses oneself in the musical presentation of the narrative and in the narrative itself.[44]

On this occasion, I am going to have to rush past many of the issues raised by the role of music in the presentation of the core narrative to note two points. First, if immersion typically consists in allowing oneself to be emotionally engaged by the content of a narrative, the emotional engagement called for in liturgical reenactment is that of responding not simply to the content of the narrative but also to features of its presentation. If this is so, what I have been calling the liturgical sequence is emotionally colored in two distinct respects: in both its content and its presentation. Both the narrative description and its musical presentation call for a range of emotional responses on the part of those assembled. Indeed, one of the more striking elements of liturgical reenactment is when these two types of colorings come apart but in complementary ways. For example, in the rite of the burial of Jesus, the content of the narrative calls for something like sorrow. Its musical presentation, by contrast, calls for that difficult-to-describe emotional reaction characteristic of being in the presence of something of great beauty. When combined, the reenactment calls for something like that state of sorrow in which we are moved by beauty. In this respect, the musical features of the presentation of some segment of a narrative may play a crucial role in understanding the narrative itself. For by presenting an episode of the core narrative such as Christ's burial as not only sad but also beautiful, two disparate elements of the episode—ones that we might not have appreciated or held together—are fused in one's experience.

The second point I wish to make is that, when applied to liturgical reenactment, any adequate account of non-fictive immersion must offer a highly nuanced account of what it is to attend to the content of the core narrative. For, if the foregoing is along the right lines, what immersion often requires is

---

[44] In this regard, perhaps the closest analogue to what I am describing occurs when watching an art form such as opera, for the response called for is one in which one enters into the narrative presented by way of its musical presentation. The crucial difference is that liturgical reenactment often takes the form of not simply listening to someone present some segment of the core narrative in song, but also engaging in the reenactment by singing the content of that narrative.

that one attend to features of the presentation of the narrative, such as its musical form, for the purpose of immersing oneself in the narrative itself. In some cases, then, the script calls for a type of dual attention that is simultaneously focused on both the content of the narrative and certain features of its presentation, much in the way that we can simultaneously attend to both the bass lines and the harmonies of a musical work.

In fact, I suspect that the type of immersion called for by the script is even more complex than this. For, arguably, what the script calls for is not simply that one simultaneously attend to the musical features of the presentation of some segment of the core narrative for the purpose of immersing oneself in that segment but also that one immerse oneself in the music itself—where musical immersion is a matter of not simply attending to the musical properties of the performance of some work, but also being absorbed by the musical properties of the performance of that work, where this consists in allowing oneself to be emotionally moved by those musical properties. If this is so, the thing to say is that often the liturgical script calls for not simply dual attention but *dual immersion*: immersion in the narrative itself and in certain features of its presentation as well.

In the last few paragraphs, I have called attention to some salient disanalogies between immersing oneself in a narrative-work, on the one hand, and liturgical reenactment, on the other, the most important of which being that liturgical immersion requires an especially nuanced sort of attending. Let me now call attention to yet another disanalogy. The core narrative with which one engages in liturgical reenactment is unusual in important respects. While it is a narrative, it is also studded with metaphors, "uncrystalized" images and tropes that resist anything like being unpacked in propositional terms without remainder—images such as wine, water, bread, and blood.[45] At one point, for example, the liturgical script blends the images of blood and water, inviting us to view the blood that flowed from Jesus's side as a river of paradise: "As though from some new river of Paradise, there flows from it the quickening stream of your blood mingled with water, restoring all to life."[46] Shortly thereafter, it invites us to view water in a much different light: "I am swimming in the deep waters of destruction and have come near to drowning. . . . save me as you saved Peter."[47]

Attending to the core narrative, then, often requires not simply that one keep track of its flow or significance but also that one engage with its uncrystalized elements, images that can unite disparate things (a river in Eden, Jesus's blood) and admit of considerable ambiguity (water as both

---

[45] I borrow the term "uncrystalized" from Wettstein (2012b).
[46] *LT*, 254. In the Orthodox tradition, some of the uncrystalized images to which I refer take a visual form in its art—the image of Theotokos with Child, for example.
[47] *LT*, 410.

life-giving and life-destroying). Here the disanalogy is not so much with reading as such as with reading narrative-works, as the attention required in liturgical reenactment is often more similar to that called for by poetry. In attending to the content of a poem, rather often one does not try so much to understand or unpack it—such content is frequently too difficult for this!—as to latch onto metaphors, images, and tropes, allowing them to settle in one's mind, resonate, and color one's experience of the fine details of the world. Having done this, these elements of the poem are now there, available to consciousness as the objects of meditation, reflection, and emotional engagement.[48]

Let me now come full circle, returning to the topic that I used to introduce the immersion model, namely, the place of target roles in liturgical reenactment. Although it is easy to overlook the point, reading narrative-works requires bodily action; one must do such things as focus one's eyes on the words of the page, for example. But, unless a narrative-work is also an instruction manual of an unusual sort, it rarely calls for, while reading, actions such as kissing, touching, or bowing. Neither, for that matter, does a narrative-work typically call for, while reading, imitating the actions depicted in the narrative that it presents. The sort of immersion that the liturgical script calls for, then, is of a different order, since it calls for precisely these sorts of activities.

Return, once more, to cases of liturgical reenactment such as the rite of foot washing, the burial of Jesus, baptism, the repetition of the words of the Publican, the Prodigal, and the Righteous Thief. In each case, the script appears to call for participants in the liturgy to immerse themselves in the core narrative by identifying to some degree or other with its characters and their situations, assuming what I've called target roles. Admittedly, not all cases of liturgical reenactment call for this sort of response. And some cases of liturgical reenactment such as the eucharistic rite are fairly difficult to characterize. In this rite, does the liturgical script call for the response that the assembled are to identify with the disciples? I am not sure. However that may be, it is worth noting that, in the eucharistic rite, the reenactment lies in large measure with the actions of the celebrant, as it is the celebrant who repeats the act-sequence attributed to Jesus in the Gospels. Once we recognize this, however, the model seems to capture important elements of even this rite. For while the script seems to call for the celebrant to identify with Jesus's actions of sharing food with those close to him, this is compatible with the celebrant's *acting on behalf* of Jesus, as there is no tension between assuming a target role in which one identifies with a figure and acting on behalf of that

---

[48] Peter Kivy (1997), 134, argues that a "full literary experience" of a work such as *Pride and Prejudice* must include some significant "literary afterlife" in which one reflects on the themes that it raises. A full liturgical experience, I believe, is similar.

figure. In fact, the reenactment that occurs in the eucharistic rite might be a case in which, in acting on behalf of someone, one identifies with the person on behalf of whom one is acting by imitating him.

4.4. WHAT REENACTMENT IS FOR

I began this chapter by noting the prominence of liturgical reenactment in the Orthodox liturgies, noting some of the different forms it can take. Along the way, I expressed dissatisfaction with various accounts of such reenactment, eventually identifying what a good model of liturgical reenactment should accomplish: it should smoothly accommodate the liturgical data, identify the behaviors the liturgical script calls for, and identify why it is that the liturgical script calls for these behaviors. When presenting what strikes me as the most promising model of liturgical reenactment—namely, the immersion model—I have mostly had my eye on the first two components of a good model, as I have been interested in illustrating the degree to which the model takes into account the liturgical data and identifies the behaviors that the liturgical script calls for. What the script often calls for, I have been claiming, is assuming target roles of various sorts, imaginatively identifying with characters in the core narrative. The remaining task is to take the next step, identifying what the purposes might be of immersing oneself in liturgical reenactment in these ways.

The topic calls for a discussion unto itself. So, let me say only this: by immersing themselves in the core narrative, participants in the liturgy fundamentally alter their relation to that core narrative. They are not outsiders to it, onlookers, or spectators of its events and characters. Rather, they inhabit the narrative, engaging with it, perhaps even wrestling with dimensions of the narrative that call for such a reaction. What might be the purpose of immersing oneself in the core narrative in this way? The short answer, I believe, is that immersion in liturgical action is in the service of receptivity and appropriation. The dominant purpose of immersion is to let participants open themselves up to and appropriate the riches of the narrative, often by identifying with its characters in such a way that they construct and revise their narrative identities.[49]

[49] This is a theme I develop in Cuneo (2015a), which is included as Chapter 5 in the present volume. I thank Tyler Doggett, Jonathan Jacobs, Lori Wilson, and Nick Wolterstorff for their comments on or discussion of an earlier draft of this chapter.

5

Liturgy and the Moral Life

If you attend the performance of most Christian liturgies, you will find the assembled reading and listening to the scriptural depiction of various events that compose the core Christian narrative. If you attend the performance of a liturgy of the Eastern Christian churches, however, you will discover that the assembled do not simply read or listen to the scriptural presentation of the events that compose the core Christian narrative but also reenact many of these events by imitating them. During the services of Holy Week, for example, the assembled will read and listen to what the Gospels say about the events surrounding Jesus's death. Then, at various points, they reenact some of these events, such as Jesus's washing of the disciples' feet and his burial. At these points, the readers and listeners become performers.

The question that I would like to pursue in this chapter is why this is so. Why would the scripts of the ancient liturgies direct those assembled for the liturgy not to merely read and listen to the scriptural presentation of various events that compose the core narrative but also to perform actions that imitate them? In raising this question, I am not interested in identifying causal or historical explanations of why the activity of reenactment figures so prominently in the ancient liturgies, as interesting as such explanations might be. Instead, I am asking what the activity of liturgical reenactment is *for*, what its contribution to the moral and religious life is supposed to be.

The answer that I am going to offer assumes that there is no single contribution that liturgical reenactment is supposed to make to the moral and religious life; there are probably multiple ways in which it is supposed to contribute to the realization of various ethical and religious ideals. Still, I suggest that we can helpfully speak of the dominant ends or goals of liturgical reenactment and that among these dominant ends is that of contributing to the construction of a narrative identity of its participants.

By an agent's narrative identity, I have in mind a sequence of events, which has that agent as a subject, to which he or she might refer if he or she were accurately to tell a story of his or her life. Suppose, for example, I were to ask you a series of questions such as: "Who are you? What made you who you are? And what do you value most in your life?" You might answer by telling me that you are the one whose love of music led to years studying the cello and whose dedication to the instrument required sacrificing a promising dancing career. Your having such properties as *being a lover of music* would be part of your narrative identity, since it would form part of a story-like sequence of events, which has you as a subject, to which you might refer were you to tell a story of your life. (I do not assume that there must be only one such story that you could offer in response to my questions, or that it would have to fall into some specific genre, or have any specific content. Such a story simply needs to be responsive to the types of questions mentioned at the outset of this paragraph.)

In focusing my discussion on the topic of narrative identity, I realize that I am joining a much larger conversation about the role of narrative in the moral life. The contribution I hope to make to this discussion is not, however, to advance another descriptive claim about the ways in which certain activities are likely to contribute to the development of one's narrative identity. So, for example, I am not going to develop a variant of the thesis that Plato railed against, namely, that imaginatively identifying with a character in some work of art, such as a drama, increases the likelihood that one becomes like that character, thereby undermining self-control. Instead, the view I defend is thoroughly normative. I am interested in the normative commitments that agents undertake when engaging in liturgical reenactment and how these commitments might contribute to the construction of a narrative identity of a particular sort.

My topic in this chapter is a large one, so I should call attention to several respects in which my discussion will be selective. Although the activity of liturgical reenactment is prominent in the ancient liturgies, I am going to focus not on these liturgies in general but only on those of the Eastern Christian churches, as these strike me as a particularly rich resource to explore. More-over, my eye will be on not the totality of the Eastern liturgies, but on the Lenten liturgies in particular, as it is in these deeply penitential services that the activity of liturgical reenactment figures most prominently. For ease of reference, I will often refer to "the" script of the liturgy, but when I do so, it is the scripts or performance-plans of these liturgies that I will typically have in mind. Finally, liturgical reenactment comes in different varieties. As will soon be evident, I will be focusing not on reenactment in all its forms but on those cases in which the performance of speech acts plays a fundamental role. The performance of these acts, I'll claim, plays an important role in the formation and sustenance of traits of character important to the moral and religious life.

In order to illuminate the way in which participating in the liturgy can contribute to the formation and sustenance of an agent's narrative identity, I'll need to engage in some stage-setting. I will dedicate the first section of this chapter to this stage-setting and then draw upon this work in the second and third sections of the chapter to directly address our topic.

5.1. LITURGICAL IMMERSION

The vesperal service of Holy Tuesday begins with a reading from the Gospel of Matthew that presents the story of the woman whom the tradition often identifies as a prostitute, Mary of Bethany.[1] According to the scriptural narrative, in the middle of a dinner party, Mary anoints Jesus with "very precious ointment," pouring the oil on Jesus's head and wiping his feet with her tears and hair (Matt. 26: 7; Luke 7: 37–8; John 12: 3). In the services that follow on Holy Wednesday, the hymnody embellishes Mary's story by putting words in her mouth, at one point having her address Jesus with this request: "'Behold me sunk in sin, filled with despair . . . yet not rejected by your love. Grant me, Lord, remission of my sins and save me . . . O merciful Lord who loves human kind, deliver me from the filth of my works.'"[2] At a different point, the hymnody then shifts from the perspective of Mary to that of the assembled, having them sing words attributed to Mary: "Like the Harlot I fall down before you, Christ my God, seeking to receive forgiveness; and instead of ointment I offer you the tears of my heart. Take pity on me, Saviour, as you had on her, and grant me the remission of my sins. For I cry like her to you: Deliver me from the filth of my deeds."[3] What then occurs in the service is that the people file forward to venerate the icon of Christ, kissing it in the way that Mary is said to have kissed Jesus himself on the occasion of the dinner party. Immediately after venerating the icon, each is anointed with oil by the priest.

The sequence of liturgical actions just described is interesting on several levels. Notice, first, that some of the actions performed by the assembled are ones in which they reenact elements of the embellished scriptural narrative by both imitating and repeating actions attributed to Mary, such as her cry to be delivered from her misdeeds. Other liturgical actions—such as when the people venerate the icon of Jesus—imitate Mary's actions but do not repeat them. Instead they reenact these actions by employing props, in this case an icon of Jesus, to perform actions that are supposed to represent Mary's action of kissing Jesus. It is clear, moreover, that the priest's action of anointing the people is supposed to connect with Mary's own anointing of Jesus, although it is not exactly clear how. One interpretation is that the rite is a commemoration of her action, a fulfillment of Jesus's words that what she had done "will be told in memory of her" (Matt. 26: 13). The "telling" in this case would not simply be an oral or a written presentation of her story, but also a dramatic

---

[1] The identification is contentious. For a discussion, see Stump (2010), ch. 12.

[2] Mary and Ware (2002), 539, 537. I have modernized the English used in the translation. In what follows, I will refer to this work as *LT*.

[3] *LT*, 695–6.

and creative extension of it, in which the priest anoints the people as she anointed Jesus.[4]

Mary is only one of a cast of characters whose actions are reenacted in the context of the liturgy. On the Sunday of the Publican and the Pharisee, for example, the people listen to the Gospel story of the Publican and the Pharisee and sing: "In our prayer let us fall down before God, with tears and fervent cries of sorrow, emulating the Publican in the humility which lifted him on high.... Let us utter the words of the Publican in the holy temple 'God be merciful.'"[5] Likewise, on the Sunday of the Prodigal Son, the people listen to the story of the Prodigal, and sing: "With the words of the Prodigal I cry aloud: I have sinned, O Father; like him, receive me now in your embrace and reject me not.... Accept me in repentance and make me as one of your hired servants."[6] In both cases, by performing speech acts of certain sorts, the people reenact parts of the Gospel story by imitating and repeating actions attributed to its characters.

I have called figures such as the Publican and the Pharisee "characters" advisedly, as neither is presented in the scriptures as being an actual historical figure. Each is instead a fictional character that Jesus employs in his parables. An interesting feature of these last examples of liturgical reenactment, then, is that when the people imitate and repeat the words of the Publican and the Prodigal, they are engaging not with a historical narrative but with a fictional one. The case of Mary of Bethany is somewhat different, since she is not presented in the scriptures as a character in a parable. Still, it is worth stressing that when the assembled imitate and repeat Mary's words, they repeat not Mary's actual words (the scriptures do not present her as saying anything when she anoints Jesus) but those attributed to her by the church's hymnody in its effort to embellish the scriptural narrative. In all the cases we've considered, then, liturgical reenactment involves reenacting either the actions of fictional characters or act-types attributed to non-fictional characters that (for all we reasonably believe) they did not perform.

Let me, for ease of reference, call actions of both these sorts *fictive actions*. Given our topic, a natural question to raise is how we should understand the activity of reenacting fictive actions. Are the reenactments themselves best viewed as a species of make-believe behavior in which the people pretend to be Mary of Bethany, the Publican, or the Prodigal? Or are they better described as cases in which the participants pretend to be present in their own person at,

---

[4] Another interpretation suggested by the liturgical script is that the act of being anointed is answering a call issued by Mary of Bethany: "The Harlot washed your pure and precious feet with her tears, and she urges all to approach you and receive the remission of their sins. Unto me also grant her faith, O Saviour, that I may cry to you: Before I perish utterly, save me, O Lord" (*LT*, 375).

[5] *LT*, 107, 108.   [6] *LT*, 116, 118.

say, the event (whether real or fictional) in which Mary anoints and kisses Jesus or when the Prodigal returns home to his father?

There are powerful trends in both philosophy and theology that would recommend that we view liturgical reenactments of both sorts as dramatic performances and, hence, behavior in which we engage in make-believe.[7] According to these views, when the assembled engage in liturgical reenactment, they should be understood to pretend that they are characters in the scriptural narrative or to be present in their own person at the events depicted by the narrative, much in the way that you or I might pretend to be Mary if we were to stage a dramatic reenactment of the Gospel of Matthew.

I do not wish to broach any empirical claims about what it is that the assembled are doing or take themselves to be doing when engaging in liturgical reenactment. I do want to claim, however, that like any script or score, the liturgical script calls for responses of certain types from participants in the liturgy. Among the responses *not* ordinarily called for by the liturgical script, I also want to claim, is that of engaging in make-believe behavior. If I am right about this, the response called for when the assembled venerate the icon of Christ is not that of pretending to be Mary of Bethany (or pretending to be present in one's own person in Mary's circumstances). Similarly, the response called for when the assembled imitate and repeat the behavior of the Prodigal is not that of pretending to be the Prodigal (or pretending to be present in one's own person in the Prodigal's circumstances). In the next section, I will offer an argument for this assessment. For now I wish to emphasize two points.

The first is that engaging with narratives—whether they be fictional or not—ordinarily requires imaginative activity on the part of those who attempt to understand or interpret them. Among other things, when we try to understand a narrative, we must fill in its gaps, project possible explanations for what occurs, creatively interpret its happenings in the light of relevant background knowledge, and so on. But we should not, I believe, equate imaginative activity with pretense; to imaginatively extrapolate from a narrative needn't be to engage in any sort of make-believe behavior. The second point is that from the fact that important parts of a narrative are presented as and recognized to be fictional, we cannot infer that imaginatively engaging with that narrative is itself a matter of engaging in make-believe. When one finds oneself imaginatively engaged by a story—even to the point of being swept away by it—one needn't be engaging in any sort of pretense or game of make-believe. To share in the pain of addiction in David Foster Wallace's *Infinite Jest*, need not require us to pretend that we, too, are addicts. There is such a thing as imaginative engagement with fictional narratives that is not pretense.

---

[7] See Walton (1990) and the references in Wolterstorff (1990), for example.

Let us suppose for present purposes that the assessment just offered is correct: when the script directs the assembled to reenact the behavior of the Publican or the Prodigal by imitating or repeating it, it ordinarily calls for the activity not of pretending to be the Publican or the Prodigal (or pretending to be present in one's own person in their circumstances) but of imaginatively engaging with the stories that involve these characters. How, though, should we understand the sort of imaginative engagement that the liturgical script calls for if it is not a species of make-believe?

The issue calls for a discussion unto itself but let me briefly gesture at what I believe is the correct answer.[8] There are, in principle, untold ways in which one could approach a work, such as a novel, that presents a narrative; one could approach for the purpose of uncovering the author's religious views, political allegiances, sexual preferences, or the like. Here, however, is a way to approach such a work with which we are familiar and on which many other approaches are parasitic: one imaginatively immerses oneself in the narrative presented by the work.

Think of the activity of immersing oneself in a narrative work (that is, a work that presents a narrative) as having two primary components: first, it involves attending to the content of the narrative of the work (what it is communicating) and properties of that content (such as how its various elements hang together) in such a way that, in engaging with the work, one prioritizes attending to this content. This means that, while immersing oneself in a narrative work is compatible with attending to features of the presentation of its narrative, such as the author's word choice or use of certain grammatical constructions, doing so is for the purpose of better attending to the content of the narrative itself. So, when reading, for example, one can momentarily marvel at the use of a striking metaphor, asking oneself why the author would use it in this context. But the point in doing so is better to engage with the content of the work in which the metaphor is being used.

Immersing oneself in a narrative work involves more, however, than simply attending to its content in such a way that one screens off or fails to prioritize certain features of its presentation, such as the author's word choice. It is also to take up a certain kind of vantage point with regard to the narrative presented by the work. Explicating the phenomenon of taking up a vantage point is not easy, but the basic idea is that when immersing oneself in a narrative work, one imaginatively enters its narrative by situating oneself within it.[9] In taking up such a vantage point, then, one does not take up the

---

[8] I have developed the view in considerably more detail in Cuneo (2014a), which is included as Chapter 4 in the present volume.

[9] Harris (2000) offers some interesting empirical data that supports this way of thinking about immersion.

stance of a dispassionate observer or critic. Rather, one attends to its content in such a way that its characters and events loom large in one's consciousness, and one becomes emotionally engaged to some significant degree with these characters and events. Still, in so immersing oneself in the narrative of the work, one does not take oneself to be a character in the work (or be present in one's own person at the events described in the work). Characters in a work do not, after all, attend to the ways in which the work of which they are a part is presented.[10]

The positive proposal I wish to make is that the liturgical script ordinarily calls for behavior similar to that in which we engage when we immerse ourselves in a literary work. When the script of the service of Holy Wednesday, for example, calls for the assembled to imitate and repeat the speech acts attributed to and behavior of Mary of Bethany, they are to immerse themselves in Mary's story. Or, to state the phenomenon from the opposite angle, when the script directs the assembled to imitate and repeat Mary's behavior and the speech acts attributed to her, it calls for the activity of allowing the assembled to be absorbed by Mary's story, engaging with its content and allowing her character and actions to loom large in their consciousness and emotional life when they reenact her behavior.

5.2. IDENTIFICATION

I started our discussion by raising the question of why the scripts of the ancient liturgies go beyond directing the assembled to simply read and listen to segments of the core Christian narrative but also to reenact some of the events it depicts. In my initial attempt to address this question, I assumed that it would be helpful to get a clearer sense of what liturgical reenactment is, the character of the sort of activity that is called for when the liturgical script directs the assembled to do such things as imitate and repeat the actions of Mary of Bethany or Jesus. The question on which we need to make progress is the contribution that liturgical reenactment so understood is supposed to make to the moral and religious life. Let me take a few more steps toward that goal by saying something more about the phenomenon of reading narrative works, canvassing what some philosophers have said about the ways in which reading literature is supposed to contribute to the moral life and the formation of character.

---

[10] Cuneo (2014a), which is included as Chapter 4 in the present volume, expands upon these points, noting that immersion typically requires moving back and forth between attending to the content of a work and ways in which that work is presented.

In the introduction to her collection of essays *Love's Knowledge*, Martha Nussbaum points out that moral philosophers have virtually ignored the role of literature in the moral life.[11] Nussbaum contends that this oversight is not trivial, for literature—and Nussbaum has in mind the novel in particular—is especially well-suited to contribute to the expansion and refinement of moral understanding. What literature does, Nussbaum suggests, is present us with rich descriptions of characters, their traits, and their often complicated predicaments, allowing us to emotionally engage them and thereby expand our powers of moral judgment, refine our abilities of ethical discernment, deepen our ethical understanding, and have access to alien points of view. In this regard, Nussbaum contends, these works are importantly different from those of philosophy. In a treatment of the virtues, a philosopher such as Aristotle or Aquinas might offer an accurate analysis of a particular virtue. But given its abstract nature, such an analysis could (for most of us) gain only limited traction in the moral life; we would gain very little appreciation for its lived character. By contrast, "showing" a virtue by means of a narrative that displays its dynamics over time—so Nussbaum maintains—offers us a much better sense of what the virtue is and how we might recognize it. In this way, the sorts of narratives regularly presented in literature make a unique and important contribution to the moral life; they often accomplish what works from other genres—and, indeed, ordinary life—cannot.

When all goes well, immersing oneself in liturgical action might expand and refine our powers of moral understanding in much the same way that engaging with literature does, at least if philosophers such as Nussbaum are right. But it would not do so because those segments of the liturgical script concerned with liturgical reenactment present us with rich and detailed descriptions of characters and their predicaments. The reason is that although these segments of the liturgical script engage with the scriptural narrative, they do so largely by re-presenting and embellishing portions of this narrative. More exactly, these segments of the script are largely a selective and stylized appropriation of this narrative that presupposes an intimate familiarity with it. When, for example, the script for the services of Holy Friday imaginatively weaves together the stories of Joseph of Arimathea and Mary Theotokos, presenting these stories from the first-person perspective of its characters, it does not follow them through an extended period of time, offering rich and detailed descriptions of these characters and the predicaments they face. Rather, it offers snapshots of their lives, creatively blending and embellishing their stories by, among other things, highlighting some of their important characteristics, such as their courage in conditions that appear to them

---

[11] Nussbaum (1990). Carroll (2001b), Part IV, and Carroll (2011a), Parts IV and V, also have some of the best discussions of the topic of which I'm aware.

hopeless.[12] But if the contribution that liturgical reenactment makes to the moral and religious life is not that of imparting moral understanding by the presentation of rich and nuanced narratives, how should we understand it?

The answer, I believe, lies in what I will call the self-reflexive character of the liturgical script. As the passages I have quoted from the liturgical script will have already indicated, the liturgy has the striking feature of casting much of its hymnody in the first-person. This technique is employed in three different although compatible ways.

In some places, the technique is employed to re-cast stories, which in their scriptural presentation are themselves not narrated from the first-person perspective, into hymns that are narrated from the first-person perspective of their characters, such as when the hymnody presents elements of the Genesis story from the perspective of Adam:

> The Lord my Creator took me as dust from the earth and formed me into a living creature, breathing into me the breath of life and giving me a soul. . . . He honoured me . . . making me companion of the angels. . . . In my wretchedness I have cast off the robe woven by God . . . and I am clothed now in fig leaves and in garments of skin.[13]

Elsewhere, the script presents hymnody from the perspective of Jesus, the so-called second Adam:

> I who am rich in Godhead have come to minister to Adam who is grown poor. I who fashioned him have of mine own will put on his form. I . . . have come to lay down my life as a ransom for him.[14]

Call the technique employed in this and other passages *narrative recasting*. If the point of these particular examples of narrative recasting were simply a matter of getting the assembled to pretend to be Adam or Jesus, their function would be more or less transparent. What better way to pretend that one is Adam or Jesus than to take up their perspectives? I have claimed, however, that we ought not to understand the liturgical script to call for the assembled to pretend that they are characters such as Adam or Jesus. If I am right about this, when the script directs the assembled to sing hymns from Adam's or Jesus's perspective, something else is going on. That something else, I would say, consists in the assembled *playing the role* of Adam and Jesus—where playing the role of these characters consists not in pretending to be them but (in part) taking up their perspective by speaking in their voices.[15]

---

[12] Eric Auerbach's classic work, *Mimesis* (Auerbach [2003]), contrasts Greek and biblical narrative on precisely this point: biblical narratives don't fill in the background in the way that Greek narratives do.

[13] *LT*, 168.   [14] *LT*, 513.

[15] It is not easy to specify exactly what it is for an agent to play a role. I say more about the matter in Cuneo (2014a), which is included as Chapter 4 in the present volume.

In other places, the liturgical script directs the assembled not to recite stories narrated from the first-person perspective of their characters, but to quote and appropriate passages from these stories, employing them to perform speech acts that express the first-person perspective of those assembled:

> let us emulate the groaning of the Publican and, speaking to God with warm tears, let us cry out: "O you who loves humankind, we have sinned. In your compassion and pity, be merciful and save."[16]
>
> Like the Thief I cry to you "Remember me"; like Peter I weep bitterly; like the Publican I call out "Forgive me, Saviour"; like the Harlot I shed tears. Like the woman of Canaan I cry to you, "Have mercy on me, Son of David." Like the woman with an issue of blood, I touch the hem of your garment. I weep as Martha and Mary wept for Lazarus.[17]

Call this activity that the liturgical script calls for *indexical appropriation*. In the cases before us, indexical appropriation consists in embedding various speech acts, such as requests that incorporate first-person pronouns ("Remember me" and "Forgive me, Saviour") in other speech acts, such as assertions ("Like the Thief I cry to you") that also incorporate first-person pronouns. Unlike the examples of narrative recasting offered above, indexical appropriation consists not in playing the role of a character but in allowing biblical persona to function as models—these models often functioning as ideals whose characteristics we try to approximate in our own behavior.

Finally, in other places, the liturgical script employs the first-person pronouns in what is perhaps an even more unusual way. Under this use, the pronoun functions not so much as a marker of who is doing the addressing as an indicator of who is the *object* of address. When the pronoun is used in this way, the liturgical script is self-referential in the sense that, when an individual conforms to it in the context of liturgical performance, she is herself the object of her own address. What is more, these uses of the first-person pronouns often figure in a certain type of construction in which the speaker refers to him or herself comparatively, as being like or identical with one or another character, such as when the assembled compare themselves to the Prodigal Son:

> I am become the Prodigal Son, and having wasted my riches I perish now from hunger. Beneath your protection I seek refuge, O loving Father: accept me as you have accepted him. Make me a sharer at your table, that I may cry to you: Before I perish utterly, save me, O Lord.
>
> I am the prodigal: conceived in sin, I dare not look up to the height of heaven. But trusting in your love for human kind, I cry: God be merciful to me and save me.[18]

---

[16] *LT*, 108.   [17] *LT*, 245, 263.   [18] *LT*, 375, 668.

Call this use of the singular first-person pronoun *comparative self-address*. Unlike narrative recasting, comparative self-address is not (in the paradigmatic case) a matter of playing a role. And unlike indexical appropriation, it is not (in the paradigmatic case) allowing a character to function as a model. Rather, I would say it consists in treating a figure function as a *type* of which the assembled declare that they are examples. In the passages just quoted, for example, the Prodigal Son functions in just this way.

The overarching question we are pursuing concerns the contribution that liturgical reenactment is supposed to make to the moral and religious life. An important clue to understanding that contribution, I have suggested, is the liturgical script's use of the first-person pronouns. Let me now move beyond noting the various uses to which the script puts these pronouns and hazard a general suggestion as to what their functions might be in the context of liturgical performance. Having offered this suggestion, I will qualify it in some important respects.

Imagine that you and I are very different people: you are a thief and I am not. Or somewhat differently, suppose that you are a collaborator with an oppressive foreign power that is occupying our country and I am not. Between you and me there is likely to be considerable psychological distance. That is, given our different stations, it is likely that you and I have rather different histories, temperaments, values, commitments, and the like. Suppose, though, it is important for me to understand you better, say, because we find ourselves invested in a joint project whose success matters to both of us. In order to understand you better, I could engage in at least two activities.

I might attempt, in the first place, to close the psychological distance between us by taking up your point of view on some matter on which I find your views puzzling or alien. Or, somewhat differently, I might attempt to identify with you, locating points of similarity between you and me, where these points of similarity could be the basis for mutual enjoyed recognition, lasting social bonds, or unified action, such as when we realize that we share a deep interest in jazz and make plans to perform some of our favorite pieces with one another.[19] A moment's reflection reveals that these activities are not identical. I could close the psychological distance between you and me to some significant degree by appreciating how you see things without identifying with you in any appreciable sense, since your ways of seeing the world might still seem too alien. Similarly, I could identify with you without having to close any appreciable psychological distance between us, since there might be none to speak of.

---

[19] A vivid example of this is found in Patrick Leigh-Fermor's book *Abducting a General* in which Fermor tells of the experience of capturing a German general in Crete and reciting an ode of Horace—in Latin—with his enemy. Thanks to Luke Reinsma for this reference.

I take it that closing the psychological distance between oneself and another is often for the purpose of identifying with that other person. At any rate, in what follows I shall understand it to have that function and will speak simply of the activity of identifying with another—where identifying with another is understood typically to incorporate the activities of both closing the psychological distance between and identifying (in the sense specified above) with that person.

The proposal I want to develop is that the liturgical script's use of narrative recasting, indexical appropriation, and comparative self-address is to facilitate the identification with the array of characters presented in the liturgical script. To appreciate the point, begin by observing that the liturgical text presents us with an array of characters whom many of us are likely to find deeply alien in important respects: criminals (the Thief), collaborators with oppressive foreign powers (the Publican), betrayers (Peter), wastrels (the Prodigal), prostitutes (Mary of Bethany), hysterics (the woman of Canaan), and the impure/sick (the woman with an issue of blood). Notably, however, the script directs the assembled not to distance themselves from these characters because they are vivid examples of the unsavory and the unclean but to imitate and repeat their actions and words to the point of identifying with them, sometimes in the strongest of terms, such as when it directs the assembled to assert such things as "I am the Prodigal."

That such identification is the activity called forth by the liturgical script is, I think, especially evident in the cases of comparative self-address that we considered. But it is also evident in the cases of indexical appropriation that we canvassed, such as this passage:

> Like the Thief I cry to you "Remember me"; like Peter I weep bitterly; like the Publican I call out "Forgive me, Saviour"; like the Harlot I shed tears. Like the woman of Canaan I cry to you, "Have mercy on me, Son of David." Like the woman with an issue of blood, I touch the hem of your garment. I weep as Martha and Mary wept for Lazarus.[20]

This passage helps us to see the self-constituting character of liturgical re-enactment: in performing the speech acts of requesting forgiveness and mercy by using the words of the Publican and the woman of Canaan, the assembled do not simply express a desire to emulate these characters; they also *bring it about* that in performing these speech acts a range of similarities now hold between them and these characters—these similarities being of such a kind that they can contribute to the project of identifying with these characters. To the question "In what way are you like the Publican?" it could fairly be responded by the assembled: I am like the Publican in imitating and following

---

[20] *LT*, 245, 263.

his example to the point of even using his words. Imitation, in this case, begets identification.

The liturgical activity of identifying with the range of characters presented in the liturgy is intriguing if only because traditional religious traditions are often intent on carving out and ratifying strict social roles for their adherents. In many such traditions, men are allowed to perform certain actions but women are not. The ritually clean are permitted to participate in certain rites but the ritually unclean are not. In the passages that we have considered, exactly the opposite dynamic appears to be at work: the script invites men to identify with characters who are women, women with characters who are men, the innocent with characters who are criminals, the faithful with characters who are betrayers, the responsible with characters who are wastrels, the healthy with characters who are chronically sick, the stoical with characters who weep, the emotionally stable with characters who are emotionally unstable, and so forth.

The intended effect seems (at least in part) to be twofold. On one level, it is to destabilize the self to some degree, inviting participants in the liturgy to expand their own self-conceptions in ways that, for many, are hardly going to seem like second nature. One could, in fact, look at the activity of identifying with the cast of characters presented in the liturgy as an exercise of autonomy of a certain kind in which agents revise certain self-understandings of themselves or call into question roles into which they have been scripted. On another level, however, the script seems intent on unifying the self-conceptions of the participants around certain ethical and religious ideals that these characters share, such as their willingness to repent of their failures and their readiness to acknowledge that they do not have it all together. In this regard, participating in liturgical reenactment of this sort has a pronounced leveling effect: whoever you might be, and whatever your station—so the script seems to say—there is considerable common ground between you, me, and these characters whose actions and behaviors we imitate and repeat. Interestingly, unlike the basis of the sort of friendship that Aristotle lauded, the common ground does not consist in acknowledging shared virtues or accomplishments. Rather, it consists in sharing deep and regrettable flaws—ways in which we are fragile and fail.

Let me now add a qualification to these points about identification, which I mentioned in passing a few paragraphs back. To this juncture, I have been speaking in general terms about the function of the liturgical script's use of first-person pronouns, suggesting that they are employed to invite the assembled to identify with these various biblical persona. But speaking in such general terms risks distortion, since terms such as "I" and "we" are indexicals and, as such, do not have a unique content that determines their reference. All else being equal, when I use the term, "I," it refers to me; when you use it, the term refers to you. Indexicals, then, have what are commonly called *characters*, which are roughly rules or functions from contexts—such as my uttering the term "I" on some occasion—to contents—in this case me. The character of the first-person indexical, then, will determine on any given occasion of use whom it picks out or refers to.

I call attention to this point about the nature of indexicals because it is important to see that in its ample use of first-person pronouns, the liturgical script allows for a great deal of flexibility concerning what is said or accomplished by the participants' use of these pronouns. Depending on who you are and what stage of your life you are in, your uttering sentences in a liturgical context that repeat those attributed to the Thief or the Prodigal Son might mean something very different or play very different cognitive roles from my uttering those same sentences in the same context. Given your history, uttering the sentence "I am the Prodigal" might function as an invitation to search for similarities that might not be obvious or to close the psychological distance between you and the Prodigal, so that you can better understand and reconcile with those who are like him in obvious respects. In contrast, given my history, uttering that same sentence might function to acknowledge a past that I would rather forget but that is important for me to come to terms with.

I would add to this that the activity of identifying with characters in the context of liturgical performance can be fraught with moral risk, as it can be an occasion to distort one's self-conception or trigger tendencies that are on the whole harmful to oneself, such as engaging in self-abasing behavior when what is needed most is assurance of one's worth. We have, then, another reason to think of the liturgical script as calling for certain types of responses not from all participants but from only those who stand to make progress in the moral and religious life by immersing themselves in the activity of liturgical reenactment. It goes without saying that whether one is such a person might require reflection and good judgment.

To this point, I have been developing the thought that, like engaging with literature, liturgical reenactment can make important contributions to the moral and religious life, helping us to realize certain ethical and religious ideals in the activity of identifying with the array of characters presented in the liturgical script. Recall, though, that my claim at the outset of this essay was stronger than this, for I said that a dominant aim of liturgical reenactment is to contribute to the construction of a narrative identity. And, it could rightly be observed that identifying with someone in some respect is not perforce to construct a narrative identity. I could, for example, discover that you and I have a shared love of jazz, and we might identify with one another because of this. But when it comes to telling a story of my life, this similarity may not be important enough to figure in my story. It is not part of my narrative identity.

That noted, it strikes me that attention to the cases of comparative self-address that we've considered, such as when the assembled assert "I am the Prodigal," strongly suggests that the liturgical script is calling for more than simply identifying with characters such as the Prodigal. It is telling, after all, in the passages I have quoted that the identification is complete; the claim is not that I am like the Prodigal in some respect or other but that I *am* the Prodigal. I am the one who has thrown away his birthright and squandered the gifts given to him. As such, the identification appears to be of such a kind and importance that it is an answer to the question "Who are you?" which is exactly the sort of question that the telling of one's story is supposed to address. In fact, I think we should be open to the possibility that what the liturgical script is calling for, when it directs an agent to reenact the Prodigal's actions and engage in comparative self-address, is for that agent to narrate or construct his or her own story in the context of the liturgy. If that is right, the activity of liturgical reenactment can be itself a kind of story-telling, a telling of one's own narrative. That is, such an activity can consist in articulating who one is or aspires to become, which would be another striking example of the self-constituting character of liturgical action, since by engaging in such an activity one would, in a certain range of cases, bring it about that one's narrative identity has a particular contour, which it shares with the Prodigal's. I would add that the telling of one's story in the context of the liturgy needn't be de novo. For many, it will be a retelling of one's story that perhaps amends, augments, or corrects a narrative that one is prone to tell in other contexts. At any rate, if these suggestions are along the right lines, we can identify yet another way in which narrative functions in the context of the liturgy: when people assemble for the liturgy, they not only read and listen to narratives but are also called to construct them while engaging in the liturgy.

5.3. COMMITMENT

The overarching question that I have been pursuing is the contribution that liturgical reenactment is supposed to make to the moral and religious life. The clue to answering this question, I've suggested, lies in the self-reflexive character of the liturgical script, as it is this feature of the script that helps us to locate the sorts of activities that the script calls for. Prominent among the activities called for by the script, I have claimed, is that of identifying with characters in the core Christian narrative, where this identification should be understood as contributing to the construction of a narrative identity.

I have, however, stopped short of broaching any empirical claims to the effect that liturgical reenactment is likely to contribute to the construction of a narrative identity. For my proposal is unapologetically normative: the construction of a narrative identity is among the activities that the script calls for. I now want to suggest that the answer to our overarching question is normative in another distinct sense.

The cases of reenactment in which I've been interested involve the performance of speech acts of various sorts in which one appropriates the words of characters presented to us in the liturgical script. Fundamental to the performance of any speech act, however, is that the speaker commits himself to the world being a certain way. In asserting, I commit myself to the world being thus and so (and to my believing it to be thus and so). In promising, I commit myself to acting in a certain way (and believing that I can act that way). In commanding, I commit myself to having the authority to direct your actions in certain ways (and believing myself to have such authority). In my view, it is the normative alteration that occurs upon committing oneself in these ways that accounts for (at least in part) why it is that certain sentence utterances count as speech acts such as asserting, promising, and commanding. Speech, under this approach, necessarily involves normative transformation of such a kind that a speaker acquires rights, responsibilities, and obligations vis-à-vis her audience and vice versa.[21]

Taking account of the ways in which speech is normative allows us to address more adequately questions that I have raised earlier in our discussion. One question—the question that I raised at the outset of our discussion—is why the scripts of the ancient liturgies go beyond directing the assembled to read and listen to the presentation of events that compose the core Christian narrative to reenacting them. The answer is that in reading or listening to a narrative, one does not thereby commit oneself to anything. But when the assembled engage in reenactment of the sort called for by the liturgical script, they perform speech acts of various sorts that commit themselves to their being certain ways, such as being like (or aspiring to be like) the Thief, the Publican, or the Prodigal.

A second, closely related question is how liturgical reenactment might make a distinctive contribution to the moral life, different from reading narrative works such as novels. The answer is that while reading a novel can be morally transformative, it is not an activity that as such calls for the activity of committing oneself to anything. Liturgical reenactment of the sort called for by the liturgical script is different since it belongs to the essence of this activity that the assembled commit themselves to ethical and religious ideals of various sorts, such as being like, say, Mary of Bethany. Of course we have excellent empirical evidence that in a large range of cases these ethical ideals do not "take." But when they do not, the failure is of a distinct kind: it is a failure to live up to the standards that have been imposed on one not by another but to

---

[21] Cuneo (2014e) defends this position. This view, which I call the *normative theory of speech*, takes its inspiration from Searle (1969), Wolterstorff (1995), Brandom (1998), and Alston (2000).

which an agent has committed herself in the context of liturgical action.[22] If this is so, and liturgical reenactment is as I have described it, then such reenactment is doubly normative: it is an activity not only called for by the liturgical script but also one in which the assembled commit themselves to various moral and religious ideals, including being like (or aspiring to be like) the characters presented in the liturgical script.

Having noted the ways in which liturgical reenactment is normatively transformative, we are now better situated to address yet another issue that I left hanging. The issue is why we should understand liturgical reenactment to be a species not of make-believe behavior but of immersion in which one imaginatively enters in the narrative presented by the liturgical script. We are better situated to address this question because it should be evident that, when one engages in pretense of a sort in which one pretends to be a character, one does not thereby commit oneself to the world or oneself being a certain way. To illustrate, suppose I were to pretend to be Mary of Bethany, repeating the words attributed to her in the liturgical script: "Behold me sunk in sin, filled with despair . . . yet not rejected by your love. Grant me, Lord, remission of my sins and save me . . . O merciful Lord who loves human kind, deliver me from the filth of my works." Were I to repeat Mary's words in the context of the liturgy while pretending to be her, I would not thereby have committed myself to being sunk in sin, filled with despair, or anything of the sort. Neither would I have requested anything of Jesus. I would have merely acted the part of Mary of Bethany much in the way that I would if I were acting a part in a theatrical presentation of the book of Matthew. If I am right to suggest that the heart of liturgical reenactment consists in *committing* oneself to being certain ways, however, then I believe that we have decisive reason to reject an account of liturgical reenactment according to which it consists in make-believe behavior. For if it did, then liturgical reenactment could not be normatively transformative—at least in the ways with which we have been concerned. Its aim would not be to transform the self by way of committing oneself to certain ethical and religious ideals.

One remaining observation deserves to be voiced, and that is the communal nature of liturgical reenactment. For, although I have not emphasized the point, liturgical reenactment is an activity that is performed not in isolation but in the context of a community dedicated to the realization of certain moral and religious ideals. When all goes well, one is aware that the liturgical script

---

[22] In the Divine Liturgy, immediately before partaking of eucharist, the assembled pray: "May the communion of your holy mysteries be neither to my judgment nor my condemnation, O Lord, but to the healing of soul and body." One way to understand this prayer is that it expresses the desire that the partaking of eucharist not be out of step with ideals to which one has otherwise committed oneself in the context of the liturgy such that partaking of the eucharist proves to be an exercise of self-condemnation, a failure to live up to these ideals to which one has committed oneself.

calls one's fellow participants to commit themselves to the very ideals to which it calls you to commit yourself. Moreover, your fellow participants are aware that the script calls you to commit yourself to the ideals to which it calls them to commit themselves. Mutual recognition, then, is yet another dimension of liturgical reenactment, and it deserves to be the subject of further reflection. It is a topic of sufficient richness, however, that exploring its role will have to await another occasion.[23]

[23] Thanks to Brad Cokelet, Christian Miller, Nick Wolterstorff, members of the University of Vermont Ethics Reading Group, and an audience at the Character Project conference at Wake Forest University for their comments on an earlier version of this chapter.

6

If These Walls Could Only Speak

Icons as Vehicles of Divine Speech

"For the silent painting speaks on these walls, and does much good"

Gregory of Nyssa

In both their private and corporate worship, Eastern Orthodox Christians do all sorts of things with icons: they adorn them with flowers, process with them held aloft, bless them with water, prostrate themselves before them, and touch and kiss them. What is more, Orthodox Christians behave in this way toward a wide variety of types of icon. They engage in more or less the same behavior toward icons that depict particular saints, such as Isaac of Syria, and those that depict particular events, such as Christ's baptism in the Jordan. In the eyes of many Western Christians, such behavior appears very strange. What is it about icons that would make such behavior appropriate? Or to state the question somewhat more precisely: Given the Christian East's insistence that icons play their proper role in the context of the liturgical life of the church, what is it about the liturgical role of icons that would make such behavior as touching and kissing them appropriate?

Two rather different proposals have enjoyed currency in the church's reflections on this matter. On the one hand, there is the understanding of the role of icons dominant in the (non-iconoclastic) Christian West. Gregory the Great articulates this view in a well-known passage, writing that "to adore a picture is one thing, but to learn through the story of a picture what is to be adored is another. For what writing presents to readers, this a picture presents to the unlearned who behold, since in it even the ignorant see what they ought to follow; in it the illiterate read."[1] Gregory's claim is that icons primarily serve a didactic purpose: they are pictorial texts for the illiterate.

On the other hand, there is the rather different understanding of the role of icons dominant in the Christian East. According to this view, icons are not

---

[1] Quoted in Thiessen (2005), 47.

primarily pictorial texts for the illiterate, but quasi-sacramental mediators of divine presence. To express this mystery, Eastern Christians resort to metaphors, claiming that icons are "windows to heaven," "visible images of mysterious and supernatural visions," as St. Dionysius the Aeropagite puts it.[2] Through these windows, that which is depicted is said to become "spiritually present to us."[3]

Neither of these approaches is likely to strike someone interested in the liturgical *ratio* of icons as particularly satisfying. The problem with the first approach is that it is too minimalist in character. Were icons primarily didactic in purpose, it would be hard to see why for nearly two millennia Christians have done such things as prostrate themselves before them, touching and kissing them. More importantly, the Gregorian view (as we might call it) fails to account for the passionate insistence on the part of the Christian East that iconoclasm is an attack not merely on a particular mode of Christian worship, but on the very substance of the Christian faith itself. In his reflections on images, Luther admitted that icons could function as a memorial or commemoration. In so doing, he identified one of their liturgical functions, also identified by John of Damascus in his defense of icons in *On the Divine Images*. Still, were the liturgical function of icons primarily one of commemoration—at least in the sense that Luther appears to have had in mind—this would not explain why the Christian East has insisted that the very essence of the faith was at stake in the struggle with the iconoclasts. To destroy or deny the legitimacy of a memorial is no light matter. But it is difficult to see why it would be tantamount to eviscerating the content of the Christian faith, as the East claimed.

But if the Western position is too thin, the Eastern view is likely to strike us as extravagant. In what way could an image make Isaac of Syria present to us? In general, the suggestion that a pictorial depiction of a thing makes that thing present looks like an invocation of magic. Perhaps even more worrisome is the fact, alluded to earlier, that so many icons depict not particular persons, but events such as Christ's crucifixion. Everyone agrees, however, that were events such as this to have taken place, then they are over with. If so, one wonders how an icon could in any interesting sense make them present to us. When used to describe icons that depict events such as Christ's crucifixion, metaphors of being present, being a window to heaven, and being a visible image of supernatural vision seem inapt. Or if not inapt, these metaphors leave us with deep questions about how to understand them in a way that their use is both illuminating and intelligible.

[2] Quoted in Florensky (1996), 65.
[3] Ibid., 69. The claim is made in nearly every theological treatment of the Eastern view of icons of which I know. By calling this the dominant view in the East, I do not wish to suggest that Eastern thinkers have not employed other models regarding the liturgical role of icons.

Texts for the illiterate or mediators of divine presence: neither suggestion sheds much light on the liturgical role of images. Neither offers a satisfactory theoretical model for understanding their appropriate role in the liturgical worship of the church. Can we do better?

I believe so. The key to identifying the liturgical function of icons, or so I shall suggest, is to understand them as vehicles of divine action, indeed, of divine speech. Understanding icons as vehicles of divine action, I shall further suggest, can help make sense of the language of presence so frequently appealed to by Eastern Christians. Between action and presence we needn't choose. Before I lay out my case for this view, however, let me preface what follows with three remarks.

The first remark concerns the relevance of our topic. I shall assume without argument that not only religious beliefs, but also many of the practices in which religious believers engage, including their liturgical practices, deserve the attention of philosophers. Still, it might be tempting to believe that the topic of the liturgical role of icons is of interest only to Christians of the East— or at least only to those interested in the practices of the Christian East. I believe that this is not so. In his excellent book *Worship: Its Theology and Practice*, the Swiss Reformed theologian Jean Jacques Von Allmen notes that among the great traditions of Christendom, the Reformation traditions alone have rejected the use of images in worship and, at that, not consistently. It is time, Von Allmen argues, for those who belong to the traditions of the Reformation to think hard about how the sense of sight can be redeemed in Christian worship and whether icons might play some role in this project.[4] If Von Allmen is right about this—and I think he is—the question I wish to pursue in this chapter is one in which the wider Christian community should have a stake. It is not one only for those interested in the Eastern church.

The second remark I wish to make concerns the type of model that I shall present regarding the liturgical role of icons. The model is one that, so far as I know, has not been explicitly defended by Eastern theologians, but is both informed by and consonant with the main lines of reflection in the East on the liturgical role of icons.[5] Call it an "expanded" Orthodox view, if you like. Accordingly, it is a model that takes seriously the East's insistence that icons are mediators of divine presence. However, as I've already noted, central to my argument is the claim that we needn't choose between thinking of icons primarily as mediators of divine presence, on the one hand, or vehicles of

---

[4] Von Allmen (1965), 276ff. Pelikan (1990), ch. 4, expands upon this theme of the sanctification of sight, arguing that the defense of images marks an epistemological shift in Christianity in which the modality of sight is given a role at least as important as that of hearing.

[5] I use the term "theologian" here and elsewhere in a wider sense than that used in the Christian East.

divine action, on the other. Indeed, thinking of icons as vehicles of action, I argue, allows us to shed light on the claim that they are vehicles of presence.

The final remark I wish to make concerns talk—talk to this point in which I have freely engaged—about the liturgical function of icons. Talk of this sort can suggest that icons have one liturgical function and that our task is to identify it. I do not, however, believe that icons have a single liturgical function. Icons have multiple liturgical functions. Still, some of their functions are arguably more central than others, in part because they unify and make sense of other liturgical functions that icons play. So, in what follows, when I speak of the liturgical function of icons, I wish to identify a central liturgical function of icons that makes good sense of the ways in which Christian believers interact with them in worship.

6.1. SALVIFIC EVENTS

In a striking passage from his book *Liturgy and Tradition*, the Orthodox theologian Alexander Schmemann writes the following regarding Christian faith:

> the faith which founds the Church and by which she lives is not a mere assent to "doctrine," but her living relation to certain events: the Life, Death, and Resurrection of Jesus Christ, his ascension into heaven, the descent of the holy Spirit on the "last and great day" of Pentecost—a relationship which makes her a constant "witness" and "participant" of these events, of their saving, redeeming, life-giving and life-transfiguring reality. She has indeed no other experience but the experience of these events; no other life but the "new life" they always generate and communicate.[6]

If Schmemann is right, Christian faith is not mere assent to a class of propositions or, for that matter, trust in a person. It is also a living relation to certain *events*, primarily, says Schmemann, the founding events of the church, which include the life, death, and resurrection of Christ. It is events such as these to which the church is called not only to bear witness, but also to participate in and experience as a source of life-giving reality.

In one sense, what Schmemann says here seems profoundly correct. The events to which Schmemann refers enjoy a certain type of primacy in the life of the church. A fundamental role of the writings and hymnody of the church is to bear witness to them; the church bears a living relation not primarily to the media that witness to them, such as scripture and hymnody, but to the events themselves. That said, there is another sense in which what Schmemann says

---

[6] Schmemann (1990), 54.

raises questions of its own. Schmemann writes that the church witnesses to various events in its history, allowing its members to participate in them. If this is right, then presumably the church does not wish its witness to these events to consist in mere commemoration. It intends for its members in some sense to participate in them. But how could we, who are thousands of years removed from these founding events of the church, become participants in them, thereby allowing them to communicate to us "new life"?

I shall turn my attention to this question in the last section of this essay. For the time being, however, let me use Schmemann's observation regarding the centrality of events in the faith of the church to throw light on the topic I wish to explore. Earlier I said it is difficult to miss the fact that so many icons depict not particular figures, but events fundamental in the history of the church. Indeed, it is difficult to miss the fact that the so-called festal icons of the church depict not particular figures, but the very events to which Schmemann refers. Suppose, to keep our topic manageable, we limit our attention to such event-depicting icons, as we may call them.[7] I want to suggest that Schmemann's reflections allow us to reframe the issue we are exploring, bringing it into sharper focus.

Central to the East's reflection on the liturgical role of icons, I have noted, is the claim that they are mediators of divine presence. But if what Schmemann says is correct, they are not just that. For the art of the church also purports to bear witness to the founding events of the church, inviting us to become participants in them. If so, we now have three interlocking ideas about the liturgical role of icons with which to work. Event-depicting icons are at once witnesses to divine action in the world, mediators of divine presence, and occasions for participation in the founding events of the church. My project in what follows is to unpack these three themes, arguing that they allow us to make progress with our leading question about the liturgical *ratio* of icons. Indeed, I shall suggest that these three themes are more closely connected than they might seem at first glance. If we understand the ways in which icons are a witness, then we shall also understand how they are both mediators of divine presence and invitations to the living relation of which Schmemann speaks.

To this let me add the following observation: if the Christian East is correct, both scripture and the art of the church bear witness to its founding events. The Eastern church, however, has never viewed event-depicting icons as midrashic commentary on scripture. The role of these icons is not, as it were, to put scripture into pictures. Rather, generally speaking, icons of this sort purport to represent the *same content* as scripture, albeit in a different medium and with

---

[7] Among the class of event-depicting icons, I shall have my eye exclusively on those that purport to represent past events and not those that purport to depict future events, such as the Last Judgment.

different interpretive emphases.[8] Scripture and icons are, according to this view, different ways of expressing or getting at the same thing. If this is right, icons and scripture do not have fundamentally different purposes. (Indeed, we should not miss the fact that the Christian East speaks not of painting, but of *writing* icons.) This suggests that if we understand how it is that scripture functions as a witness, then we shall also understand how icons do the same. In the next section, I shall pursue the parallel between these two instruments of witness.

6.2. WITNESS

Having spent fifteen chapters exploring the notion of divine speech, Nicholas Wolterstorff, in the Afterword to his book *Divine Discourse*, raises the issue of what reason there is to believe that scripture is actually a medium of divine discourse.[9] Wolterstorff notes that the dominant type of rationale offered for this claim within the broadly Protestant tradition, found in both Calvin and Barth, is a-historical. Scripture, according to such views, is self-authenticating or authenticated by the internal testimony of the Holy Spirit. On its own, Wolterstorff contends that this type of approach will not work. Any plausible justification of the claim that scripture is an instrument of divine speech will have to proceed historically, taking into account the historical pedigree of the text. However, when one does proceed historically, Wolterstorff suggests, a pattern of justification emerges. The pattern is one that proceeds from divine authorization to divine appropriation.

The divine authorization consists in a chain of authorization-conferring events. The initial event is one in which the apostles are deputized by God the Father through Christ to be witnesses to and representatives of Christ and his salvific work. What emerges from this commission is a body of apostolic teaching and practice, which incorporates what Jesus taught them and what they remember of Jesus's ministry, all of which is formulated under the guidance of the Holy Spirit. Substantial parts of this body of teaching is, over a period of time, then incorporated not only into the church's worship, but also into a series of books and letters composed by the apostles or their close associates—the apostolicity of these texts lying in the fact that they express the mind of those commissioned to be witnesses to Christ. The final

---

[8] The exception to the identity-in-content claim is those icons that depict events not recorded in scripture, such as the dormition of the Theotokos. The identity-in-content-claim is, I believe, best understood to be a claim about what Wolterstorff (1995) calls *designative content*. Two claims that purport to represent some event have the same designative content just in case they designate or refer to the same event.

[9] Wolterstorff (1995), ch. 16.

link in the chain of authorization is the process of canonization, wherein the church designates that a single text, Holy Scripture, is divinely authorized.

The book that emerges from this process of canonization is, in the mind of the church, the word of God. But how is it that the writings of Luke, John, and Paul have this status? How can it be that scripture is an instrument of divine speech? The answer that Wolterstorff offers is this: it cannot simply be because their writings are inspired by God. Nor can it merely lie in the fact that in these writings God reveals God's will to humanity. For it is perfectly possible for something to be inspired by someone and yet not count as his word. Likewise, it is possible for something to reveal something about someone without its being the case that that thing is a case of that person's speech. So what brings it about that the scriptural texts are God's word, God's speech to humanity?

Simplified somewhat, Wolterstorff's suggestion is that the writings of Luke, John, and Paul count as divine speech because God appropriates their writings as God's own.[10] An analogy might help to understand the proposal: suppose you and I serve together on a school board. And suppose, in the context of a meeting, you enter a motion. I agree heartily with the content of this motion and second it. In so doing, I have made your speech act my own. I have appropriated your speech. In much the same way, Wolterstorff contends, God appropriates the discourse of those God has commissioned to speak, thereby making their discourse God's own. Scripture is a case in which one person speaks by way of the speech acts performed by another. To use Wolterstorff's terminology, it is a case of double-agency discourse.

The position just articulated is a blend of the old and the new. By insisting that the books that belong to the scriptural canon must be apostolic, the position is identical with that defended by the ancient church, including the church of the East. By offering a model of what brings it about that the apostolic writings count as divine speech, however, the position goes beyond anything explicitly said by the Church Fathers. Nonetheless, as I shall suggest in a moment, I believe it to be a natural extension of what the Fathers say and, perhaps, what they would've said had they reflected on the matter using the conceptuality of speech acts.

At any rate, according to the view we're exploring, scripture is a witness to the founding events of the church. The witness, if Schmemann is correct, is the church's. But it is not only the church's. It is also God's. In a large range of cases, by both authorizing and appropriating the speech of the apostles, God vouches for the historicity of these events, calls attention to their centrality in salvation history, and communicates God's present intentions toward

---

[10] Wolterstorff himself distinguishes between deputized discourse, cases in which one person is authorized to speak for another, and appropriated discourse, cases in which one person appropriates the discourse of another. Here I emphasize the latter sort of double-agency discourse.

humanity. In this double-agency witness, one sees a theme deep in the theological reflection of the East rising to the surface. For fundamental to the Eastern view is the conviction that, at its best, the divine-human interaction is a *synergos* or a synergy between God's will and work and ours. The synergy between the divine will and the human, according to the church, is present most explicitly in the person of Christ. It is also present in that process that the church calls salvation, the aim of which is to become participants in the divine life. Finally, if the model that Wolterstorff proposes is correct, the synergy is also present in the message of the scriptural texts, as it is also the joint product of human and divine speech. *Synergoi* of the word, both incarnate and written.

The witness of scripture, according to the model that we've been exploring, consists (at least in part) in the fact that it is a text both authorized and appropriated by God. Let me now move to the second part of the parallel I am pursuing, which concerns the art of the church. Over and again, in their struggle with the iconoclasts, the Church Fathers speak of icons as witnesses to God's salvific work. What is the character of their witness? The Seventh Ecumenical Council states the matter thus:

> To make our confession short, we keep unchanged all the ecclesiastical traditions handed down to us, whether in writing or verbally, one of which is the making of pictorial representations, agreeable to the history of the preaching of the Gospel, a tradition useful in many respects, but especially in this, that so the incarnation of the Word of God is shown forth as real and not merely fantastic....
>
> We, therefore, following ... the authority of our Holy Fathers and the.... Holy Spirit ... define with all certitude and accuracy that just as the figure of the precious and life-giving Cross, so also the venerable and holy images, as well in painting and mosaic of other fit materials should be set forth in the holy churches of God.... For by so much more frequently as they are seen in artistic representation, by so much more readily are men lifted up to the memory of their prototypes, and to a longing after them; and to these should be given due salutation and honourable reverence, not indeed that true worship of faith which pertains alone to the divine nature; but to these, as to the figure of the precious and life-giving Cross and to the Book of the Gospels....
>
> Thus we follow Paul, who spake in Christ, and the whole divine Apostolic company and the holy Fathers, holding fast to the traditions which we have received.[11]

The argument of this passage comes in two layers. In the first layer, the authors of the council maintain that the icons of the church are, first and foremost, vehicles by which the church witnesses to the incarnation. What makes them legitimate vehicles of witness? They are apostolic; they express the mind of the church and, in particular, of "Paul, who spake in Christ." But why think that

---

[11] Seventh Ecumenical Council. I quote from the translation in the Christian Classics Ethereal Library. Available at <www.ccel.org/ccel/schaff/npnf214.toc.html> (accessed August 21, 2015).

the icons genuinely have this status of being legitimate apostolic witnesses to the incarnation? Here we come to the second layer of the argument, which is an argument from the liturgical practices of the church. No Christian, the authors of the council claim, denies the legitimacy of displaying both the cross and the Gospels. And no Christian denies that it is appropriate to show great reverence toward them by, among other things, touching and kissing them. These practices also express the mind of the apostles; if not explicitly taught by the apostles, they are actions that the apostles would have instructed us to perform were they aware of our situation. But if so, how could one legitimately treat objects such as the cross and the Gospels with great reverence and not the images of Christ and his salvific work? "Why do you worship the book and spit upon the picture?" asked John of Damascus. Since the content of the icons and scripture is identical, John continues, "if the one is worthy of honor, the other is worthy of honor also."[12]

By pressing these points about the practices of the church, the authors of the council took themselves to be on firm polemical ground. For they were well aware that arguments similar to these had won the day in the first council of Nicea over four hundred years earlier. When unable to settle the issue of Christ's divinity by appeal to the writings of the apostles alone, the response was to look at how the apostles had taught the followers of Christ to pray. The followers of Christ, the architects of the first Nicean council pointed out, are to pray in the name of the Trinity. Were Christ not divine, the argument continued, this practice would be bizarre. Why would we pray in the name of the one true God and also in the name of two other created sub-deities? Were Christ a creature, to pray as the apostles had taught would be idolatrous. Such idolatry would be unacceptable, however, especially were it to come from the mouths of the apostles. The best explanation of why the apostles instructed us to pray in this way—so the argument continues—is that they assumed that Christ himself is divine in the same manner as the Father.

Let us now take the argument a further step. John of Damascus writes that the icons are "not our gods, but are like books which lie open in the churches in the sight of all." These visual books are helpful, for "all of us alike, whether learned or uneducated, benefit from what is painted in the icons. What the written word proclaims through letters, iconography proclaims and presents through colors." Lightly admonishing his readers, John continues, "now use your mind with precision. It is not I who am speaking, but the Holy Spirit who declares plainly through the holy apostle Paul, 'God spoke of old in various

[12] Quoted in Pelikan (1974), 131. Later, I'll indicate why John's argument goes through only if one adds several other assumptions, including the claim that the content of both types of text is presented with the same illocutionary force. Perhaps it is also worth adding that I do not interpret John to claim that because icons and scripture share the same content, they thereby have the same authoritative status in the church.

ways to our fathers by the prophets.'" To which John then adds this point of emphasis: "note that God spoke *in many and various ways.*"[13] The implication that John wishes his readers to appreciate is clear: do not be surprised by the fact that God speaks in many and various ways. Do not, furthermore, be surprised that God speaks through the art of the church as well as through the Gospels themselves. For, once again, if these two media genuinely express the same content, it is difficult to see how one could at once maintain that God speaks through the one but not the other.

Had we not explored how it might be that the scriptural texts are instruments of divine speech, John's suggestion that icons are also media of divine discourse might have seemed baffling. How could a work of art count as a case of divine speech? But at this point, we can see how to expand upon John's observation. Suppose that agents can perform speech acts not only by writing and speaking sentences, but also by composing works of visual art. Suppose, further, that the church's use of icons, like the writing and the canonization of scripture, has been not only guided by the work of the Holy Spirit, but also divinely authorized in virtue of its apostolicity. Suppose, finally, that by both authorizing and guiding the composition of the icons these works of art have been appropriated by God as a vehicle by which God expresses God's intentions with respect to humanity. (We might think of the Spirit's act of guidance functioning like a divine signature, appropriating a speech act that has been divinely authorized.) By appropriating these works, God does such things as vouch for the historicity of the events they depict, draw attention to their centrality in salvation history, and communicate God's present intentions toward humanity. If we assume these things, then the parallel between the Gospels and icons that both the authors of the seventh ecumenical council and John of Damascus wish to emphasize is close. Both media function as witnesses to divine action in the world—and this in a twofold sense: both media are the product of those authorized to witness or testify to Christ's salvific work. Moreover, both media themselves represent events central to the life of the church as having certain features, thereby testifying to their occurrence. If the model that we have been exploring is correct, then God appropriates what is said by way of the composition of these works. This is what renders them the book and the art of the church.

6.3. PRESENCE

Few of us communicate by hand-written letters these days. For better or worse, electronic media have won the day. But most of us know what it is like to receive

---

[13] John of Damascus (2003), 44, 54.

a hand-written letter from a friend, spouse, or loved one. The shapes of the letters on the page, the phrases and idioms used, as well as what is said all bear the marks of the author. They express his or her person. Art is often similar. The materials and colors used, the use of space and, more broadly, the choice of what to present in a work of art also bear the mark of the artist. They, too, express his or her person. When the author or artist is no longer alive, often his or her writings or works of art are the closest thing we have to being with that person. Such is the degree to which these media can express who we are.

Several times now I have drawn attention to the Christian East's claim that icons are mediators of divine presence, raising the question of what this claim could amount to. I would like to suggest that the answer to this question is now before us. The key is to understand the ways in which icons mediate divine presence along the lines of how a letter communicates the intentions of its author.

Letters are vehicles of communication. By performing the action of writing a series of sentences, an author thereby performs speech acts of various kinds such as asserting that one thing is the case, asking about something else, and promising to act in a certain way. These speech or illocutionary acts are not produced haphazardly. It is in virtue of having illocutionary act intentions of various kinds that an author performs them. Of course we are all familiar with cases in which an agent's illocutionary act intentions fail to correspond to the speech act performed. Jane means to praise another's work but inadvertently voices criticism. We are also familiar with cases in which an author's illocutionary act intentions no longer represent her considered opinion, as when a person changes her mind about what she said earlier about someone else's work. Still, when all goes well, the two correspond. In these cases, when an author intends to assert that the Rocky Mountains are magnificent, she succeeds in asserting this about the Rocky Mountains. When all goes well, then, there is a perfectly straightforward sense in which a letter expresses the intentions of its author. For by authoring this letter she thereby expresses her illocutionary act intentions with regard to her audience. And when all goes well, these intentions are manifest to her audience. They are, to use an equivalent idiom, present to her audience. The letter, in this way, is a vehicle of presence.

Let us return once again to the claim that icons are mediators of divine presence, keeping in mind the appropriation model of speech with which we have been working. By composing an icon according to the conventions of icon writing, what does its creator wish to communicate? The question raises complexities. Consider the person who composes (or "writes") a particular copy of Christ's baptism in the Jordan. In so composing this icon, that person may have no illocutionary act intentions whatsoever. She may be simply engaging in an exercise of copying one thing from another, thereby honing some of her artistic skills. Or she may compose the icon simply because she enjoys creating fairly abstract art. And indeed something similar may be true of the person who composed the original icon from which this particular icon is copied. It is possible that in depicting, say, Christ's baptism in the Jordan, he did not intend to claim that Christ was baptized at all. And yet I've claimed that it's the church's view that icons are vehicles of speech. If so, then illocutionary act intentions must somehow be operative if an icon is to testify to this event. But whose intentions?

Well, suppose that over time a system of composing icons emerged that had many features similar to that of a natural language: certain colors are used to represent particular attributes of persons represented, particular artistic tropes are used to help the viewer recognize where the event depicted took place, certain symbols are used to communicate that a depicted person who bears them has a particular standing such as being a martyr, certain acronyms and monograms are used to identify particular figures, and so forth. Call this *the communication system* of icons. Suppose, furthermore, that this communication system is a component of the wider social practice of writing icons, a social practice in which only certain people are appointed to write icons, only certain materials are used to compose them, and only certain media are employed to display them. This social practice evolves and is fluid. For example, some who work within the practice add new emphases to established patterns of using the communication system; others introduce entirely new elements to the communication system. Although there is a tight connection between elements of the communication system and that which they communicate, there is, however, nothing like a one-to-one correspondence between them. The system can be employed by competent participants in the social practice in various and creative ways to communicate different things. The same thing can be represented in different ways and the same elements of the system can communicate different things. Given this fluidity, when we examine an icon, how are we to determine how the communication system is being used?

In principle, there are several available answers to this question. Without arguing for the position here, let me simply remark that appeal to something akin to authorial or speech act intentions appears unavoidable at this point.[14] To determine how an element of the communication system is employed in the composition of a given icon, we need to know something about how the person employing it intended it to be used. But this leads us back to our initial question: Whose intentions?

The answer, I suggest, lies in distinguishing the composer of an icon from its author. Those who compose icons are the practitioners of iconography, those who engage in the social practice of composing icons, employing what

---

[14] A fuller defense of the issue in play can be found in Carroll (1992), and Wolterstorff (1995), ch. 11.

I've called the practice's communication system. The author of an icon, by contrast, is the one to whose intentions we must appeal in order to determine how the composer's employment of the communication system should be interpreted (on the assumption, of course, that it admits of a determinate interpretation). According to the Christian East, the church is the author of its icons. If this is right, the intentions of the church have not only formed and informed the social practice of iconography; they also determine how these texts should be read. Obviously, we touch here upon deep and controversial issues about whether there can be collective intentions and how we should understand them. But suppose for argument's sake that there can be.[15] Then the position of the East is evident: when the East claims that icons are the art of the church, at least part of what is meant is that the church is the author of these pictorial texts.

What should now be added is that, if the appropriation model is correct, the church is not the only author of these texts. For fundamental to a position such as that defended by John of Damascus is that icons are vehicles of divine speech. If so, God uses them as instruments of speech. The appropriation model tells us how this might be so: God appropriates the intentions of their author—in this case, those of the church—to communicate various things to humanity. If so, then the icons of the church also express God's communicative intentions toward us. Here we have double-agency discourse once again. Indeed, we have dual authorship as well. The icons have dual authors, both human and divine.[16]

Let me now tie this together. At the outset of this section, I suggested that there is a perfectly intelligible sense in which a letter makes its author present to us. Inasmuch as that letter is a vehicle of that author's illocutionary act intentions, it not only informs us about them, it also expresses these intentions, making them (when all goes well) manifest to us. It is in this sense that a letter is a vehicle or mediator of presence. The Eastern Church's puzzling claim that icons are mediators of divine presence, I am now suggesting, should be understood along similar lines. For suppose the appropriation model is correct, and

[15] For a defense, see Gregory Mellema (1997).

[16] The dual authorship of icons and scripture opens up various possibilities regarding the nature of divine speech, among which are these: suppose we distinguish an agent's intention to perform an illocutionary action of a given type, such as asserting, from her intention to perform an illocutionary act of a certain type that has a particular meaning or noematic content, such as *that the Rocky Mountains are magnificent*. According to the appropriation model, when God appropriates human speech, at least two things could occur. First, God could appropriate both the human author's intention to perform an illocutionary act of a particular type and the noematic content that that agent intended to express by the performance of that act. Second, God could appropriate the intention to perform an illocutionary act type, but not the noematic content that that agent intended to express by the performance of that act. In this case, by appropriating illocutionary act intentions, God performs an illocutionary act of the same type performed by its human author, but endows it with a new meaning.

icons are vehicles of their author's illocutionary act intentions. Their primary author, if I have interpreted the main line of thought in the Christian East correctly, is the church. Still, God appropriates what the church says via its art, thereby also becoming its author. If so, the art of the church expresses God's illocutionary act intentions to us, their audience. Icons are mediators of divine presence, then, in the sense that they mediate God's illocutionary act intentions toward humanity. Or more exactly, in some cases, they are the mediators of God's *present* standing illocutionary act intentions with respect to humanity. The presence in question also has a temporal dimension.

To this line of argument let me add a caveat. I have said that we ought to think of the way in which icons communicate divine presence along the model of the way in which a letter communicates the intentions of its author. By saying this, however, I do not mean to offer a view that provides an exhaustive account of the manner in which an icon communicates divine presence. I mean only to draw attention to one, albeit a central, way in which an icon might do this. For all that I've argued, there are other ways in which icons communicate modes of divine presence that prove to be much more difficult to elucidate in any sort of philosophically articulate way. That said, I do understand the dimension of presence on which I've had my eye to be robust. Sometimes—think once again about cases in which one is separated from another whom one loves—a vehicle of another's intentions, such as a letter, is the most vivid way by which he or she can be present to one.

6.4. PARTICIPATION

At the outset of his defense of images, John of Damascus writes that "things which have already taken place are remembered by means of images. . . . These images are of two kinds: either they are words written in books . . . or else they are material images, such as the jar of manna, or Aaron's staff, which were to be kept in the ark as a memorial."[17] Icons, John continues, belong to the second category. They are memorials. But they are memorials of a curious sort. For their role is not merely to testify to what has occurred, but also to gesture toward what is to come. Odd as it may sound, because they depict what has occurred in certain ways, icons are memorials that point in multiple temporal directions. Paying attention to this feature of iconography, I now want to suggest, will help us to unpack the last of the three themes I wish to explore, which is the claim that icons are means by which one can participate in the events they depict.

---

[17] John of Damascus (2003), 21.

To get our bearings with respect to this issue, let us return once more to the idea that event-depicting icons function as a witness. The witness consists in the fact that icons of this sort accurately represent events central in the life and history of the church. But it does not wholly consist in this. One can, after all, accurately represent an actual event but not thereby intend to testify to its historicity. In books of historical fiction, for example, authors often depict actual events but make no claims about whether they actually occurred. Rather, by representing these events, an author invites his audience to consider or imagine them as part of a larger fictional world that is projected by the text. If the East is correct, however, icons do not function like the propositions presented in a text of historical fiction (although, as I shall point out in a moment, there are similarities to appreciate). Rather, in a large range of cases, in depicting an event in a certain way, the author of an icon wishes to vouch for the fact that the event depicted actually occurred. To employ the idiom of speech acts, in depicting an event in a certain way, the author of an icon thereby intends to assert or *testify* that that event has actually occurred and has many of the properties that it is depicted as having.

Suppose, then, we pair the commemorative function of icons with assertive illocutionary act intentions: by pictorially depicting an event, the (human) author of an icon thereby asserts, testifies, or witnesses to the fact that that event has actually occurred and has properties of various sorts. If the appropriation model of speech is correct, these assertoric speech intentions are also ones that God expresses toward us by appropriating the art of the church. A moment ago, however, I pointed out that icons have the distinction of at once pointing in multiple temporal directions. Their function is not simply to testify to what has occurred, but also to gesture toward what shall occur. Consider, in this regard, an icon of the Last Supper that depicts Christ surrounded by his apostles. In one sense, this icon is supposed to be historically accurate, for it purports to depict an event that actually occurred. But, in another, it takes considerable liberties with the history, for this icon does not endeavor to depict Christ and the apostles at the Last Supper as they actually appeared. Rather, faces are elongated, mouths are closed, eyes are enlarged, nimbuses are introduced, and perspective is inverted. And yet this icon is not badly executed realist art! Rather, the emphases and distortions are used to present the figures depicted in the icon as transfigured. The icon depicts Christ as he appeared to the apostles later in the upper room and the apostles as they appeared to each other on Pentecost, brimming with light. Echoing a theme deep in the liturgical life of the East, the commemoration of a past event contains within itself anticipations of a future one.[18]

---

[18] Dozens of examples could be given from the church's hymnody. Here is the Troparian from Lazarus Saturday, which is also sung on the Sunday of Palms: "O Christ God, when you raised Lazarus from the dead before Your passion, You confirmed the universal resurrection.

So, there is a sense in which event-depicting icons testify not only to what has occurred, but also to what shall occur. But here the significance of the Christian church's claim that we are all called to be disciples of Christ should not be lost from view. The depiction of the disciples not as they were but as they would become is both an invitation and a promise. The invitation is to become as the disciples were to become: bearers of the divine light who are transfigured by their interactions with Christ. Icons invite us to imagine what this might be like. The promise is that transformation indeed shall occur if the invitation is accepted. If icons do indeed point in multiple temporal directions, we can render the idea that they are vehicles of divine presence still more concretely. In the art of the church, what are made present to us are God's illocutionary act intentions. These are intentions whereby God not only testifies to what has occurred, but also invites us to be transformed, promising that the transformation shall take place. By pairing the broadly eschatological dimension of icons with those illocutionary act intentions expressed by invitations and promises, we can come to a fuller view of the presence that icons are intended to communicate.

But what has any of this to do with our final task, which is to make sense of the idea that icons allow us to participate here and now in the events they depict? Well, suppose that icons do function to express a divine invitation and promise. Then there is certainly a sense in which by recognizing this invitation and promise, we can thereby presently participate in the reality of the events depicted. When reflecting on the church's frequent use of the "liturgical present"—its use of the indexical term "today" in its hymnody—Schmemann puts the matter like this:

> To be sure, the Virgin does not give birth today, no one "factually" stands before Pilate, and as facts these events belong to the past. But *today* we can remember these facts and the Church is primarily the gift and the power of that remembrance which transforms facts of the past into eternally meaningful *events*.
>
> Liturgical celebration is thus a re-entrance of the Church into the event, and this means not merely its "idea," but its joy or sadness, its living and concrete reality.... We were not there in Bethany at the grave [of Lazarus] with the crying sisters. From the Gospel we only know *about* it. But it is in the Church's celebration today that an historical fact becomes an event for us, for me, a power in my life, a memory, a joy.[19]

Distinguish, Schmemann suggests, between an event and its significance. An event itself is a dated happening that, unlike a property or state of affairs, does not admit of multiple instantiations. There is no intelligible sense in which an

Like the children with palms of victory, we cry to You: O Destroyer of Death, Hosanna in the Highest! Blessed is He who comes in the name of the Lord!"

[19] Schmemann (1969), 82–3.

event such as Christ's baptism in the Jordan can reoccur. Nor is there any sense in which one can today literally be a participant in this event, for it has already occurred. By contrast, the significance of an event is a property that that event has. Roughly speaking, the significance of an event for a person is the import it has or should have for that person given his commitments, interests, or values. While there is no literal sense in which we can participate in a past event, we can presently "participate" in it inasmuch as we can presently allow its significance to shape our lives. To use language often appealed to by contemporary theologians, we can participate in an event inasmuch as we allow it to shape our narrative identity.

The point is worth expanding upon. Consider what Augustine does in his *Confessions*. An unmistakable feature of Augustine's telling of his life-narrative is that it is couched in the language of the scriptures. Indeed, at various points, Augustine invites his audience to view events in his own life, such as his anguishing in the garden, as ones that parallel those in the Gospels. In doing so, Augustine makes the Gospel narrative his story; the Gospels provide the framework in which he understands the significance of the events that compose his life. There is also, however, an unmistakable sense in which by appropriating aspects of the Gospel narrative, Augustine thereby expands this narrative itself, presenting his own life-story as an extension of it. This allows Augustine to situate his own life-narrative within a larger, more cosmic narrative of redemption that highlights the scope and power of the Gospel narrative itself. We could think of these two ways in which Augustine connects his life to the events of the Gospels as an inward and an outward movement: the inward movement is one in which Augustine appropriates the Gospel narrative to illuminate events in his own life, while the outward movement is one in which Augustine situates his own story within a larger, more cosmic narrative. The point that is important for my purposes is that these two different ways in which Augustine connects his life with the Gospel narrative are ways in which he participates in the events depicted by the Gospels. To use the language from the passage quoted from Schmemann earlier, they are two ways in which Augustine comes into a living relationship with these events.

In any case, if Schmemann is correct, to participate in the founding events of the church is not, as some Orthodox theologians have suggested, to enter into a liturgical time machine in which the past mystically becomes present.[20] Rather, it is to do something very much like what Augustine does in writing

---

[20] For example, in his book *Time and Man*, the Greek theologian Georgios Mantzaridis maintains that there is a unique dimension of time, which he calls liturgical time. In this dimension, we are "freed from the restraints of time." Whatever is repeated in time is "not confined to time but extends into eternity." "Liturgical time" not only "transcends time," but also "transfigures physical time and transports us from symbol to truth, from the transient to the eternal." So, in some sense that lies beyond understanding, in liturgical time, these events become present to us here and now, allowing us to participate in them (Mantzaridis [1996]).

his *Confessions*. It is to order one's life around the founding events of the church, taking stock today of the full significance of these events for us here and now. But it is also to view one's life as a part of a larger narrative, which includes the founding events of the church. It is to come into living relationship with these events by doing such things as celebrating them in the liturgical life of the church, living in expectation of further events they anticipate, and comporting one's life in recognition that they have transformed human history.

Understood thus, there is nothing particularly mysterious about the claim that icons are vehicles by which we participate in the founding events of the church. They are the visual means by which the church invites us to shape our narrative identities by connecting them in various ways with the founding events of the church. It may bear emphasizing that, if the appropriation model is correct, the invitation is issued not merely by the church, but also by God.

Let me add to this a final observation. In his reflections on faith, Schmemann speaks both of participating in the founding events of the church and coming into living relation with them. I have offered an account of what he means by the first claim, thereby also dropping clues about what it would be to come into living relation with these events. What should now be added is that the art of the church can also be an occasion for coming into living relation not simply with the events they depict, but also with their author. As philosophers of art such as Noël Carroll have emphasized, when we engage with a work of art such as an icon, there is a sense in which we enter into a relationship with its author.[21] For to genuinely engage with a piece of art is not simply to arrive at clever construals of its significance. Rather, it is to attempt to understand its author, discerning what he is trying to say by way of the creation or presentation of that work of art. This is surely a natural extension of what Schmemann himself had in mind when he speaks of coming into living relation with the events that the art of the church depicts.

6.5. CONCLUSION

If you were to walk into a traditional service in the Dutch Reformed tradition you might find that immediately after the sermon, there is a long period of intentional silence. If you were to ask about the significance of this practice, someone knowledgeable would tell you that the people view the sermon as an occasion in which God speaks to the congregation. The silence is an

---

[21] Carroll (1992), 118ff.

expression of grateful acceptance of what has been proclaimed.[22] To my knowledge, there is no similar practice in the Eastern church. Rather, at various points in the liturgy, Eastern Christians do such things as kiss a copy of the Gospel itself and prostrate themselves before icons. At the outset of our discussion I asked about such behavior: What is it about the liturgical role of icons that would render such behavior fitting or appropriate?

The answer I have offered to this question falls into two parts. The first part, which has occupied most of my attention, has been to identify the liturgical function of icons. Only if we understand this, I have assumed, can we begin to understand the behavior in which Orthodox Christians engage. Admittedly, the account of the liturgical role of icons I have offered is not general in character; it pertains only to the role of event-depicting icons.[23] Still, its main lines should be clear enough. According to this answer, icons are best viewed as vehicles of both divine action and presence. By appropriating the speech actions performed by the human authors of these texts, God does such things as vouch for the historicity and importance of the events these texts depict, invite us to be transformed by them, and promise that we shall see both redemption and transformation.

If this is right, however, the second part of the answer more or less falls out of the first. Eastern Christians prostrate themselves before icons, touching and kissing them for much the same reason that the Dutch Reformed keep silent after the sermon. It is their way—demonstrative by Western European standards—of expressing gratitude toward the divine witness, invitation, and promise they communicate. To say this, admittedly, is not to settle the issue of whether such behavior is fitting. We are all aware of cases in which gratitude and affection are expressed in mawkish or inappropriate ways. That said, one needn't cast far to discover parallels to the ways in which Eastern Christians comport themselves with respect to icons. Visit a work of art such as Maya Lin's Vietnam War Memorial and you will find people doing such things as touching and kissing the names of fallen soldiers, etched in marble. Evidently, the touching and kissing are organic—indeed, uniquely human—responses that these people find that this work of art calls forth. Why should it be any

---

[22] In saying this, I don't wish to hazard a brutely empirical generalization. Rather, I wish to proffer what Gadamer would call a descriptive account of understanding. The behavior in question is what takes place when participants in the practice have grasped its *ratio*, conforming their behavior to it.

[23] I believe, however, that the account can be naturally extended to apply to icons of other sorts. Very briefly, I would say this: first, many icons that we might not initially categorize as event-depicting actually are—think here of icons in which Christ raises his hand in blessing or judgment or when the Theotokos holds the Christ child. Second, as Orthodox thinkers such as Leonid Oupensky point out, icons of the saints are ones in which these individuals are presented as transfigured. What is presented in these images, then, is something like a point in a narrative: among other things, icons of this variety invite us to explore the details of that person's life that either led to or have been the result of such a transformation. See Oupensky (1992).

different with the icons? By touching and kissing them, Eastern Christians find themselves expressing, in as fitting a way they know how, gratitude toward the extraordinary witness, invitation, and promise that the icons communicate. In doing so, they express gratitude, love, and laud toward the One who, if the church is correct, is their author.[24]

[24] I thank Sarah Coakley, Jamie Smith, Reinhardt Hütter, Peter Ochs, and Nicholas Wolterstorff for their feedback on the ideas that eventually made their way into this chapter. (Those familiar with Wolterstorff's work in both aesthetics and hermeneutics will recognize its influence on the line of argument developed here.) Tom Flint, Jonathan Jacobs, Luke Reinsma, two anonymous referees, the philosophy department at Calvin College, and an audience at the conference "Philosophy and Liturgy: Ritual, Practice, and Embodied Wisdom," Calvin College, May 2008, also offered helpful input on a version of this essay. Finally, I owe special thanks to both Matt Halteman and Anne Poortenga for puzzling through these issues with me.

7

The Significance of Liturgical Singing

It is a striking feature of the Eastern Christian liturgies that they are almost entirely sung.[1] With the exception of the homily, almost nothing in these liturgies is merely spoken. Moreover, aside from the occasional gesture, such as when the priest bows to the assembled, virtually none of their actions are performed in silence. Instead, singing accompanies nearly all the actions that constitute these liturgies, including the action around which they revolve, namely, eating the eucharistic meal.

To my knowledge, the Eastern liturgies are unique among the Christian liturgies in this regard; none of the other Christian liturgies incorporates singing to the extent to which the Eastern liturgies do. Why is that?

A satisfactory reply to this question would be complex, but let me gesture toward the beginnings of an answer. All the liturgies in the Christian tradition exhibit an orientation, emphasizing certain activities rather than others. Many of the liturgies that belong to the Reformed traditions, for example, emphasize proclamation, placing the sermon at the center of the service; any singing that occurs in these liturgies is supposed to complement the sermon. Other liturgies, such as those of the Eastern churches, are oriented not toward proclamation but worship, moving through multiple episodes of petitioning, praising, and thanksgiving. Of course proclamation is not absent from the Eastern liturgies (any more than worship is absent from the Reformed liturgies). Nevertheless, proclamation does not lie at the heart of these liturgies; worship does.[2]

Once one appreciates the orientation of the Eastern liturgies, however, then it's apparent why singing figures so prominently in them. There is no more fitting way to express worship than in song. Yet it is one thing to say that singing in the liturgy fits its structure and orientation; it is another to identify

---

[1] Unless I indicate otherwise, when I speak of the Eastern liturgies, I'll have the eucharistic liturgies in mind. I should also note that I am, to a certain extent, working with a semi-idealized type of these liturgies in which many portions of the liturgical script are sung by the congregation (and not simply the choir, chanters, or celebrant).

[2] Here I echo von Allmen (1965) and Wolterstorff (1983), both of whom locate themselves within the Reformed tradition.

what it is about singing that makes it so fitting. In this chapter, I would like to address this last issue, exploring the topic of what (at least in part) the fittingness of liturgical singing consists in. By focusing on this issue, I realize that I am wandering far off the beaten path of topics standardly addressed by philosophers. Topics such as liturgy and ritualized activity—let alone the role that singing plays in such activities—are hardly the stuff on which philosophers cut their teeth! Be that as it may, I hope to show that the topic can bear philosophical fruit.

My discussion divides into four sections. In the first (Section 7.1), I engage with recent work in the philosophy of literature, exploring the theme that the form of a work is not incidental to its content but deeply shapes the sorts of information that it can express or that we can assimilate. I then turn in Section 7.2 to the Eastern liturgies themselves, paying special attention to several themes that figure prominently in their content. Section 7.3 engages with work in collective action, highlighting what is distinctive about the action of group singing. The last section (7.4) of the chapter ties together the topics introduced earlier in the discussion, arguing that singing the text of the Eastern liturgies is an activity of such a kind that its form guarantees that those who engage in it instantiate important elements of its content. Somewhat more specifically, in this section, I'll suggest that the fittingness of liturgical singing consists (at least in part) in the way that it exemplifies the understanding of *shalom/eirene* that the liturgical text itself calls for its participants to enact. I should stress at the outset that while my attention is focused on the fit between the form and the content of important and pervasive elements in the Eastern liturgies, I believe that the points I make here can be applied to other liturgies that I do not discuss.

7.1. FORM AND CONTENT

The overarching theme of Martha Nussbaum's collection of essays *Love's Knowledge* is that, while moral philosophy has largely ignored the role of literature in achieving moral understanding, it can no longer afford to do so.[3] The reason, Nussbaum claims, is not that those who write literature tend to explore important topics that moral philosophers ignore but that literary *forms*—in particular, the novel—can communicate truths about how we should live in ways that the academic journal article or monograph cannot. In the Introduction to *Love's Knowledge*, Nussbaum specifies more clearly

---

[3] Nussbaum (1990). I will insert page references to Nussbaum's book parenthetically in the text.

what she means by these claims, identifying two theses about form or "style" that she wishes to defend:

> My first claim insists that any style makes, itself, a statement: that an abstract theoretical style makes, like any other style, a statement about what is important and what is not, about what faculties of a reader are important for knowing and what are not. There may then be certain plausible views about the nature of the relevant portions of human life that cannot be housed within that form without generating a peculiar implicit contradiction. The second claim is, then, that for an interesting family of such views, a literary narrative of a certain sort is the only type of text that can state them fully and fittingly, without contradiction. (7)

Anglo-American analytic philosophy, Nussbaum continues, has rejected these claims, since it has either ignored "the relation between form and content altogether, or, when not ignoring it, to deny the first of our two claims, treating style as largely decorative—as irrelevant to the stating of content, and neutral among the contents that might be conveyed" (8).

As an illustration of what Nussbaum is driving at, consider the topic of friendship. If one wanted to better understand the nature of friendship, there are any number of philosophical texts to which one could turn, including Aristotle's discussion in book VIII of the *Nichomachean Ethics*. There one would find Aristotle distinguishing different types of friendship and specifying the conditions that any genuine friendship must satisfy, such as that friends be virtuous, have wealth to share, and so forth. Reading Wallace Stegner's depiction of friendship between two couples in his novel *Crossing to Safety*, in contrast, would be a very different experience. Stegner's text presents not only a rather different understanding of friendship—one in which good but less than virtuous characters are genuinely friends—but also a narrative in which we witness friendships, with their imperfections and limits, develop over time. *Crossing to Safety*, like other excellent novels, doesn't defend any sweeping claims about the nature of friendship; instead, it presents in rich detail a particular set of friendships in a context in which its characters must navigate illness, strong personalities, lack of ambition, jealousy, and the like. Of course Stegner doesn't simply present the everyday details of these friendships; his presentation is thoroughly stylized, selecting from the lives of his characters those details that contribute to his story.

In Nussbaum's view, books such as Stegner's make rather different demands of their readers than do (most) philosophical texts. Readers of a contemporary philosophical essay, says Nussbaum, are called upon to exercise their intellectual powers, to critically analyze whatever claims or lines of argument the author might be presenting. In contrast, readers of Stegner's book are supposed to immerse themselves in its narrative in such a way as to better appreciate the various forms that friendship might take, to calibrate their expectations regarding friendship, to deepen their understanding of friendship, and so forth. It's on the basis of this contrast that Nussbaum defends an additional pair of claims, which are considerably more ambitious.

The first is that literary forms such as the novel are particularly hospitable to Aristotelian conceptions of ethics that emphasize the particularity, open-endedness, complexity, and emotionally laden character of the ethical life. The second claim, which is an application of a thesis that Nussbaum voices in the passage quoted at the outset of this section, is that there is a kind of "contradiction" inherent in attempts to address topics such as friendship in the prose of Anglo-American analytic philosophy. The "contradiction," in Nussbaum's view, is that, on the one hand, philosophical prose calls readers to exercise their critical powers by analyzing whatever claims or arguments that an author may be presenting; this typically requires putting one's emotions at bay. But, on the other, such prose is employed to examine topics such as friendship, which are such that to understand them, readers need to exercise their ethical imagination and allow their emotions to be engaged. Thus, the "contradiction" between the form of the genre and its content.

By calling these claims of Nussbaum's "ambitious," I have already signaled some hesitation about them. To be acceptable, I believe that they would have to be heavily qualified. However that may be, I want to take very seriously Nussbaum's thesis that the form of a work can shape what it communicates to such an extent that there are types of understanding that it would be very difficult and perhaps impossible to impart by employing some other form. And, while I doubt there is any contradiction between the form of contemporary philosophical discourse and much of its content, Nussbaum seems to me clearly right to point out that the form of a work can have better or worse types of fit with its content. The question to pursue—as I mentioned earlier—is to locate what such fittingness might consist in.

To that end, let me introduce some terminology that will prove useful. In her discussion, Nussbaum has her eye exclusively on texts and the relations between their content and form. Rather than focus exclusively on texts, I would like to broaden the discussion and focus on *works*, whose examples include not only texts but also symphonies, operas, plays, dances, and the like.[4] A particularly important feature of works, given my purposes, is that agents can perform illocutionary acts of various sorts by the selection or creation of a work. By composing *Crossing to Safety*, for example, Stegner performed various illocutionary acts such as asserting, questioning, and praising, many of them in the fictive-mood. Given that works such as *Crossing to Safety* are used to perform illocutionary acts, they have content, where the content of an illocutionary act is simply what its speaker seeks to communicate in performing that act—anything that its audience must grasp in order to understand

---

[4] The *locus classicus* regarding works is Wolterstorff (1980).

what the speaker is saying. This is, admittedly, a broad understanding of content, incorporating the illocutionary force of a speech act, what is pragmatically conveyed by the performance of a speech act, and its propositional content. Although broad, this is the understanding of content that will be most suitable for our purposes.

With the notions of a work and its content in hand, we can now distinguish different types of form that a work can have. In the first place, works have what I'll call *primary form*. The primary form of a work is what is often called its *genre*. A text, for example, can be a case of a novel, an epic poem, or a philosophical essay—these all being different literary genres. Works that exhibit some primary form, however, can be presented in various ways. An epic poem can be sung, a short story can receive a dramatic reading, a symphony performance can be presented in film. These ways of presenting works are what I'll call their *secondary form*. A thesis for which I'll be arguing is that in addition to there being fittingness relations between the primary form of a work and its content, there are fittingness relations between the secondary form of the performance or occurrence of a work and its content. To lay out the case for this claim, however, we'll first need to explore important dimensions of the content of the Eastern liturgies.

7.2. THE VISION IN THE LITURGY

I started our discussion by noting that the Eastern Christian liturgies have the striking feature of being almost entirely sung. That is, in addition to having a primary form—which is an amalgamation of, among other things, poetry, prayer, narrative, and creedal declarations—the liturgy has the secondary form of being sung. In this section, I want to take a closer look at some prominent themes expressed in its content. Before I do so, I should acknowledge that the content of the liturgy is not exhausted by what the assembled verbalize in the performance of the liturgy, since the assembled perform illocutionary acts such as thanking by performing non-linguistic acts, such as eating. That noted, my attention in what follows will be focused primarily on the contents of the linguistic acts performed in the liturgy, although I'll also draw attention at various points to non-linguistic acts in which the assembled perform illocutionary acts.

Those familiar with the liturgy of St. John Chrysostom know that, after the priest declares the kingdom of the Father, Son, and Holy Spirit blessed, it begins with a series of petitions, the Great Litany. These petitions have the curious feature of not only presenting requests to God but also instructing the assembled how they are to perform these requests. The assembled are to pray not only "for the peace of the whole world," but also "in peace" and "with one accord."Later in the liturgy, the assembled receive similar instructions. In the Anaphora ("the lifting up"), for example, the deacon directs the assembled to not only offer the "holy oblation" or the eucharistic gift but also to do so in peace. And at the liturgy's conclusion, the priest directs the people not only to depart from the liturgy but also to do so in the same way that they began the liturgy, namely, "in peace."

If this is right, phrases such as "In peace, let us pray to the Lord," which are used repeatedly in the liturgy, function as exhortatory directives, both instructing and exhorting the assembled to perform liturgical actions, such as praying, in a certain way. There is evidence in the liturgical script, however, that phrases such as this are not simply directives but also play additional illocutionary roles. A clue that they do lies in a line that the deacon recites during the Litany before the Lord's Prayer, where he comments on what the assembled have accomplished thus far in the liturgy: "Having asked for the unity of the Faith, and the communion of the Holy Spirit, let us commend ourselves and each other, and all our life unto Christ our God." When read in conjunction with the text from the Great Litany, in which the assembled ask for such things as unity, this comment suggests that phrases such as "In peace, let us pray to the Lord" function not simply as instructions directed toward the assembled, but also as requests that the assembled direct toward God—among these being that the assembled present their petitions in peace and in unity. The suggestion seems to be that fulfilling the directives voiced by the deacon is not something that is entirely in the power of the assembled. Rather, their fulfilment is a corporate endeavor between the people and God, something that is accomplished by (and only by) joint divine and human activity. In a moment, I'll have more to say about the general phenomenon of corporate or collective action. For now, let me also note that the deacon's comment also suggests that the peace requested is not a state that pertains to the assembled alone. What has been requested, according to the deacon, is also "communion with the Holy Spirit."

Before reflecting on these features of the liturgy, there is another dimension of what the deacon says that deserves mention. For note that, in addition to commenting on what has been accomplished in the liturgy, the deacon exhorts the assembled with these words: "let us commend ourselves and each other, and all our life unto Christ our God." In English, this sentence is striking. By pairing the singular noun "life" with a verbal phrase that incorporates the first-person plural pronoun, this sentence communicates the idea that the assembled enjoy a common, unified life. And this phrase is not an isolated case. Later in the liturgy, the assembled recite other lines that employ the same construction: "let us all say with all our soul and all our mind, Lord have mercy" and "Unto you we commend our whole life and our hope, O Master who loves humankind."

As it happens, what is striking in the English translation of the liturgy is not so striking in the original Greek. Idiomatic Greek often pairs singular nouns such as "life" with verbal phrases that incorporate the first-person plural pronoun; the English translation of the liturgy simply preserves this grammatical construction, which is idiosyncratic by the standards of ordinary English. A closer look at the liturgical script, however, reveals that the use of images of unity is not merely an artifact of an unusual Greek grammatical construction. For, in addition to the phrases just quoted, there are phrases that express the idea that the assembled are, in the liturgy, to be united in their action: "Let us love one another that with one mind we may confess Father, Son, and Holy Spirit" and "Grant that with one mouth and one heart we may praise your all-honorable and majestic name." (Later, I'll comment on the aptness of the phrase "with one heart.")

Interspersed throughout the liturgy, then, are exhortatory directives that the assembled perform the actions that compose the liturgy in peace and in a state of unity. These directives, I believe, are best understood as expressing adequacy conditions for the performance of the liturgy: a performance of the liturgy is adequate only to the extent that the assembled actually perform actions that satisfy these directives, such as the action of requesting peace of the world and doing so in unity. Under this interpretation, were some performance of the liturgy not to satisfy these conditions, then it would thereby be defective. For example, if the assembled were to recite the words of the liturgy but not thereby engage in the activity of requesting such things as peace for the world, then their performance of the liturgy would be defective.

At this point, fascinating and difficult questions bubble to the surface. For, if what I've said is correct, the liturgy, like a symphony, admits of adequate and defective performances. But the conditions of adequacy for the performance of a symphony differ markedly from those for the performance of the liturgy. In one sense, the conditions for the adequate performance of a symphony are considerably more stringent than those for the adequate performance of the liturgy. If a performance of a symphony is to be adequate, after all, each of its members must follow the symphonic score rather closely; only minor deviations are allowed. In contrast, if a performance of the liturgy is to be adequate, it needn't be the case that each of the assembled follow the liturgical script rather closely, for a performance of the liturgy can be adequate when some of the assembled do not or cannot perform such actions as requesting peace for the world. Rather, what renders a performance of the liturgy adequate is that *the assembled* make such requests, where the assembled cannot be identified with the totality of people assembled.

But in other ways, the conditions for the adequate performance of a symphony are considerably less stringent than those for the adequate performance of the liturgy. The conditions of adequacy for the performance of a symphony do not dictate that the members of the symphony be at peace with one another (or anything of the sort). All they need do is follow the symphonic score. In contrast, the conditions of adequacy for the performance of the liturgy require that the members of the assembled bear relations to one another such as being at peace and being in unity.

On this occasion, let me bracket the question of what brings it about that the assembled (as opposed to those assembled) perform such actions as requesting, focusing on the issue of what the frequent directives to pray in peace could mean. None of us, I imagine, is tempted to interpret the directive that the assembled pray in peace to mean that the assembled are to enact a *truce* among themselves; even if this were something that the assembled needed to achieve, its achievement wouldn't imply that the assembled are in any interesting sense unified. Given, however, other directives voiced in the liturgy—such as the exhortatory directive voiced in the Cherubic Hymn "to cast aside all earthly cares" and Jesus's directives not to worry about what tomorrow may bring—it would not be implausible to understand these directives as instructing the assembled to offer their petitions from a state of inner-peace or tranquility. It would, after all, be a rare case in which none of the assembled attend the liturgy with troubled hearts.

While not implausible, I think that this understanding of the directive to perform liturgical actions in peace could be only partially correct. Let me explain why.

A central contention of Nicholas Wolterstorff's *Until Justice and Peace Embrace* is that a comprehensive vision animates the Hebrew and Christian scriptures, one according to which the ideal for which we are to strive is *shalom* or *eirene*—translated in English as "peace."[5] As Wolterstorff understands it, shalom/eirene is not a state of individual agents—a state of inner-tranquility—but a state that supervenes on normative *relations* that agents bear to themselves and other things, including other agents. Specifically, shalom/eirene is a state that supervenes on agents being rightly related to themselves, others, the natural world, and God. A theme that Wolterstorff stresses in his presentation is that when the scriptures offer us images of shalom/eirene—such as in passages from the Hebrew prophets—these images are ethically infused; they include images in which the downtrodden are lifted up, the oppressed are treated with dignity, and the weak receive just treatment. According to the scriptural presentation, the effect of agents standing in these ethically infused relations is twofold. In the first place, when agents stand in these normative relations, states of harmony and unity take hold—harmony among the animals, harmony among human beings, harmony between nature and human beings, harmony between human beings and God, and so forth. Second, when agents stand in these right relations, there is no fissure between

---

[5] Wolterstorff (1983), especially ch. 6.

duty and delight. Rather, the people delight in standing in these ethically infused right relations and the harmony in which they result. An implication of this last point is that to delight in shalom/eirene is itself also a component of shalom/eirene.

When viewed against the comprehensive vision of shalom/eirene, liturgical actions take on new significance; they are not empty gestures but ways in which the assembled enact the vision of shalom/eirene. Think, for example, of the various actions of the liturgy in which the people interact with elements of (or products of) the natural world, such as when the priest blesses the people with water or the assembled kiss a cross of wood at the conclusion of the liturgy. When they perform these actions, these natural elements are treated not with indifference but with reverence. As the Orthodox theologian Alexander Schmemann has repeatedly pointed out, when they are so treated, these natural elements function as points of contact, means of communion with God.[6]

On this occasion, I am going to have to postpone a fuller discussion of the various ways in which the variety of liturgical actions enact the vision of shalom/eirene, settling instead for voicing a general proposal, which is that we understand the liturgy's frequent directives that the assembled perform actions in peace as speech acts that direct the assembled to perform these actions in such a way that they enact and enhance shalom/eirene. If this proposal is correct, the injunction to pray in peace is not, in the first instance, a directive to pray *for* peace or to *be at* peace with oneself when one prays. Nor, for that matter, is it a directive to pray *from* a state of peace. Rather, it is a directive that the assembled pray in a shalom-enacting and enhancing way—a way such that their praying contributes to the realization of important elements of shalom/eirene, such as being rightly related to one another and God. In what remains, the question that I want to pursue is why corporate singing in the liturgy would be a shalom-enacting and enhancing action. To do that, we need to explore the character of group singing.

7.3. MUSICAL UNITY

Reading texts such as novels is for most of us a solitary activity. Although these texts are communal in the sense that they are the subject of joint exploration and discussion, the activity of reading is itself not something we typically perform together. The same is not true of singing, however. We often sing

---

[6] Schmemann (1969) develops this theme.

together. Indeed, we intentionally form and participate in groups such as choirs precisely because we enjoy it so much.

As it happens, the phenomenon of group singing has recently caught the attention of a group of diverse thinkers interested in musical cognition.[7] In a discussion of Stacy Horn's book on group singing, *Imperfect Harmony*, the neuroscientist Daniel Levitin comments that he finds two aspects of group singing particularly striking. The first is that when we engage in group singing, "it brings us outside ourselves. It forces us to think about what another person is doing.... We have to pay attention to what someone else is doing" and "coordinate our actions with theirs." This, says, Levitin, pulls us "out of ourselves" to see how we "fit into a larger whole." For to competently engage in group singing, "you're not just...executing your part. You're trying to make it merge with the parts of others."[8] The second thing that Levitin notes is that group singing has profound physiological effects on those who participate in it; we have evidence, for example, that when people sing together, it not only releases oxytocin—the so-called "social bonding hormone"—but also (among other things) increases the production of immunoglobulins that enhance our immune system.[9]

In calling attention to the first aspect of group singing, Levitin seems to suggest that while group singing is a collective action, it is also a collective action of a distinctive sort. Since Levitin's observations directly bear upon the thesis that I would like to defend, I suggest that we pursue the issue of whether Levitin is right about this, beginning with the notion of a collective action.

Common to all accounts of collective action is the thesis that, if the behavior of some group of people counts as a collective action, it is not enough that members of that group perform the same act-type.[10] To use John Searle's well-known example, suppose a group of people is sitting on the grass when a storm rolls through. If each member of the group performs the action of running for cover to a nearby gazebo, theirs is not a collective action. It would count as such only if the members of the group had shared intentions of a particular sort: in this case, the intention that we, who belong to this group, perform the action of running to the gazebo together (say, because we are engaged in a piece of performance art).

But even sharing a "we intention" of this sort is not enough for some action that expresses such an intention to count as collective, since collective action requires that our intentions fit together in the right way. To see why, suppose

[7] See, in particular, Levitin (2006), Horn (2013), and the BodyScore project run by Gothenberg University.

[8] Available at <http://www.npr.org/2013/06/03/188355968/imperfect-harmony-how-chorale-singing-changes-lives> (accessed August 21, 2015).

[9] Horn (2013), 147. In her discussion, Horn specifies other physical and psychological effects of group singing.

[10] In what follows, I borrow primarily from Searle (1990) and Bratman (2009).

that you and I share the intention to travel to New York City together. If you intend to go there with me "mafia style" by throwing me in the trunk of your car and I intend to go there with you "mafia style" by throwing you in the trunk of my car, then our shared intentions don't fit together in the right way for us to perform a collective action. For our action to be genuinely collective, we both need to take into account each other's relevant intentions, taking each other to be intentional co-participants in the performance of the action. I must intend to get to the city (in part) by way of the execution of your intention and you must intend to get to the city (in part) by way of the execution of my intention. What is more, if we intend to go to New York City together by taking into account each other's relevant intentions, then we must intend to do so in a way that our sub-plans mesh in this further sense: our intentions must be co-realizable. If we are to perform the collective action of travelling to the city together, I cannot plan to get there with you by car and you cannot intend to get there with me by train. This last point highlights the fact that, in order for ours to be a collective action, we must not only share intentions of the relevant sort (related in the right ways), but must also be aware that we do.

Return, now, to the passages in which Levitin claims that group singing is a type of collective action. Recall that, when he does, Levitin says that group singing is a type of collective action that pulls us "out of ourselves" in a way that we "fit into a larger whole," "merging with the parts of others." Suppose, for the moment, that we understand well enough the phenomena to which Levitin gestures when he uses these phrases. With the preceding sketch of collective action in hand, the question to raise—it seems to me—is whether Levitin is correct to suggest that group singing is a distinctive sort of collective action, which has features that other collective actions lack, or whether the features to which Levitin adverts are simply implications of performing a collective action. Painting a house together and collectively producing a hollandaise sauce, for example, are collective actions. Are they also the sorts of actions that, in virtue of being collective, pull us out of ourselves, forcing us to merge with the actions of others simply in virtue of being collective?

Let me address this question by engaging with a book that I mentioned a moment ago, namely, Horn's *Imperfect Harmony*, since it complements what Levitin says in some instructive ways. In her discussion of the dynamics of group singing, Horn includes some fascinating reflections on the character of group singing offered by members of a choir of which she is a member. One fellow choir member tells Horn that singing harmonies together is

> like going from two dimensions to three. What is flat takes shape. And when the harmonies are just right, it's like you've created a hologram out of thin air. But it's ephemeral, so you have to keep infusing it with energy for it to stay alive. Physically, the sensation is of connection . . . [it's] a buzz. You make a contribution of sound waves and air-waves, and something more complex, something you couldn't possibly produce on your own, comes back to you. You constantly adjust

your contribution. And it's focusing—or getting lost—in this feedback loop of producing sound and enjoying your labor at the same time. It requires more concentration than if you were producing sound or singing on your own . . . and thus you really do get lost—in the sense that you can't worry about anything else in your life at that moment.[11]

Using a different series of metaphors, another choir member explains the experience as one in which "physically it feels like there is a space above my head that we all meld into, that is the purest form of together, a spiritual unworldly space."[12]

Admittedly, it would be unusual for a philosopher to use many of these images ("a space above my head that we all meld into") when describing the character of group singing. Still, I want to suggest that, when combined with what Levitin says, these passages give us a better sense of why group singing is a collective action of a distinctive sort.

Before I explain why, however, let me narrow our focus, so as to bring out more clearly what these passages communicate. Group singing is something that can be done poorly or well. Clearly, the passages just cited concern the activity when it's performed competently. I'll follow them in this respect, focusing on the competent performance of group singing. Moreover, group singing can take various forms; it can be improvised or scripted, can take a call-and-response form or that of singing in harmony simultaneously. The passages cited above clearly concern scripted group singing in which participants sing in harmony. I'll also follow them in this regard, focusing on singing of this sort.[13] In addition, group singing can take more or less paradigmatic forms, ranging from singing along with the radio, to singing along with a recording of a live performance of group singing, to actually singing along with others in a live setting. I'll have cases of the last sort in mind, which I take to be paradigmatic. Finally, when engaging in group singing, we can rehearse some musical work, which might require that we frequently stop to fine tune our singing by discussing or experimenting with our parts, or we could perform it, which would require that (all else being equal) we not do this. In what follows, I'll have not rehearsing but performing in mind. These points noted, let's turn to that which these passages are drawing our attention.

Group singing clearly seems to satisfy the criteria for collective action specified above: it requires the requisite "we intentions," that these intentions fit together in the right ways, and awareness of one another's intentions. Specifically, it requires that the members of a group follow some musical score for the sake of performing some musical work. The question that I'm interested in pursuing is whether there is more to it than this. As a first step

---

[11] Horn (2013), 120.   [12] Horn (2013), 121.
[13] This last assumption, I should add, is compatible with a musical score being such that it calls for various sections to be improvised.

toward addressing this question, begin by noting that you and I can paint a house together or execute a football play together and, while we do so, pay virtually no attention to one another's activities: while painting, I can be on one side of the house and you on the other; while executing the play, I can be on one side of the field, and you on the other. What matters for the competent performance of these actions is that we execute our intentions and that these intentions mesh in the right way. Group singing is much different, since it requires not only this but also that, while I sing, I pay attention to your singing, and while you sing, you pay attention to my singing. Call this activity that is required in order to engage in group singing *full divided attention*—"full" because one's attention is entirely devoted to the singing that is occurring and "divided" because one's attention is simultaneously directed at one's own singing and others' singing. Although the point may seem obvious, the way by which we engage in full divided attention is crucial: we do so by *listening* to the sequences of sounds that each of us is producing while we produce them. In a moment, I'll have more to say about the role of listening in group singing.

As the passages quoted earlier indicate, however, to engage in group singing also requires that I adjust my singing to yours and that you adjust your singing to mine in "real time," often in ways that are not dictated by the score that we are following. You may, for example, hold a note longer than I anticipated or syncopate a phrase in an unusual way; if we are singing together, then, all else being equal, I will try to match the length for which you hold the note or blend the rhythm of my singing with yours. In contrast, suppose that you and I are making a hollandaise sauce together side-by-side in the kitchen. Doing so will require that we respond to each other's actions but it doesn't require that we do so more or less simultaneously. What this highlights is that while there are important diachronic elements in group singing—we must, for example, anticipate what each other is going to do—the sort of responsiveness that is required in group singing is fundamentally synchronic: what I sing right now must fit with what you are singing right now by being responsive to it. For ease of reference, let's call this characteristic of group singing *coordinated real-time responsiveness*—or simply *real-time responsiveness*. Importantly, real-time responsiveness needn't involve the meshing of intentions in the sense that when I respond to the way in which you sing something, I intend to match the way that you intend to sing it. But it must involve a meshing of *actions*. You might, for example, unintentionally sing a sequence of notes more loudly than usual; for my singing to fit with yours, I need to respond to what you do and not to what you intend to do.

When we combine these two points about attention and responsiveness, the importance of the sensory modality primarily at work in group singing—namely, hearing—comes to the fore. Engaging in some comparisons can help us to see the point.

Imagine, once again, that you and I are engaged in the shared activity of producing a hollandaise sauce together. In principle, we could both simultaneously attend to the flavors, texture, and aroma of the sauce. But, given the nature of these sensory modalities, there's no way for (i) me to respond to your action of adding some ingredient at time t by my tasting, feeling, or smelling the sauce at t while (ii) you respond to my adding some ingredient at t by your tasting, feeling, or smelling the sauce at t. We cannot, that is, attentively taste, feel, or smell together in the sense that what I do at some time is more or less simultaneously responsive to what you're doing at that time simply by each of us employing one or another of these sensory modalities. Rather, if we're using the modality of taste, I must first taste the sauce and then respond to what I've tasted. You must too. In this imagined scenario, in which we are both attending to the flavors of the hollandaise sauce and responding to changes in the flavors, the closest analogue to singing would be a call-and-response format in which one person at one time responds to what another person does at another time. The same would be true if we were introducing new ingredients to our sauce by both attentively smelling or touching the sauce.

I suppose the closest we could come to a case in which we exercise full divided attention and real-time responsiveness by the use of another sensory modality would be a case involving vision. Imagine, then, that we are painters who decide to paint some work together—say, a still life—by reference to some agreed upon performance-plan. Could there be times at which, when we're side by side at an easel, when my painting proceeds by my attending to and responding to what you paint at (more or less) those same times? And could the same be true of you? Could my painting with a particular stroke and color at a time be something that I accomplish by paying full attention to what you are painting at that time? I suppose so—although the case is difficult to imagine because of the motor skills and skills of attention that it would require. Indeed, even if there were times in which we could execute our plan, the primary difficulty would be whether we could sustain it for any length of time, since the coordination of our actions would be incredibly difficult.

In contrast, attending to and responding to some sequence of sounds you produce by listening to them at more or less the same time as you sing them while I also attend to the sequence of sounds I am singing is something that, with a minimal amount of training, we find relatively easy to do. What I want to further suggest is that it's this ability of ours to at once exercise full divided attention and real-time responsiveness to each other when singing that accounts (at least in part) for the experience, in group singing, of "connectedness," "merging," and "melding," to which figures such as Levitin and Horn call our attention. The modality of hearing allows us to exercise these capacities when singing, rendering it possible to synchronize our efforts in ways that would be very difficult using other sensory modalities. I would stress that this ability of ours to exercise full divided attention and real-time responsiveness would only partially account for the phenomenology characteristic of group singing. The fact that those who participate in group singing are aware of their shared intention to perform a work by their mutual contribution is also important. And, as Levitin points out, the fact that our bodies release oxytocin when engaging in group singing and that the heart rates of those who sing together almost immediately synchronize are probably also part of the explanation.[14] Fascinatingly, and important for my purposes, when the heart rates of singers are synchronized, this effect is most pronounced when they sing slower music, such as hymns.

Is there, then, something about the character of group singing that renders it a distinctive sort of collective action, distinguishing it from the many sorts of other collective actions that we perform? I've claimed that there is. While it is a paradigmatic case of a collective action, group singing also requires the exercise of capacities such as full divided attention and real-time responsiveness. It is the exercise of these capacities, I further claimed, that explain (in part) the phenomenology of group singing, which is characterized by an experience of connectedness or unity so often adverted to by those who engage in the activity.

7.4. PULLING THINGS TOGETHER

Our discussion opened with the observation that none of the Christian liturgies incorporates singing to the extent that the Eastern Orthodox liturgies do. We noted that while singing is a particularly fitting way to express worship, it would be worthwhile to pursue the question of what this fittingness consists in. Using Nussbaum's discussion as a guide, we observed that the form of a work can bear fittingness relations of various kinds to its content. A closer look at the Eastern liturgies revealed that themes of shalom/eirene figure heavily in their content—where shalom/eirene is a state that supervenes on agents bearing normative relations of various kinds to one another and the natural world. Specifically, the liturgical script repeatedly directs and exhorts the assembled to perform liturgical actions, such as praying, in peace (shalom/eirene) and unity. In this regard, the liturgy, or so its text indicates, is to be a shalom-enacting and enhancing activity. Having taken account of these themes, we then turned to the topic of singing, interacting with literature on the nature of collective action. While group singing is a paradigmatic collective action, it is also distinctive in various respects, requiring attention and

---

[14] NPR. Available at <http://www.ckh.gu.se/english/research/bodyscore/more-about-bodyscore> (accessed August 21, 2015).

responsiveness of special sorts on the part of its participants. The types of attention and responsiveness that group singing requires, I conjectured, account (at least in part) for the pronounced phenomenology that so often attends group singing, which is that of being united or merging with others.

Let me pull these various strands of our discussion together by engaging once again with Nussbaum, who, you'll recall, defends the thesis that, when it comes to literary works, there are various sorts of fittingness relations that hold between their content and what I've called their primary form. The primary form of works in academic moral philosophy, says Nussbaum, fails to fit much of their contents, at least when those works concern how we should live. A philosophical article, for example, might argue that "the emotions are essential and central in our efforts to gain understanding of any important ethical matter; and yet it is written in a style that expresses only intellectual activity and strongly suggests that only this activity matters for the reader in his or her attempts to understand" (21). The primary form of literary works, such as the novel, in contrast, fits remarkably well with their content. When Stegner presents a narrative regarding two pairs of friends in *Crossing to Safety*—to return to an earlier example—his discussion calls forth from the reader an engagement with the text that is directed toward the particulars of these relationships. The text raises questions about these relationships and leaves them unresolved; by the employment of both imagination and sentiment, the reader is presented with the task of trying to work through the complexities of these relationships, assessing where they fall short, why they are so resilient, and so forth.

In my view, the liturgy can function in ways similar to the ways in which Nussbaum holds that literature functions, calling forth from its participants such activities as imaginatively identifying with characters presented in the liturgical script that are alien in important respects.[15] While the similarities between literature and liturgy are important, I want here to focus on some prominent differences.

Call an activity *content-engaging* if it is such that by performing it one engages that content by doing such things as presenting it, trying to understand it, evaluating it, or the like. Reading is a content-engaging activity; in the ordinary case, we read texts in order to understand them, be edified by them, be entertained by them, and the like. But, in the ordinary case, reading is not an activity such that by engaging in it one instantiates important properties expressed by the content with which one engages. In the ordinary case, when reading about friendship, one does not thereby instantiate friendship. In the ordinary case, by reading about a character's foibles, one does not thereby instantiate those foibles. In contrast, participating in liturgical singing is,

---

[15] See Cuneo (2015a), included as Chapter 5 in the present volume.

I want to suggest, a content-engaging activity such that, in the paradigmatic case, one instantiates important elements of the content with which one is engaging. Such participation is, I shall say, *content-instantiating*.

For, at various junctures of the liturgy, I've pointed out, the assembled do such things as pray for the shalom/eirene of the world, are enjoined to be at shalom/eirene with one another, ask for "one heart and mind," and so forth. They perform these activities by singing together. A theme that emerged in our discussion is that group singing is not only a paradigmatic collective action that requires its participants to have shared intentions of the right sort that bear the right sorts of relationships to one another; it also requires that its participants carefully attend to each other's actions, responding to them in "real time" in such a way that they fit together for the sake of contributing to the performance of a work.

If this is right, when the assembled engage in group singing, they thereby instantiate important elements of shalom/eirene—elements that form important and pervasive elements of the content of the work that they are singing. Shalom/eirene, after all, does not descend upon us from out of the blue; it is something that is achieved by doing such things as being attentive to the actions of the other, responding in appropriate ways to these actions, and acting together for the purpose of actualizing something commonly recognized to be of worth. If this is true of shalom/eirene, then singing the liturgical script together is content-instantiating, as these are the very qualities that those who engage in singing the liturgy instantiate. It may also be worth remembering that, according to the scriptural presentation of shalom/eirene, it is a state that is characterized by delight; those who stand in these right relations delight in being so related. In the paradigmatic case, group singing has the additional feature of being something in which its participants delight. To the extent to which shalom/eirene is characterized by delight in these right normative relations, then this is another, extended sense in which the performance of the liturgy is content-instantiating. Nor should we overlook the fact that when the assembled ask to pray with "one heart," their heart rates are, in the paradigmatic case, actually synchronized!

When Levitin and Horn write about singing, they repeatedly draw attention to its phenomenology—what it's like to engage in the activity. Indeed, they often do so in quasi-religious terms; such singing, they point out, has the effect of effacing differences that might otherwise divide those who sing together, whether political, racial, or socio-economic. And here, perhaps, we touch on one of the more important dimensions of liturgical singing. The liturgical script does not present the assembled with an abstract description of shalom/eirene. It presents them with images of shalom/eirene—such as those in the Psalms—and directs them to enact important elements of it. Most importantly for my purposes, it affords the assembled the experience—a taste—of *what it's like* to be in a state of shalom/eirene. When all goes well, to engage in liturgical singing is not simply to instantiate important elements of the content of the liturgical text but also to experience what one is singing about.

The sort of experiential understanding of shalom/eirene that participation in the liturgy affords is not only unique but, I believe, also significant to the religious life. Let me close by suggesting why.

In our day-to-day lives, we commonly distinguish different ways in which we can understand something. It is one thing, we say, to understand that child-rearing involves various tasks and responsibilities; it is another thing altogether to experience having and raising a child, carrying out these tasks and being subject to these responsibilities. Articulating the difference between these two types of understanding in anything but the most abstract terms proves, moreover, extremely difficult; there is something what it's like to have and raise a child that is difficult to communicate to others. Among other things, there is the experience of what it's like to have someone else's well-being more or less completely depend on you. Those committed to the religious life have been telling us something similar for millennia. According to these people, it is one thing to understand that this life involves devotion to God and the biblical vision of shalom/eirene; it is another thing altogether to experience this way of life "from the inside," to have experiential acquaintance with elements of the vision of shalom/eirene that animates it. Articulating the difference between the two types of understanding in anything but the most abstract terms is, moreover, extremely challenging; it proves to be no easy task to communicate to another who lacks the experience what it's like to engage in this way of life.

Although articulating the difference between these two types of understanding is difficult, we can perhaps say this much: when we talk of experience providing understanding, we sometimes mean that it has provided greater depth of insight into some topic, person, relation, or event—perhaps because this experience has expanded our conceptual repertoire or refined our conceptual expertise. At other times, when we speak of experience providing understanding, we mean to draw attention to the fact that this experience has expanded our vision; we now see what we had failed to see, or see better how things hang together than we did previously—once again, perhaps because we have expanded our conceptual repertoire or refined the employment of our concepts.

Experiencing what it's like to be in a state of shalom/eirene, I want to suggest, is precisely the sort of state that affords understanding of both types. We can know in the abstract that standing in right relations with ourselves, others, the natural world, and God is valuable, something worth pursuing. But understanding what it's like to stand in these relations can offer a unique sort of experiential acquaintance with their worth, offering us experiential insight into why such relations are worth cherishing and pursuing—although, once again, articulating this depth of insight can be very difficult. Correlatively, we can know in the abstract that standing in right relations with ourselves, others, the natural world, and God are interrelated in various ways. But actually experiencing a state in which one simultaneously enjoys such states can help us be acquainted with what it's like for these states to mesh, helping us to appreciate that often there is no sharp division between being in unity with one another, the natural world, and God.

In drawing attention to the experiential dimensions of liturgical singing, I have entered into the territory occupied by discussions of religious experience. Philosophers of religion have not ignored religious experience. On the contrary, some of the most probing discussions in the contemporary literature concern it. But almost always these discussions concern mystical or "uncanny" religious experience. In contrast, the experience of being in a state of shalom/ eirene, which I am suggesting so often accompanies liturgical singing, is not (in the ordinary case) mystical or unusual but fairly common. It is religious nonetheless, belonging to the unduly neglected category of *ordinary religious experience*.[16]

[16] My thanks to David J. Clark, Randall Harp, Eleonore Stump, Nick Wolterstorff, and an anonymous referee for their comments.

8

Ritual Knowledge

Christian belief has faced and continues to face no shortage of challenges. Some challenges are broadly internal, generated by the Christian tradition itself. An example of such a challenge would be the controversy that animated the fourth-century discussion regarding what to believe of the person of Jesus. Other challenges, by contrast, are broadly external, typically generated not by the Christian tradition itself, but by those who stand outside of it. An example of such a challenge would be the charge that death cannot be due to human sin, as the Christian scriptures teach, since long before there were human beings who could sin, other animals suffered and died, often at remarkable rates.

The contemporary discussion of the epistemology of religious belief is driven by not an internal but an external challenge. While the challenge takes a variety of forms, each of its versions accuses religious belief of being epistemically defective in some way: irrational, unjustified, unwarranted, or the like. Over the last twenty-five years, this challenge has met stiff resistance. According to the resisters, it is not religious belief that is defective but the challenge itself. For nearly always, the resisters maintain, the challenge incorporates a commitment to inflated or otherwise unacceptable accounts of what epistemically meritorious beliefs would be. Given a more nearly adequate account of what such beliefs would be—so the resisters continue—we can see that religious beliefs can and often do exhibit epistemic merits such as being entitled, justified, warranted, and the like.[1]

The project of responding to this external challenge strikes me as eminently worthwhile. We have learned a great deal about what it is for beliefs to exhibit epistemic merits from it. But the project also carries risks. One such risk is that, in focusing almost exclusively on this external challenge to religious belief, philosophers have paid insufficient attention to both the variety and the roles of the religious attitudes, neglecting to ask questions about their

---

[1] The most prominent work of the resisters includes Plantinga and Wolterstorff (1983), Wolterstorff (1984) and (2010b), Alston (1992), Plantinga (2000), and Swinburne (2005).

character and purpose in the religious life. The result is often a lopsided picture of religious life "on the ground."

Let me illustrate what I mean. In his book *Warranted Christian Belief,* Alvin Plantinga develops an account of religious belief-formation that he calls the Aquinas/Calvin or "A/C" model. According to the A/C model, we human beings are endowed with an array of epistemic faculties, among which is the *sensus divinitatis* or "sense of the divine." Like our other indigenous epistemic faculties, the *sensus divinitatis* operates according to a design plan, which is itself calibrated to form true beliefs in congenial circumstances. When the *sensus divinitatis* operates according to its design plan in such circumstances, it yields warranted religious beliefs and, indeed, religious knowledge.

How does the *sensus divinitatis* yield such beliefs? According to the A/C model, it does so when various types of experiences occasion beliefs with theistic content. For example, when you or I contemplate the starry skies above, we might find ourselves forming the belief *that God is the designer of the universe.* Or, to enrich the model somewhat, when you or I hear the Gospel proclaimed, we might find ourselves forming the belief *that Christ has atoned for the sins of humanity.* What distinguishes beliefs of this last kind from beliefs of the former kind is not simply their distinctively Christian content. If Plantinga is right, these specifically Christian beliefs can also be viewed as having been evoked by divine action, what Plantinga calls (following Aquinas) the "internal instigation of the Holy Spirit."[2] Plantinga is quick to emphasize that all this is merely a *model* of religious-belief formation in the paradigmatic case. Still, he also maintains that were Christian theism true, it would be unsurprising if something close to the A/C model (in both its generic theistic and expanded Christian form) were to capture the way in which things actually go for many religious believers.[3]

Two features of the A/C model leap to the eye. The first is that human agency seems to play almost no role in the formation of warranted religious belief. When, for example, Plantinga presents cases in which ordinary people might form religious beliefs, these people hardly do anything. For their beliefs to be formed, they need do only such things as look up into the starry sky above or hear the Gospel proclaimed, at least in congenial circumstances. At no point does the A/C model hint at the fact that, in the paradigmatic case, religious beliefs might be the fruit of extended effort, including engaging in those activities that are so often central to religious life, such as prayer, meditation, fasting, and what the Eastern Fathers call "watchfulness."[4] Nor, for that matter, does the model hint at the fact that these practical activities might play a crucial role in determining whether religious beliefs enjoy

[2] Plantinga (2000), chs. 8–9.   [3] Ibid., 285.
[4] See the section attributed to St. Hesychios the Priest (ca. eighth–ninth century) in Palmer, Sherrard, and Ware (1979), 162.

warrant. *Warranted Christian Belief* includes an entire chapter dedicated to the topic of the cognitive consequences of sin. Still, it never broaches the topic of whether engaging in the religious disciplines might be the very sort of activity that removes various impediments to (or abets) the proper working of the *sensus divinitatis*. As the A/C model presents things, these activities seem merely to be that which *occasion* the formation of warranted religious beliefs but not that which *determine* (even partially) whether these beliefs are warranted.

The second striking feature of the A/C model is that it presents the outputs of the *sensus divinitatis* as beliefs whose objects are propositions concerning God (or God's activity), such as *that God is the designer of the universe* or *that Christ has atoned for the sins of humanity*. Plantinga develops the idea that, in the paradigmatic case, when these beliefs constitute religious faith, they are accompanied by conative states of various sorts such as desiring and enjoying God's presence. The paradigm case of religious faith, says Plantinga, is "sure and certain knowledge" of God that is "sealed to the heart . . . in the having of the right sorts of affections."[5] Taken at face value, this formulation tells us that the role of the affections in faith is to cement or more deeply entrench the state of knowing various propositions about God.

I think we should find this striking. When, for example, the writer of *Hebrews* presents to the reader what it is to have faith, he presents what are not primarily reports regarding the mental lives of persons of faith but *action narratives*, stories of what these people have done. These narratives suggest that paradigmatic religious faith consists not merely or even primarily in a person's being certain of propositions regarding God (or having certain affections that seal this knowledge) but rather in his being practically oriented toward the world in certain ways, such as being disposed to engage in acts of gratitude toward God.[6]

My purpose in making these observations is, as I say, not to pour cold water on the contemporary discussion of the religious attitudes. Nor is it to suggest that the A/C model could not be amended to accommodate these observations. It is rather to illustrate the point that, by largely omitting the practical dimensions of the religious life, the contemporary discussion threatens to offer a distorted picture of the religious attitudes and, more generally, what it is to be a religious believer. Given the character of Christianity, it could not be otherwise. Christianity is not a body of propositions. Its fundamental aim is not to produce agents that form warranted beliefs about God. Nor is its aim to

[5] See Plantinga (2000), 291, 323.
[6] Although Plantinga comes close to entertaining a more expansive account of faith on p. 293, it's clear that his eye is on not the role of acting, but the role of the affections in faith: the "difference between believer and devil . . . lies in the area of *affections*" (ibid.). For reasons that will emerge later in this discussion, this seems to me incorrect.

increase the likelihood that its adherents will have mystical experiences of God. Christianity is, rather, a way of life that is thoroughly practical. It is dedicated to *engaging* God in various ways by doing such things as blessing, petitioning, and thanking God—activities about which, I should add, philosophers have said virtually nothing.

Although the aim of the Christian way of life is practical, there is nevertheless a perfectly good sense in which it aims to provide knowledge of God. But the knowledge in question, I suggest, is often not knowledge *that* one or another proposition regarding God is true but knowledge *how* to engage and live in communion with God. "If you wish to behold and commune with Him who is beyond sense perception and concept," writes the fourth-century monastic Evagrios of Pontikos, then you must engage in such activities as prayer, singing the Psalms, giving alms, and engaging in the rites of the church.[7] Under the approach that Evagrios advocates, knowing God is fundamentally a practical activity.

Appreciating this point about the practical aim of the Christian way of life, I believe, opens up new vistas in the epistemology of the religious attitudes. For it helps to bring together two sides of the Christian tradition that do not often meet in contemporary philosophical discussion. On the one hand is the insistence, which lies deep in the Christian tradition, that the Christian way of life includes as one of its central components ritualized activity, such as participating in the liturgical actions of the church. Gregory of Nyssa voices this conviction when he writes that the power of Christianity resides not in its philosophical sophistication but in the "power of regeneration by faith" and the "participation in mystical symbols and rites."[8] On the other hand is the conviction that a central aim of the Christian life is not to theorize about God but to know God. Were we to view knowing God as (in part) a species of practical knowledge, this would—or so I suggest—help us to see how these two sides of the Christian tradition fit together. It would allow us to see that knowing how to engage in ritualized activity is, when all goes well, a way in which we know God.

This last claim does not wear its meaning on its face, so let me unpack it. When I speak of knowing God, I have in mind a considerably broader notion of knowing than that employed by most epistemologists, who tend to think of knowledge as a species of knowing that or having acquaintance with an object. The sense of knowing that I have in mind is not easy to articulate, but it is probably best described as *being in rapport* with someone. When one is in rapport with another, one does not simply enjoy some sort of privileged epistemic contact with that person. One also knows how to engage that person and, often, what that person cares about. In this respect, the concept of

---

[7] Palmer, Sherrard, and Ware (1979), 57.   [8] Gregory of Nyssa (1979), 18.

knowing with which I am working belongs more nearly to a cluster of virtue-theoretic notions according to which knowing someone is not only a mode of understanding but also an achievement, typically accomplished only with time, familiarity, effort, and discernment. It goes without saying that knowing of this sort is often implicit—one needn't be able to articulate one's know-how—and acquired by osmosis when participating in practices in which such know-how is modeled by others. Under this understanding, then, the dictum that knowing God is a species of practical knowledge is the claim that knowing God (in the sense just specified) consists in (although is not exhausted by) knowing how to engage God.[9]

My project in this chapter is to explore the contribution that knowing how to engage in ritualized activity plays in knowing God (in the sense just specified). Specifically, it is to explore the contribution that knowing how to engage in ritualized *liturgical* activity makes to knowing God (in the sense just specified). Engaging in this project will, however, require laying some conceptual groundwork. I'll begin by discussing the notion of knowing how, staking out a position on this issue that seems to me plausible. I'll then turn to the ancient Christian liturgies, developing the idea that it is by participating in these activities that we acquire and exercise ritual knowledge, which is a type of knowing how. In my judgment, it is not helpful to discuss Christian liturgical practices in the abstract. So, I shall focus on a liturgical tradition in which the theme of practical knowledge of God is especially prominent, namely, the Eastern Christian tradition in which figures such as Evagrios and Nyssa developed their own views. However, much of what I say about the Eastern liturgies can, I believe, be applied to other liturgical traditions in which ritualized forms of action are prominent.

It might be worth adding a final observation before diving into our topic. When compared to mainline philosophy of religion, my discussion will be thoroughly unorthodox. I will have almost nothing (more) to say, for example, about the rationality of religious belief. And I will have a good deal to say about various elements of Christian ritual. In these respects, my discussion has something in common with the approach taken by so-called Wittgensteinian philosophers of religion, who have chided philosophers for paying insufficient attention to the fact that the religious attitudes are embedded in and have their distinctive roles in religious ways of life. Still, unlike the Wittgensteinians, I have no interest in defending a noncognitivist account of the religious attitudes, according to which the religious attitudes fail to express full-fledged

---

[9] A word about how I am using the phrase "to engage God." We engage those around us in all manner of ways: by catching their attention, addressing them, and embracing them, for example. What these various activities have in common is that, when all goes well, they effect mutual recognition. I am using the phrase "to engage God" in a way that analogically extends our ordinary understanding of what it is to engage another. It is, when all goes well, to effect a state of divine-human mutual recognition.

beliefs about God.[10] In my view, the religious attitudes come in a great variety of forms, including full-fledged religious belief. It is also my view that full-fledged belief needn't be a component of knowing how to dwell in communion with God, but this is a topic that I will broach only at the end of this chapter.

8.1. KNOWING HOW

Suppose Christianity is a way of life, incorporating activities such as prayer, fasting, and ritualized activity. If it is, then the thesis that some religious knowledge is (to some significant degree) a species of knowing how should have immediate appeal. For to engage in a way of life is to have a certain kind of competence or know-how. But what is it to know how to do something, to engage in those activities that constitute a way of life?

In this section, I sketch what seems to me a promising account of what it is to know how to do something. For reasons that will become apparent soon, I will call this position the *moderate view*. Roughly stated, the moderate view tells us that to know how to perform some activity Φing is to stand in a knowing or understanding relation to a way of Φing.[11]

In the next few sections, I will conduct my discussion as if something close to the moderate view is correct. Nonetheless, I do not want the general project in which I engage—namely, to explore the contribution that knowing how to engage in ritualized liturgical activity makes to knowing God—to depend on the particularities of the moderate position. So, those unsympathetic with the moderate position—say, those who identify knowing how with a special sort of knowing that—should feel free to attempt to translate what I say into the idioms that belong to their favored version of knowing how. Let me also add that, although I will speak as if I am unpacking *the* concept of knowing how, it might be that there are multiple conceptions of knowing how. Some might be very thin, expressing the idea that knowing how to perform an activity is simply a matter of being able to perform it. Others might be thicker, expressing the idea that knowing how to perform an activity requires a lot more than this, such as understanding what one is doing. As will become evident, the moderate view expresses a thicker notion of knowing how (although there are accounts that are still thicker). If you prefer to work with a thinner concept of knowing how, then think of the moderate view as one that articulates a fairly advanced state of knowing how. Finally, I should emphasize that my aim is

[10] The most thorough engagement with the Wittgensteinians of which I am aware is Wolterstorff (2010a).

[11] This is the view defended in John Bengson and Moffett (2011). In what follows, I borrow liberally from their fine paper. I have also been helped by Noë (2011).

simply to sketch the main features of the moderate view so as to have an account of knowing how with which to work. A full presentation of the view would introduce nuances and refinements that I am going to ignore.

The Moderate View

The best way to understand the moderate view is to begin with the notion of a *way of acting*. A way of acting is a sequence of act-types that an agent can perform. Performing a work of music, swimming the crawl stroke, and offering thanks are all ways of acting. If, for example, an agent knows how to perform a work of music or offer thanks to God, that agent grasps a way of acting that is a way of performing that work of music or thanking God. If this is right, knowing how to perform an action is a species of objectual knowledge, having as its object not a proposition but a way of acting.

The thesis that knowing how is not a species of propositional knowledge or knowing that is controversial. Here, however, are several considerations in its favor. First, note that when an agent knows a proposition, this relation can be "upgraded" in certain ways. If you are in excellent epistemic position with regard to the proposition *that your mother's maiden name is "Smith,"* for example, you might say, "I not only know that her maiden name is 'Smith,' but I'm also certain of it." Knowing how, by contrast, cannot be upgraded in this way. When you know how to engage in an activity such as performing John Coltrane's "Giant Steps," you wouldn't say, "I not only know how to perform 'Giant Steps,' I am also certain of it." This is because when knowing how gets upgraded, it is often upgraded to the level of not certainty but *mastery*. When you are in excellent position with regard to performing an activity such that you know how to perform it, you would say, "I not only know how to perform 'Giant Steps,' but I've also mastered it."[12]

A second consideration in favor of the claim that knowing how is objectual is that states of knowing how are not susceptible to Gettier-style cases in the way that states of knowing that are. Suppose, for example, I am a pianist who wishes to perform "Giant Steps." I consult a written score that I recently purchased, thereby grasping how to play the piece. Suppose, though, that I were extraordinarily lucky to consult this particular score, since all other

---

[12] See Bengson and Moffett (2011), 184. I say that knowing how is "often" upgraded in this way because one could distinguish between *excellence* in knowing how and *mastery* in knowing how. As I understand this distinction, one has excellence in knowing how to act in some way when one has understood to a sufficiently high degree how to act in that way. This is compatible, however, with not being able to act in that way. I could, for example, have excellence in knowing how to swim the crawl stroke, since I know all its ins and outs, but be too uncoordinated to perform it well. By contrast, one has mastery in knowing how when one has excellence in knowing how to act in some way and can perform that activity well.

available written scores are defective on account of including badly incorrect information regarding how to play the piece, such as including the wrong time signature and melody. Although I am very lucky to have the correct score, I know how to perform "Giant Steps" nonetheless. The fact that I was lucky enough to hit upon the correct score seems irrelevant to whether I have come to know how to perform the piece. This is in sharp contrast to the standard way in which philosophers think of knowing that. When an agent knows that something is the case, most philosophers believe, it cannot be due to a fluke, but must have been the upshot of a reliable belief-forming process operating in a congenial environment.[13]

These are, I believe, important considerations in favor of the moderate view's thesis that knowing how is not a species of knowing that. Still, knowing how to perform some action, such as performing Coltrane's "Giant Steps," requires more than merely grasping or apprehending that way of acting, as an agent's grasp or understanding of a way of acting can be deficient in several important respects.

Consider the following pair of cases. Imagine, first, a case in which I have not previously performed "Giant Steps," but gotten my hands on a score of this piece. If my copy of this score is incomplete in important respects, leaving out vital information about how to perform this piece, such as how to play its head, then I do not know how to perform it. Although there are actions that constitute performing this piece of music, they are unavailable to me. Alternatively, imagine a case in which I know how to perform some activity, such as playing a chord progression that consists in a progression of minor thirds, but I am unaware that performing that very activity is a way to perform the chord progression of "Giant Steps." If so, while I grasp a way of acting that is in fact a way to perform this work, I do not know how to perform it.

Not all deficiencies, however, are ones in which an agent's understanding of a way of acting is incomplete, as an agent's grasp of a way of acting can be deficient when it incorporates a mistaken understanding of how to perform that action. To stay with our example, suppose that I have been instructed to perform "Giant Steps" in 6/8 time and in the key of C#. Imagine, furthermore, that while I take myself to be doing exactly what I have been taught when I perform the piece, I in fact perform it in 4/4 time and visit several different tonal centers, which is the correct way to perform the piece. Do I know how to perform the piece? Arguably not. I have a mistaken understanding of how to perform it, since I am confused about its time signature and key. While I might in fact perform the piece correctly, I do not know how to perform it.

If this is right, for an agent to know how to perform some action, that agent's understanding of it must satisfy some threshold of completeness and

---

[13] The case is borrowed from Cath (2011).

accuracy. What is that threshold? It may be impossible to say. Indeed, the issue may be context sensitive, as so-called contextualists about knowledge claim. However that may be, let me now make several observations about the moderate view.

First, if knowing how to perform an action requires having a sufficiently complete and accurate understanding of a way of acting, knowing how to do something is not simply a matter of being reliably disposed to do it, as philosophers such as Gilbert Ryle claimed.[14] The moderate view, then, is aptly titled, as it implies that knowing how is neither a species of knowing that nor a matter of being reliably disposed to act in a certain way. For, to say it once again, the moderate view implies that knowing how to do something implies having a sufficient degree of understanding concerning how to do something. Second, while the moderate view tells us that knowing how to perform an activity implies having a certain type and degree of understanding of that activity, the view does not imply that knowing how to perform an activity implies that one can actually perform it. It may be that one can know how to perform "Giant Steps" even when one has suffered paralysis. Nor, finally, does the moderate view imply that knowing how to perform some activity implies that one is able to articulate how to perform it. Knowing how to do something can be implicit.

To this point, I have spoken of knowing how to perform relatively discrete actions such as performing the musical work "Giant Steps." Often, however, these ways of acting are embedded in complex social practices, such as the social practice of playing jazz piano, which have their own histories, standards of excellence, and methods of evaluation. And, often, knowing how to perform some activity is part of the larger endeavor of learning how to engage in and navigate these social practices. Take, for example, the social practice just mentioned, namely, performing jazz piano. To be inducted into this practice involves learning not simply how to perform various musical works, such as works by Coltrane, but also learning how to listen to them—noticing their nuances and differences from one another. It involves, moreover, knowing how to interpret musical scores, motifs, chord progressions, and rhythmic patterns in such a way that one develops a certain degree of facility with performing musical works in the genre. Importantly, for my purposes, knowing how to engage in the practice of performing jazz piano involves knowing not only how to evaluate compositions and performances, but also how to engage with works of music in such a way that one cares about how they are interpreted and performed. All this suggests that the best way to talk about the complex phenomenon that I am describing is probably not to speak of it as knowing how to navigate a social practice, so much as knowing how to

---

[14] See Ryle (1949).

navigate and inhabit a certain *life-world*—the world of jazz piano. For the latter way of talking has the advantage of conveying the idea that there is a musical reality with which one engages when one navigates a social practice.

Let me summarize: knowing how to perform some activity is, according to the moderate view, to stand in an understanding relation to a way of performing that activity. Knowing how is thus neither a species of knowing that nor merely a disposition to perform some action correctly. While understanding is crucial to knowing how, it is exceedingly difficult to identify some threshold of completeness and correctness that an agent's grasp of a way of acting must satisfy to count as a case of knowing how. Finally, the ways of acting that we grasp when we know how to perform them are often embedded in complex social practices. Because they are, the aim of knowing how is often not simply knowing how to perform relatively discrete activities but knowing how to navigate and inhabit a certain life-world of which these activities are a part. This last point will be important to the discussion of the Christian liturgy, which is my topic in the next section.

8.2. LITURGY

To the untrained eye, the ancient liturgies of the Christian East are a jumble of disconnected actions. Were you to observe one for the first time, you would see people doing such things as kissing, standing, bowing, prostrating, chanting, singing, anointing, processing, praying, kneeling, sensing, reading, listening, eating, washing, vesting, crossing themselves, and even spitting. With increased exposure, you would also recognize that, in many cases, these are not impromptu or improvised but scripted actions.

Call a repeatable sequence of actions that has a narrative structure— roughly, a proper beginning, middle, and end bound together in certain identifiable ways—a *narrative event*.[15] Everything from family dinners to works of music are, according to this understanding, narrative events. Narrative events often have performance-plans or scripts. And when they do, these scripts can issue two rather different types of directives. They can prescribe, first, that some narrative event-type is to be performed on some regular basis, such as once a year, once a week, or once a day. Second, they can prescribe when, during the performance of that narrative event-type, which actions are to be performed, by whom, and in what manner. For example, a script might

---

[15] Thus understood, the concept of a narrative event is normative. It has appropriate beginnings and endings bound together in the right ways. While I will have to leave discussion of the senses of "appropriate" to some other occasion, Carroll (2011b) is a good place to start.

prescribe that bells are to be rung at the outset of the performance of a musical work.

Call a script that issues both sorts of directives a *ritual script*. In the sense I understand it, a *ritualized action* is one that is prescribed by a ritual script. The actions that constitute the liturgies of the Eastern Christian church are, under this account, ritualized. For not only are these liturgies repeatable narrative event-types; the scripts that govern them also issue both sorts of directives, indicating when these narrative events are to be performed and when, during their performance, which actions are to be performed, by whom, and in what manner. The script that governs the Liturgy of St. John Chrysostom, for example, prescribes that it is to be performed every Sunday (and at most once per day by some assembly). It also prescribes that when this liturgy is performed, it begins with a Trinitarian blessing. Both the performance of the liturgy itself and the various actions that constitute it are, under the account offered, ritualized actions.

The Christian tradition has long stressed the importance of ritualized actions. I noted earlier that, at one point, Gregory of Nyssa writes that the power of Christianity resides not in its philosophical sophistication but in the "participation in mystical symbols and rites." I have also suggested that there is an important sense in which knowing how to perform ritualized activities contributes to knowing God. But how could that be so? It is easy enough to see that knowing how to play a certain chord progression could positively contribute to knowing how to play a musical work, since playing that chord progression might count as playing that musical work. But how could knowing how to perform ritualized actions such as kissing, prostrating, and eating contribute to knowing God in any similar way?

The answer that I will develop comes in several stages. In outline, it tells us that the liturgy furnishes both a strikingly wide array of ritual actions and ways of understanding them such that, when all goes well, knowing how to perform these actions under these ways of understanding contributes in important ways to knowing God. Since the first stage concerns the performance of ritualized actions, let us start with these. I will then go on to discuss conceptions of God as they are presented in the liturgy.

Liturgical Actions

At one level of description, the actions that constitute the liturgy, such as prostrating, kissing, chanting, and eating, are diverse enough that one would be hard-pressed to discern what unites them; they look like a rag-bag of different activities. At another level, however, these actions are not disconnected but unified in a certain way, being the constituents of an identifiable pattern. This pattern, which is primarily constituted by the activities of blessing, petitioning, and offering thanks to God, is what I will refer to as the *central pattern* of the liturgy. Since the central pattern is especially apparent in the eucharistic liturgies of the Eastern church, especially those of St. Mark, St. Basil, and St. Chrysostom, let us take a closer look at the way it takes shape in them.

Each of these liturgies begins with the declaration that the Kingdom of the Father, Son, and Holy Spirit is blessed. After the celebrant declares this, the deacon, priest, and people engage in a pattern of call and response. In the liturgies of St. Basil and St. Chrysostom, for example, a Deacon offers a series of petitions for peace and safety:

> For the peace from on high and for the salvation of our souls, let us pray to the Lord.
> For the peace of the whole world, for the welfare of the holy churches of God, and for the union of all, let us pray to the Lord. . . .
> For travelers by land, by sea, and by air; for the sick and the suffering, for captives and their safety and salvation, let us pray to the Lord.[16]

To each of these petitions, the people answer "kyrie eleison" or "Lord, Have Mercy." Having completed this initial series of petitions, the congregation sings Psalm 103 ("Bless the Lord, O my Soul"), which is followed by a petition for deliverance. This, in turn, is followed by the singing of Psalm 143 ("Praise the Lord, O my Soul"). Although punctuated by the reading of the scriptures, the commemoration of the saints, and various prayers of repentance, this pattern of petitioning and blessing continues throughout the liturgy, segueing into a sequence of actions in which the people offer thanks to God, which itself culminates in the action of eating together. In its structure, the analogue that comes to mind is that of a work of music, such as a rondo. Much like a rondo, the liturgy introduces themes—and variations on themes—in an alternating structure, punctuating them at certain points with still other themes. (Perhaps there is another sense in which the liturgy is the work of the people!)

It is tempting for philosophers to think of activities such as blessing, petitioning, and offering thanks to God as things that we primarily do with words. But in this case the temptation must be resisted. While the liturgical script prescribes the performance of linguistic acts that count as blessing, petitioning, and thanking, it also prescribes actions such as kissing, prostrating, and eating. Actions of these latter sorts do not merely *accompany* the linguistic acts prescribed by the liturgical script, as if their function were merely to add emphasis to these linguistic acts. Rather, in the context of the liturgy, the kissing, prostrating, and eating also count as cases of engaging God by blessing, petitioning, and thanking God. In fact, these bodily actions are

---

[16] I am using the translation of the Liturgy of St. John Chrysostom found in Thyateira (1995).

vivid cases of act-types by which a person can simultaneously perform multiple actions with expressive import without saying a thing. In the context of the liturgy, for example, prostrating is often simultaneously an act of petitioning, repenting, blessing, and offering thanks. Likewise, in the context of the liturgy, kissing is often simultaneously an act of greeting, blessing, adoring, and thanking. I should add that the act of eating, which stands at the center of all the eucharistic liturgies, is understood to be not simply one expression of thanksgiving among others. Rather, it is understood to be the paradigmic case of expressing thanks to God.

The central pattern of the liturgy, I have said, is constituted by acts of blessing, petitioning, and thanking God. Actions such as these have expressive import, since their function is not to state propositions but to express respect, affection, gratitude, and the like. Let me make a pair of observations about actions with expressive import.

The first is that there is no type of mental state such that for an agent to successfully perform an action with expressive import, that agent must be in that mental state. Thanking, when all goes well, expresses gratitude. But to thank someone at some time, one needn't be feeling gratitude at that time. Honoring, when all goes well, expresses respect. But to honor another at some time, one needn't have any thoughts to the effect that the recipient of one's action has worth of one or another sort.[17]

Call that which is expressed by the competent performance of an action with expressive import, its *expressive content*.[18] The second point I would like to make is that the expressive content of an action can be evaluated along different dimensions of fittingness. Consider thanking, for example. Suppose I write you a note thanking you for a gift that you have given me. If the writing of this note is accompanied by feelings of gratitude toward you, the expressive content of my action perfectly fits the mental state I am in when I write the note. As such, the performance of my action is especially apt.

Things might be otherwise, however. I might write the note while being deeply resentful toward you. If I do, then my action's expressive content fails to fit the mental state I am in when I write the note. It is thus an especially inapt or defective case of thanking. Between the two extremes of feeling gratitude and resentment are, of course, various other grades of aptness. Thanking can be done absent-mindedly, mechanically, reluctantly, indifferently, or with one's focus entirely on performing the action well, such as when

---

[17] What about the state of intending to perform an action of that sort? Isn't that a mental state one must be in to perform an act of the relevant kind? Perhaps, but I doubt it. I hint at why at the outset of the next section.

[18] Philosophers often distinguish between the semantic content of the performance of a speech act (roughly, what is said, its propositional content) and what is pragmatically conveyed (information not contained in what is said but conveyed nonetheless). I use the phrase "expressive content" to capture both sorts of content.

one focuses on what words to say because choosing them carefully matters a great deal. When agents are in these mental states, these actions can be more or less apt. Especially important for my purposes is the observation that actions with expressive import can enjoy high degrees of fittingness even when the expressive content of those actions fails to fit the mental states of the agents who perform them. I might, for example, form and reliably execute the resolution to write your family a thank you note every year because of some great kindness they performed toward my family before I was alive. But I may often fail to feel gratitude when I write them; their actions may seem so remote in time that they fail to engage me emotionally. Still, arguably, my actions of thanking are highly apt. They are not apt because their expressive content fits the mental state I am in when I write these notes. Rather, they are apt because they are appropriate responses to what you have done on my family's behalf, which flows from a state of being resolved to express my family's gratitude.

The first thing to notice about the eucharistic liturgies, then, is that they make available a vast array of actions by which—and a context in which—we can do such things as bless, petition, and offer thanks to God—actions that can be assessed along various dimensions of fittingness.

Liturgical Images

It is one thing to perform an action that counts as expressing thanks; it is another to know how to do so. In the context of the Eastern liturgies, small children perform actions such as kissing a copy of the Gospels and eating the eucharistic meal. Arguably, in that context, their actions count as cases of offering thanks to God. But these children do not know how to thank God by doing such things as kissing a copy of the Gospels. It is noteworthy, then, that the actions that constitute the liturgy do not stand alone. The liturgical script furnishes an equally wide array of images for thinking about or conceiving of God and God's activity that are connected with these actions—images that often pull against one another in puzzling and striking ways. Here is a sample.

Just prior to the Trinitarian blessing that begins the eucharistic liturgies, the celebrant offers the Trisagion prayers. These prayers, which are a rare instance of a prayer whose primary addressee is the Holy Spirit, begin with the invocation:

> O heavenly King, the Comforter, the Spirit of Truth, who is everywhere, filling all things; Treasury of Good and Giver of Life, come and dwell in us, cleanse us from every stain, and save us, O Good One

This fairly abstract presentation of God as the One Who Fills All Things is given an even more pronounced expression in the Anaphora ("the lifting up"), which occurs immediately prior to the eucharistic meal. In the Anaphora, the assembled address God in the following way:

> It is right and fitting to hymn you, to bless you, to praise you, to give thanks to you, and to worship you in every place of your dominion: for you are God ineffable, inconceivable, invisible, incomprehensible, ever existing and eternally the same.

This is apophaticism in high gear. God is addressed as the utterly Transcendent One. Yet the liturgical script repeatedly juxtaposes these descriptions with a very different set of images that presents God as the Immanent One, "the lover of humankind" who has acted in history. For example, soon after addressing God using the description just quoted, the assembled address God as the "Helper of the helpless, the Hope of the hopeless, the Saviour of the storm-tossed, the Haven of the voyager, the Healer of the sick." The One who "did not turn away" from Creation, Ruler of Heaven and Earth, Author of Life, Conqueror of Death, the One Who Holds All Things Together—the list of images of God in the liturgical script continues on and on.

A moment ago, I noted that the liturgies make available a vast array of actions by which (and a context in which) we can do such things as petition, bless, and express thanks to God. I now want to emphasize that they furnish not only these act-types and contexts, but also a rich array of conceptions regarding God and God's activity that agents can incorporate into a "mental file"—this being, roughly, a system of conceptions that an agent has with respect to an object, a repository of information that an agent takes to be about it, some items of which play a dominant role in an agent's thinking about it. These informational components allow agents not simply to think of God and God's activity in various ways, but also to perform liturgical actions such as chanting the Psalms, kissing a copy of the Gospels, or eating the eucharistic meal *under* these conceptions. Think of things this way: these conceptions provide specific ways of thinking about God and God's activity such as the One Who Delivers, the One Who Fills All Things, and the One who "did not cease to do all things on our behalf" (Liturgy of St. Basil). When all goes well, these conceptions of God are incorporated into complex action-conceptions. When they are, agents conceptualize act-types such as prostrating before an icon of Christ as a case of petitioning the One Who Delivers, blessing the One Who Fills All Things, and thanking the One who "did not cease to do all things on our behalf." In this way, the grasp and employment of these complex-action conceptions *guides* liturgical action.

There is a great deal of controversy over how to think about how the term "God" functions in religious discourse in the monotheistic traditions— whether, for example, it functions as a proper name or a cluster of definite descriptions. One view, which is defended by Mark Johnston, is that the name functions as an abbreviated title: The One from Whom Our Salvation Flows.[19] If Johnston is right about this, then one could think of the various conceptions of God presented by the liturgical script as specifications of this title or name, indicating ways in which God is the highest one or ways in which God has acted as the agent of salvation. Under this way of thinking, the conceptions of God presented in the liturgy, while incredibly diverse, are united (in part) by the fact that they are specifications of or variations on this title—the title itself being an abbreviated way of thinking about God's role in the Christian salvation narrative.

Let me summarize the line of thought that I have developed in this section. The Eastern eucharistic liturgies, I have claimed, are constituted by a vast array of scripted or ritualized actions, such as chanting Psalms, kissing a copy of the Gospels, and eating together. Is there anything that unifies them? Yes, these ritualized actions, I have claimed, are all ways in which participants in the liturgy engage God by actualizing the central pattern of the liturgy of blessing, petitioning, and offering thanks to God. In addition to prescribing actions such as these, the liturgical script presents a vast array of ways of thinking about God and God's activity, which appear no more unified than the actions that constitute the liturgy. Is there anything that unifies them? Yes, these images are the components of an overarching narrative regarding God and God's salvific activity, which is itself presented in the liturgies and perhaps encapsulated in the title "God." When competently employed, these conceptions allow an agent to perform actions such as prostrating, kissing, and eating as ways of intentionally enacting the central pattern of blessing, petitioning, and thanking God as the One Who Has Acted on Our Behalf.

The fundamental contribution of the liturgy, then, is to provide act-types and conceptions of God such that by performing those act-types under those conceptions one can engage God by doing such things as blessing, petitioning, and thanking God. In a moment, I will explain why this is important for knowing God. For now, let me return to a point made earlier, namely that learning how to perform certain actions is often not simply to gain facility at performing them. Rather, it is to learn how to navigate and inhabit a certain life-world in which those actions have their home. This is no less true of

[19] See Johnston (2009), ch. 1. I should add that I find Johnston's case that "God" does not function as a proper name unconvincing. Johnston writes: "In the scriptures, no one actually turns up and says anything like 'I am to be called by the name "God."' No one says anything like 'I hereby introduce the name "God" as the name of THIS very impressive being.' There is no original dubbing someone or something as 'God,' a dubbing we can hope to fall back on" (6). But it is highly controversial that such dubbings are necessary for a term to function as a proper name. Moreover, one would have to have an extraordinarily pinched understanding of how the scriptures function in the theistic traditions to infer from the fact that since the scriptures do not contain a record of any such episode, the best way to understand the scriptural talk of God is that there has been no such episode.

performing those ritualized actions that constitute the liturgy than it is of performing those actions that are cases of performing works of music. It is worth elaborating upon this observation, since to fail to do so would be to fail to take us to the heart of liturgical action.

At various points, I have drawn attention to the fact that liturgical action is not primarily a series of mental actions such as thinking certain thoughts or manufacturing certain feelings at certain times. Rather it is thoroughly bodily, involving actions such as bowing, kissing, and eating, which are oriented toward one's physical surroundings. In many cases, these physical surroundings are utterly ordinary: they include metal, wood, bread, wine, and water. Why, then, in the context of worship, would the liturgical script direct those who participate in the liturgy to orient themselves toward these materials by doing such things as kissing them?

Here the liturgical scripts themselves are instructive. Consider the following bit of Byzantine theological poetry, which the celebrant recites during the Theophany or the blessing of the waters:

> Today the grace of the Holy Spirit has descended on the waters in the likeness of a dove.
>
> Today has shone the sun that does not set, and the world is lighted by the light of the Lord.
>
> Today the moon shines with the world in its radiating beams.
>
> Today the shining stars adorn the universe with the splendor of their radiance.
>
> Today the clouds of heaven moisten humankind with showers of justice.
>
> Today the waters of the Jordan are changed to healing by the presence of the Lord.

This series of proclamations is remarkable if only because it forcefully presents the idea that, although we may in the context of the liturgy regularly engage with ordinary matter such as water, this matter is really not so ordinary. And, so, in the liturgical context, it is not treated as ordinary stuff but is the object of blessing, the vehicle of blessing, and the subject of poetry. (In the rite of the Theophany, the people not only bless, but are also blessed with the water by the celebrant.) In effect, the liturgical script of the Theophany prods those assembled to understand the salvation narrative that lies at the core of Christianity expansively. Not only is humankind being restored by the actions of God in time, but so also is matter, inasmuch as it too has become a means of God's presence, a source or point of contact with God. Indeed, as the Trisagion prayers illustrate, a prominent theme in Eastern Christianity is the omnipresence of God. God is the One Who Fills All Things, permeating the world with the divine energies. Because of this, some have described the tradition as advocating a version of panentheism.[20] However that may be, the tradition

---

[20] Ware (2004), 157–68, discusses the issue.

maintains that the relation between God and matter is intimate—so intimate, in fact, that to engage with matter *is* to engage with God.

The upshot is that ritualized activity such as the blessing of the waters has the effect, when things go moderately well, of honing one's sensibilities in such a way that one begins to view, experience, and treat matter differently than one would in one's day-to-day life. The analogue with music with which I have been working is, I believe, helpful in this respect. Being introduced to the performance of a musical work often has the effect of expanding one's ears, allowing one to hear things differently than one did in the past. Often, moreover, the expansion does not come easily to the listener; only with significant and repeated exposure on the listener's part does she begin to hear sounds differently, make connections with music with which she is familiar, and value these new types and sequences of sounds. Indeed, such exposure is often not enough. Sometimes the expansion occurs only with significant work on the listener's part, which might include intently focusing on the sounds and seeking ways to understand them, such as trying to understand their mathematical relations. These activities are part of immersing oneself in the life-world of musical performance and listening. The parallel with engaging in liturgical action and immersing oneself in the life-world of the Christian narrative, I trust, is obvious. A central aim of immersing oneself in liturgical action is often to alter one's sensibilities. Often, moreover, this process requires repeated exposure and effort; it can be difficult to achieve.

8.3. RITUAL KNOWLEDGE

There is a famous passage in the *Pensées* in which Pascal offers advice to those who have been persuaded that it is prudentially rational to accept that God exists. If you want to believe, says Pascal, then go do things. In particular, engage in liturgical actions such as taking holy water and attending mass. The natural interpretation of Pascal's advice is that engaging in these activities is the sort of thing that will increase the likelihood of coming to believe that God exists; the activities are simply the means to achieve this desirable cognitive state. But another interpretation of Pascal's advice is available, which is that engaging in the liturgical activities he mentions is not primarily a means to forming beliefs about God but that knowing God (in something like the virtue-theoretic sense identified earlier) *consists* in engaging in them.

This interpretation approximates the thesis that I have been interested in developing. But now it is time to pull together the strands of our discussion. To that end, let us begin with the conviction that has animated our discussion, which is that our thinking about the religious attitudes should be guided by the observation that Christianity is a way of life. This observation has not in fact guided the contemporary discussion of the epistemology of the religious attitudes. And because it has not, I have suggested, this discussion has threatened to produce a distorted picture of the nature and roles of the religious attitudes and, more generally, religious life "on the ground"—a picture in which the practical dimensions of religious life drop out. If, however, the Christian way of life is fundamentally practical in its orientation, it is natural to inquire: What would it be to engage in this way of life, to know how to engage in its central activities, such as thanking God?

The moderate view of knowing how can help to answer this question. It helps us to understand what it is to know how to do something—knowing how, if the view is correct, consisting in the understanding of not propositions but ways of acting. Still, the moderate view gives us only an abstract account of what it is to know how to do something. We also want to know what it is to know how to perform those actions that are central to the Christian way of life, such as engaging God by doing such things as blessing, petitioning, and thanking God.

To address these questions, I have suggested, we should look more closely at Christian liturgical practice, which is a central component of the Christian way of life. Using the Eastern Christian liturgies as our focal point, we saw that the contribution of the liturgy to engaging God is twofold. First, the liturgy makes available act-types of a certain range such as chanting, kissing, prostrating, and eating that count in the context of a liturgical performance as cases of blessing, petitioning, and thanking God—these last act-types constituting what I have called the central pattern of the liturgy. And, second, the liturgy furnishes an array of conceptions of God and God's activity under which to perform actions such as chanting, kissing, prostrating, and eating. When all goes well, these conceptions guide one's performance of these actions by being the components of complex action-conceptions in which the assembled do such things as petition God as The One Who Delivers, bless God as the One Who Fills All Things, and thank God as the One who "did not cease to do all things on our behalf."

If this is correct, the liturgy provides the materials for not only engaging but also knowing how to engage God. Or more precisely: the liturgy provides the materials by which a person can acquire such knowledge and a context in which she can exercise or enact it. For if one grasps these ways of acting in such a way that one understands them to be ways of blessing, petitioning, and thanking God, then one knows how to engage God by performing actions such as blessing, petitioning, and thanking God. Or more precisely yet: to the extent that one grasps and sufficiently understands these ways of acting, one knows how to bless, petition, and thank God in their ritualized forms. One has ritual knowledge.

A further nuance is worth noting. There are, I have claimed, many ways to do such things as bless, petition, and thank. Suppose I ask you to pass the salt when eating dinner together. I could do that by writing a formal request. Or suppose I thank you for writing a letter of recommendation. I could do that by slapping you hard on the back, despite your suffering from a degenerative back condition. These actions could even be expressions of practical knowledge, since I can understand them to be ways of petitioning and thanking. But they are egregiously inapt ways of acting. The liturgical script, interestingly, repeatedly draws attention to the fact that the ways of acting that it prescribes are not inapt. Mostly this is done by noting that the sacrifice offered to God in the liturgy consists not in shedding blood but rather in praising God and that the bowing that occurs is not to "flesh and blood" but to God, the Ruler of All (Liturgy of St. John Chrysostom). If the liturgical script's assessment of the very actions it prescribes is correct, the liturgy furnishes not simply ways of acting that are ways of engaging God, but also ways of acting that are apt ways of engaging God. Ritual knowledge, when all goes well, is knowing how to engage God in ways that are fitting.

Let me now draw out some implications of our discussion. One implication is that the conditions for knowing how to engage God are, in one regard, demanding, as an agent's knowing how to perform an action such as thanking God requires that there be a way of acting such that (i) that agent can engage in that way of acting with respect to the being who is God (if any such being exists) (ii) that way of acting counts as thanking God and (iii) that agent has a sufficiently complete and accurate understanding of that way of acting. Given the ontological distance between us and God to which the liturgy draws our attention, achieving this sort of know-how would not be a trivial matter.

But, as I indicated earlier in this chapter, there are also respects in which the conditions for knowing how to perform such actions as thanking God are considerably less demanding than the conditions for knowing various propositions about God. One such respect concerns the role of belief. Imagine that you are a high-level theoretical physicist who suspects that there is a type of subatomic particle—hitherto undiscovered—that is responsible for various happenings in the quantum world. You devise various types of experiments to determine whether there is such a particle. The evidence that there is such a particle is promising but not decisive; consequently, you do not find yourself believing that such a particle exists. Still, when you devise and conduct your experiments, you act on the assumption that it does exist and proceed with your work on this assumption. Suppose, for argument's sake, that the particle does exist and has many of the properties that you suppose it has. Do you know how to do such things as discover it, manipulate it in various ways, and make evident its properties? Presumably, yes. For to have the relevant sort of know-how, you must have a sufficiently comprehensive and accurate understanding of how to manipulate the relevant particle. And, by hypothesis, you have that. To have the relevant sort of know-how, though, you do not have to believe (and, hence, know) that the object of your actions exists. In this regard, there is a crucial difference between knowing that and knowing how. If this is so, then one can understand why certain strains of Christianity have placed emphasis on knowing how to engage God by doing such things as blessing and thanking God rather than being in or trying to manufacture certain doxastic states. The relevant sort of knowledge how does not require being in these doxastic states.

Still, under the standard interpretation, figures such as Pascal have been especially concerned that their interlocutors form religious beliefs. The contemporary discussion of the religious attitudes, likewise, has been almost exclusively focused on the epistemic status of these beliefs, as if being in this type of state holds a special prominence in the Christian way of life. I have been suggesting that this tendency threatens to offer a distorted picture of the religious life, as this way of life is fundamentally concerned not so much with being in this type of doxastic state with respect to propositions about God as with conducting oneself in certain ways with respect to God that count as engaging God, and knowing how to conduct oneself in those ways.

Suppose that one were to grant the point. A satisfactory account of the religious attitudes, you agree, would have to pay considerably more attention to their practical dimensions. It is still natural to wonder what is so special about those actions on which I have focused—those that constitute the central pattern of the liturgy. Why does their performance deserve a type of priority in the religious life, as the Eastern tradition holds?

The narrative that lies at the heart of the Christian way of life, I believe, points toward an answer to this question. At the heart of this narrative is a story of falling away, one that is wrapped in images of dust, fruit, reptiles, and nakedness. The story of falling away describes how it is that human beings have come to be at such deep variance with God and each other. In the Christian tradition, both the origin and the nature of this state are often presented in terms of disobedience—specifically, being in a state of disobedience with regard to God. In the narrative of salvation history in St. Basil's liturgy, for example, it is described along these lines.

But this is not the only or arguably the most penetrating way to understand the nature of the rupture. In his book *For the Life of the World*, the Orthodox theologian Alexander Schmemann writes that the falling away is not so much the result of disobedience as the consequence of living a "noneucharistic life in a noneucharistic world."[21] "Not giving thanks," writes Schmemann is the "'vital essence' of evil . . . the sin that tore" human beings "from God."[22] If Schmemann's diagnosis is correct, it holds the key to understanding why it is that enacting the central pattern of the liturgy enjoys such prominence in the Christian way of life: it is how we repair the rupture. For in knowing how to do

---

[21] Schmemann (1969), 18.   [22] Schmemann (1987), 187.

such things as bless, petition, and thank God, one thereby knows how to engage God in such a way that one can know God in the sense of knowing how to live in communion or be in rapport with God. That, I believe, is where the importance of ritual knowledge lies.[23]

[23] My thanks to David Manley, Mike Rea, Luke Reinsma, Lori Wilson, Lindsay Whittaker, Nick Wolterstorff, Tom Flint, and two anonymous referees for their comments.

9

Transforming the Self

On the Baptismal Rite

It is easy to see why philosophers find the eucharistic rite of such great interest. Not only is the rite (for many) central to the Christian life, it also generates exactly the sort of puzzle into which philosophers can sink their teeth. For, by all accounts, there is a time such that the bread and the wine placed on the altar during the eucharistic rite are ordinary bread and wine. And yet the ancient Christian tradition has unanimously affirmed that there is some other time during the rite in which this bread and wine are the body and blood of Christ. Hence the puzzle: How could that be so?

In contrast to the eucharistic rite, philosophers have paid almost no attention to the baptismal rite. Indeed, one would be hard-pressed to identify a single article written on the topic by a philosopher in the last fifty years.[1] Why this is so, I am not sure. The answer cannot be that the baptismal rite has fallen into disuse or is peripheral to the Christian life. For the rite has not fallen into disuse; to the contrary, many Christians consider baptism a sacrament, the rite by which one is received into the church. Nor can the answer be that the rite is not complex or puzzling enough to be of philosophical interest. For the rite, especially in its ancient forms, is extraordinarily rich, complex, and puzzling.

Consider, for example, the rite as it is practiced by Eastern Orthodox Christians. To those unfamiliar with it, the text and actions of this rite can seem baffling. I say this not simply because the rite incorporates activities such as exorcisms, which strike many as the vestiges of a primitive worldview. Nor is the rite puzzling simply because it seems to skirt close to magic, appearing to express the conviction that words can endow material things such as oil and

---

[1] I have been surprised to discover that, even among theologians, the issue is under-theorized. See K. T. Ware's opening remarks in his "The Sacrament of Baptism and Ascetic Life in the Teaching of Mark the Monk" (1972).

water with supernatural powers. The rite is especially puzzling because it seems to make audacious claims about what its performance accomplishes.

What I am calling the audacity of the Orthodox baptismal rite manifests itself in various passages, such as the following prayer of thanksgiving offered toward the end of the rite:

> Blessed are You, O Lord God Almighty, Source of all good things...who has given to us, unworthy though we be, blessed purification through hallowed water, and divine sanctification, through life-giving Chrismation; who now, also, has been pleased to regenerate your servant that has newly received illumination by water and the Spirit, and granted unto him/her remission of sins, whether voluntary or involuntary. (159)[2]

In the space of a sentence, the text ascribes to the one baptized an impressive array of states: purification, sanctification, regeneration, illumination, and remission of sins—what I'll call, for ease of reference, the *regenerate states*. These states, this passage makes evident, are acquired upon and by the performance of the baptismal rite—"by water and the Spirit." But how could that be? How could a person be illumined or enlightened as a result of being baptized? And isn't there good empirical evidence that the imposition of the regenerate states is not in fact accomplished in the vast majority of cases? After all, more often than not, those who are baptized tend not to behave much differently from those who are not baptized; those belonging to the former group seem no more illumined or enlightened than those belonging to the latter. Moreover, when one considers the further fact that the regenerate states are typically predicated of infants and young children who are baptized, the predications are paradoxical, even unintelligible. In what sense could an infant be sanctified, illumined, or enjoy remission of her sins? On a straightforward reading, the text appears to make a series of serious category mistakes.

Call this cluster of concerns regarding the baptismal rite the *Intelligibility Puzzle*. My main project in this chapter is to propose a way of understanding the baptismal rite that helps to dissolve this puzzle. As will already have been evident, my focus will be on the Eastern Orthodox baptismal rite, not simply because it is the most ancient of the baptismal rites presently used by Christians, but also because it is the most lush and audacious baptismal rite of which I am aware. If we could make sense of this rite, then we will have taken important steps toward understanding the baptismal rite in what is perhaps its most provocative and puzzling form.

---

[2] I am using the English translation of the rite as it is found in *Service Book of the Holy Eastern Orthodox Catholic and Apostolic Church according to the use of the Antiochian Orthodox Christian Archdiocese of North America* (2002). I have modernized the language used. Page references to this text are inserted in the body of this chapter.

9.1. THE TWOFOLD TRANSFORMATION

The structure of the Orthodox baptismal rite can hardly be considered common knowledge, so let me start by saying something about it. As it is presently practiced, the rite is actually composed of three separate sub-rites: the reception of the catechumens, the baptism itself, and the chrismation (the confirmation by anointing with oil) of the one(s) baptized. For ease of reference, I will refer to this constellation of rites as the *baptismal rite*.[3] Given that the components of the baptismal rite were historically performed at different times and on different occasions, one has to be cautious about simply assuming that there is some way to characterize the point of the rite in a general and illuminating way. We have to look and see if the rite itself provides us with any such characterization.

Thankfully, the text of the rite provides such a characterization. In a passage that echoes the one quoted earlier, the celebrant addresses God with the following words:

> Master of all, show this water to be the water of redemption, the water of sanctification, the purification of flesh and spirit, the loosing of bonds, the remission of sins, the illumination of the soul, the laver of regeneration, the renewal of the spirit, the gift of adoption to sonship, the garment of incorruption, the fountain of life. For you have said, O Lord: Wash and be clean; and put away evil things from your souls. You have bestowed upon us from on high a new birth through water and the Spirit. Therefore, O Lord, manifest yourself in this water, and grant that he/she who is baptized therein may be transformed. (155)

It is the last line to which I want to draw attention: the point of the baptismal rite is to *transform* the person who is baptized. In the eucharistic rite, the emphasis falls on the transformation of the bread and wine—the imposition on them of a new function. In the baptismal rite, by contrast, the emphasis falls on the transformation of the one baptized. The task that faces the one who wants to understand this rite is to get a better picture of the nature of the transformation that is supposed to occur.

To that end, let's start at the beginning of the rite and work our way forward. During the reception of the catechumens, the liturgical script instructs the celebrant to pray as follows: "And make" the one to be baptized "a reason-endowed sheep in the holy flock of your Christ, an honorable member of your Church, a child of the light, and an heir of your Kingdom" (148). During the litanies, in the middle of the rite, the priest asks that the one to be baptized "may prove him/herself a child of the Light, and an heir of eternal good things" (153). Finally, during the last section of the rite, just prior to

---

[3] For the history of the rite, see Schmemann (1974), 158, and the essays in Shaughnessy (1976).

marking the newly baptized with chrismation oil, the priest addresses God, asking that the newly baptized would "please you in every deed and word, and may be a child and heir of your heavenly kingdom" (159).

The progression of the text seems to be this: there are three separate requests that, through baptism and chrismation, the one baptized be made a member of the church, a child of the light, and an heir of the kingdom. Then, at some point—presumably by the very acts of baptizing and anointing—the complex status of being a member of the church, a child of the light, and an heir to the kingdom is conferred on the one baptized.

The text of the baptismal rite is not a theological treatise. Phrases such as "child of the light" and "heir to the kingdom" do not have some specific technical sense that the text communicates. Rather, they are phrases that have multiple connotations which, in the context of the baptismal rite, express the idea that the one to be baptized will undergo a specific and significant type of normative alteration. Although the alteration to which the text draws our attention is remarkable in its own way, there is nothing deeply mysterious about it, as we are familiar with dozens of analogues. Imagine, for example, that at an early age, you had been orphaned and that I, through the standard legal processes, adopted you as my child and heir. When you became my child and heir, a profound normative transformation occurred. Prior to being adopted, you had no rights against me that I care and provide for you on a day-to-day basis and that all my worldly belongings would pass into your hands at the appointed time. But with the adoption—effected, in this case, by the act of signing legal documents—you acquired all these rights against me and a good many more besides. Correlatively, with the signing of these papers, my normative standing was altered as well. Prior to signing these papers, I did not have an obligation to provide and care for you on a day-to-day basis and to give you all that is mine at the appointed time. But with the signing of these papers, I acquired these obligations and a good many more besides. A consequence of this alteration is that if I were to fail to care and provide for you out of negligence, then I would wrong you and you would have a right against me to seek reparation.

Many would balk at the idea that we have any rights against God, let alone rights conferred at baptism. It seems impious! And it should be admitted that many contemporary Orthodox writers seem set against using "juridical" concepts to understand our relation to God.[4] But I think the language of the baptismal rite gives us powerful reason to believe that the early church was comfortable with the idea that the normative transformation that occurs during baptism consists in the acquisition of a series of new rights vis-à-vis God, some of these being privileges of various sorts, such as the right to

---

[4] Schmemann (1974), 43, is a notable exception in this regard.

address God in certain ways and to act on behalf of God by speaking and acting in God's name.[5]

Of course the normative alteration that occurs does not simply consist in the acquisition of rights; it also consists in the acquisition of new responsibilities and obligations to God, including responsibilities and obligations to care for the well-being of the subjects of God's concerns, such as the poor. And, given some plausible assumptions, it may be that some of these normative features are acquired gradually with maturation and time. When baptized, an infant may, for example, acquire only conditional obligations—obligations of such a kind that when she is of the age of maturity, she has various actual obligations and responsibilities to the church. To which it is worth adding that the rights, responsibilities, and obligations acquired do not have only God as their direct object; in baptism, the one baptized also acquires rights, responsibilities, and obligations vis-à-vis the church and vice versa. Indeed, the Orthodox are alone in their insistence that anyone baptized has a right to all the ministrations of the church, including partaking of eucharist.[6] This is why if you were to go to an Orthodox baptismal liturgy, you will see not only infants and young children being baptized but also taking eucharist, for they are deemed full members of the church in virtue of being baptized. Were the church to refuse to commune these members on account of their age, it would (by its own lights) wrong them.

I have said that we should understand the baptismal rite as one in which the one baptized is understood to undergo a transformation. We have identified the first element of that transformation, which is an alteration in the normative standing of the one baptized (and, correlatively, of those who baptize). But as intimated earlier, there is a second element of the transformation that is more difficult to puzzle through.

In several places, I have quoted passages from the text of the baptismal rite in which seemingly audacious things are said about the baptized. Given our purposes, it is instructive to pay close attention to the language used in these passages. Consider, first, the text of the litany that immediately precedes the instruction to perform the baptismal event. In this text, a series of requests have as their object the water and oil used in the baptismal rite, such as the request that the water be "sanctified with the power (*energeia*) of the Holy Spirit." The text then turns its attention to the one to be baptized, saying:

> For him/her who is now come unto holy Baptism, and for his/her salvation, let us pray to the Lord.

---

[5] "As a friend talking with a friend," writes St. Symeon the New Theologian, "we speak with God, and with boldness we stand before the face of Him who dwells in light unapproachable" (quoted in Ware [2000], 59–60).

[6] The Roman church, apparently, discontinued this practice in the Middle Ages, around the thirteenth century.

That he/she may prove himself/herself a child of the Light, and an heir of eternal good things, let us pray to the Lord.

That he/she may be a member and partaker of the death and resurrection of Christ our God, let us pray to the Lord.

It is difficult to simply read off the illocutionary force of the speech acts performed by the utterance of these sentences in the context of the performance of the baptismal rite. In principle, in this context, these sentences could be used to perform multiple speech act types. Under the most obvious interpretation, by the utterance of these sentences, the assembled perform a series of petitions directed toward God: "Grant the one to be baptized salvation. Grant that he or she may be a child of the light. Grant that he or she may be made worthy of the kingdom." (In the Greek, the grammatical mood of these sentences is, interestingly enough, that of an hortatory or a polite command.) Under a somewhat less obvious interpretation, by the utterance of these sentences, the assembled also performs blessings directed toward the one to be baptized: "May you (who are to be baptized) have salvation. May you (who are to be baptized) be a child of the light. May you (who are to be baptized) be worthy of the kingdom." Under yet another interpretation, the speech acts performed by the utterance of these sentences are so-called exercitives akin to nominating or adjourning whereby those who perform them confer a status on someone or other: "Let it be that you (who are to be baptized) be saved. Let it be that you (who are to be baptized) are a child of the light. Let it be that you (who are to be baptized) are worthy of the kingdom."

This last reading of the text might strike some as far-fetched. How could the assembled impose what I earlier referred to as the *regenerate states* on the baptized? Drawing upon Nicholas Wolterstorff's work, I've suggested elsewhere that we have models to help us to make sense of how they might do this.[7] For it may be that by the performance of these (and other) speech acts, God confers the regenerate states on the baptized. This would be a case of what Wolterstorff calls *double-agency action*—action in which one agent acts by the actions of another. If this were correct, the church would be intimately implicated in God's creative activity, as it would be the agent whereby God imposes the regenerate states on the one baptized. I would add that this reading gains some plausibility—and this is the second point I wish to make—from a passage later in the text that I've already quoted.

The passage I have in mind is this:

Blessed are You, O Lord God Almighty, Source of all good things . . . who has given to us, unworthy though we be, blessed purification through hallowed water, and divine sanctification, through life-giving Chrismation; who now, also, has

[7] In Cuneo (2015b), included as Chapter 10 in the present volume. See Wolterstorff (1995), ch. 3.

been pleased to regenerate your servant that has newly received illumination by water and the Spirit, and grants unto him/her remission of sins, whether voluntary or involuntary. (159)

When I quoted this passage earlier, I did not draw attention to the verb tenses of the sentences that compose it. But now take another look at the tenses used. Whereas earlier in the rite, the text uses a combination of the subjunctive and indicative moods when speaking of the regenerate states, in this passage, it uses the (present) perfect tense. Addressing God, it says *you have given* the one baptized purification, sanctification, regeneration, and the like, presumably through the actions of the assembled. A straightforward explanation of this confident affirmation that the one baptized has been transformed is that the activity of transforming *consists* (at least in part) in the activity of baptizing, much in the way that acquiring the status of being legally adopted consists in the activity of signing the relevant legal documents.

The text of the baptismal rite does not itself answer the question as to whether the one baptized acquires the regenerate states simply as an answer to the assembled's request that God confer these states or as the result of the performance of a divine/human exercitive speech act in which these states are imposed on the baptized. Nonetheless, while the answer to this question would, I believe, have important implications for how we understand the nature of the baptismal rite, the more important point for present purposes is that we have identified a second element of the transformation that is supposed to occur by the performance of the baptismal rite, which is the imposition on the baptized of the regenerate states.

Two alterations, then, appear to lie at the heart of the baptismal rite. One alteration consists in the imposition of a normative standing, the other in the imposition of the regenerate states. If the first alteration is familiar and intelligible in its basic structure, the second—as I noted earlier—is baffling. It generates what I earlier called the *Intelligibility Puzzle*, this puzzle consisting not simply in the concern that it is difficult to see how the regenerate states could be conferred on someone, as opposed to acquired over time with effort. It also has an empirical dimension, since the behavior of those who are baptized rather often strongly indicates that they have not had these states conferred on them. The problem only gets worse, moreover, when we consider the fact that it is often infants and small children who are baptized. In this case, it just doesn't seem to make any sense to predicate the regenerate states of infants and small children, as the language of the rite licenses.

In what follows, I am going to develop an interpretation of the baptismal rite that addresses the Intelligibility Puzzle in a way that is, I believe, close to satisfactory. I say that this strategy is "close to satisfactory" because it is incomplete and raises questions of its own—questions that will have to be tackled on another day. Let me add that I am aware that there are strategies for addressing this puzzle that fall short of anything like a solution to it. For example, one might point out that the baptismal rites were originally composed for inducting adult converts into the church. The church, it might be said, has seen fit not to alter the rite or compose an alternate rite when infants and children are baptized. But, it might be continued, this may simply be because it has assumed that there is no harm done when, in the baptismal rite, we operate with an analogue to a legal fiction. That is, it might be that the church has assumed that there is no harm done when it says of infants and children things that are false in the context of the baptismal rite for the purpose of expediency, or of edifying the faithful, or of expressing hopeful expectation.

In my judgment, the appeal to harmless fictions deserves to be taken seriously when interpreting parts of the baptismal rite. For example, at the very outset of the rite, when the celebrant prays that Christ "remove from him/her his/her former delusion and fill him/her with the faith, hope and love which are in you" (146), it is clear that these words could not truly apply to an infant. Yet the church has chosen not to omit the utterance of these sentences when baptizing infants. One explanation of this practice is that the utterance of these sentences functions as a harmless fiction.[8] Still, even if this were correct, the appeal to such a fiction would only be a partial solution to the Intelligibility Puzzle, for it offers no answers to how we could truthfully say of adults that they enjoy the regenerate states by way of the performance of the baptismal rite.

9.2. ADDRESSING INTELLIGIBILITY

In his book *Of Water and the Spirit*, the Orthodox theologian Alexander Schmemann contends that there are important differences between the way that Patristic theology conceived of the baptismal rite, on the one hand, and the way that post-Patristic thought has construed it, on the other. In virtually every manual of post-Patristic systematic theology, Schmemann writes:

> the two essential references in explaining Baptism are *original sin* and *grace*. Baptism, we are told, removes from man and liberates him from the original sin,

---

[8] This is not, however, the only available explanation. Another explanation is that, in these utterances, nothing is said of (or even taken to be said of) the infant baptized. An analogue: at a certain point in the Orthodox Divine Liturgy, the deacon utters the sentence "Catechumens depart!" Were you to attend this service, however, you would see that any catechumens present do not in fact depart. Nor are they expected to. In the context of the liturgy, the utterance of the imperatival sentence "Catechumens depart!" no longer has (or is taken to have) the force of a command.

and it also bestows upon him the grace necessary for his Christian life. As all other sacraments, Baptism thus is defined as a "means of grace," as a "visible sign of an invisible grace." It is absolutely essential, to be sure, for our salvation; but in these definitions and explanations, it is no longer presented as being truly—in essence and not only in external symbolism—*death* and *resurrection.*[9]

By contrast, says Schmemann, when explicating the baptismal Mystery, the Patristics tended to employ as their central categories not original sin and grace but death and resurrection. And indeed the text of the baptismal rite seems to confirm Schmemann's point: there are no allusions—let alone references to—original sin in the text.[10] And while references to grace abound, it is clear that when the concept of grace is employed, the dominant theme of the text is that of the passage from the old to the new via baptism:

> You have bestowed on us from on high a new birth through water and the spirit. For this reason, O Lord, manifest yourself in this water, and grant that he/she who is baptized therein may be transformed; that he/she may put away from him/herself the old man/woman . . . and may be clothed upon with the new man/woman, and renewed after the image of Him who created him/her; that being buried, after the pattern of your death, in baptism, he/she may, in like manner, be a partaker of your Resurrection and having preserved the gift of your Holy Spirit, and increased the measure of grace committed to him/her, he/she may receive the prize of his/her high calling. (155–6)

Passages such as this present the themes of newness, regeneration, and resurrection as being at the heart of the Baptismal Mystery. But they also raise puzzles of their own—ones similar to those that constitute the Intelligibility Puzzle. For clearly, the one baptized does not, in virtue of the performance of the baptismal rite, die a physical or (what the tradition terms) a spiritual death, entering into a state of deep alienation from God. Nor is the one baptized, in virtue of the performance of the baptismal rite, resurrected in any identifiable sense. But if not, just what is the text trying to communicate with this imagery of death and resurrection?

Strictly speaking, the text that I have just quoted says not that the one baptized dies and is resurrected. Rather, it says that, in baptism, the one baptized is buried and resurrected *after the pattern* of Christ's death and resurrection. What does this mean? For his part, Schmemann wants nothing to do with a deflationary approach according to which, when the one baptized is lowered into and emerges from the water, this merely symbolically represents Christ's death and resurrection. Schmemann's suggestion is, instead, that the pattern of Christ's death consists in this: Christ went voluntarily to his

---

[9] Schmemann (1974), 54.
[10] Schmemann may overstate his point, however. Ware (1972) makes it plain that some Patristic commentators, such as St. Mark the Monk, one of the few Patristics to write extensively on the baptismal rite, thought of it in terms of the dynamic between original sin and grace.

death in obedience to God the Father. Christ, says Schmemann, *desired* to die out of love, "to destroy the solitude, the separation from life, the darkness and the despair of death," by which Schmemann means not the death of the body but spiritual death.[11] The way in which baptism is a pattern of Christ's death, then, is that the action of baptizing (or, perhaps, the state of undergoing baptism) expresses the same type of desire as Christ's: the action (or state) expresses a desire to obey, love, and overcome alienation from God.[12]

I have pursued Schmemann's discussion of this issue not simply to highlight important ways in which the Orthodox understanding of the baptismal rite is different from other understandings of the rite prominent in Western Christendom. I have pursued it also because Schmemann employs a strategy for handling attributions made in the context of the baptismal rite that are deeply puzzling, such as the claim that in baptism, the one baptized is "a partaker of the death" of Christ (153). The strategy is roughly this: when faced with an attribution concerning the one baptized that looks literally false, look for an interpretation of that attribution which comes out true because there is an agent active in the baptismal event and a state of that agent such that that agent's being in that state accounts for the truth of that attribution under that interpretation.

In his discussion of the issue of the imagery of death and resurrection, it is true that there are passages in which Schmemann seems to say that the one baptized must desire to die to self. But this is not Schmemann's considered view. For Schmemann is keenly aware that, in the case of infant baptism, there is no sense in which the infant has the relevant desire. And, though Schmemann doesn't mention the point, something similar holds true of those performing the baptismal rite itself. Aside from intending to follow the script of the baptismal rite, they needn't be in any particular mental state when performing the baptismal rite; they could be simply going through the motions. (One could, of course, maintain that baptisms of this sort are "invalid." Schmemann, however, has no interest in trying to distinguish "valid" from "invalid" baptismal rites.)[13] Instead, in a move that prefigures some of N. T. Wright's work on the topic of justification, Schmemann proposes a different answer: the agent in question is Christ and the relevant state of Christ

---

[11] Schmemann (1974), 64. "In baptism, man wants to die as a sinful man and he is given that death, and in baptism man wants the newness of life as forgiveness, and he is given it" (Schmemann [1973], 78).

[12] Schmemann (1974), 66.

[13] Schmemann (1974), 67. Consider, though, what Gregory of Nyssa writes: "If, when the washing of baptism is applied to the body, the soul does not cleanse itself from the stains of the passions, but our life after initiation continues to be the same as it was before—then, though it may be a bold thing to say, yet I will say it without shrinking: in such cases the water remains water, since the gift of the Holy Spirit is nowhere manifested in what has taken place." Quoted in Ware (1972), 448.

is Christ's *faith*. It is Christ's faith, says Schmemann, on which baptism "totally and exclusively" depends—by which Schmemann means Christ's *faithfulness* as it is expressed in the life of the church.[14]

It is difficult to see, however, how this proposal makes any headway on the issue before us. The issue before us, recall, is in what sense the one baptized could "partake" in the death of Christ or her baptism be "after the pattern" of Christ's death. Telling us that Christ's faithfulness is manifested in the actions of the church during the baptismal rite does not shed any light on how, in the baptismal rite, the one baptized partakes in the death of Christ. Presumably, it is something about Christ's faith and the relationship that the one baptized bears to it that renders the activity of baptism "after the pattern" of Christ's death and resurrection. To make progress on the issue before us, however, we need to have a better sense of what that something is and what relation the one baptized bears to it.[15] I would add that an appeal to Christ's faith also fails to illuminate the more general issue of how, in the baptismal rite, the regenerate states are imposed on the one baptized.

We need to strike out in a different direction.

9.3. A DIFFERENT APPROACH

We are looking for a way to understand the predications of the regenerate states of the one baptized that does not imply that these predications are clearly false and captures the church's conviction that in baptism the one baptized undergoes a fundamental transformation. The way forward on this matter, I believe, is to attend to an ambiguity in the language of the baptismal rite. To that end, return to the passage I quoted at the outset of our discussion in which, I said, the baptismal liturgy seems at its most audacious:

> Blessed are You, O Lord God Almighty, Source of all good things . . . who has given to us, unworthy though we be, blessed purification through hallowed water, and divine sanctification, through life-giving Chrismation; who now, also, has been pleased to regenerate your servant that has newly received illumination by water and the Spirit, and granted unto him/her remission of sins, whether voluntary or involuntary. (159)

[14] Schmemann (1974), 67–9, 31.

[15] I find what the Orthodox theologian Georges Florovsky writes no more satisfactory. In his short article "Baptismal Symbolism and Redemptive Reality" (n.d.), Florovsky writes that the one baptized "is transformed through following and imitating; and thus what was foreshown by the Lord is realized." Without being told more, I fail to see in what sense imitating Christ's death would be to partake in the death of Christ. Although I have reservations about his interpretations of the Church Fathers, Finn (1976) canvasses views of various Church Fathers on the matter.

This passage, and others like it, appears to predicate of the one baptized the regenerate states of being purified, being sanctified, being regenerated, being illumined, and having remission of sins. This, I have emphasized, is puzzling in multiple respects, not the least of which is that it is difficult to see how infants and small children could be in any of these states. Another look at the passage, however, reveals that each of these states admits of a process/product ambiguity, which the English translation masks to a certain degree. In the English translation, in fact, we are naturally drawn to the "product" interpretation of these states: as a result of the performance of the baptismal rite—we read the text as affirming—the one baptized is now purified, sanctified, regenerated, illumined, and released from sin. But the text admits of a different "process" reading: as a result of the performance of the baptismal rite, the one baptized, is now *being* purified, *being* sanctified, *being* regenerated, *being* illumined, and *being* released from sin. Under this reading, which receives qualified support from the writings of figures such as Mark the Monk and Gregory of Nyssa, the fundamental alteration that occurs in the baptismal rite is that the performance of the rite has *instigated* these processes in the one baptized.[16]

While I doubt that this reading can be vindicated on linguistic grounds alone, it might be worth emphasizing that the Greek text indicates that something like a process interpretation is along the right lines. Take, for example, petitions that figure in the rite's text such as:

> That this water may be sanctified with the power, and effectual operation and indwelling of the Holy Spirit, let us pray to the Lord.

In the Greek, the object of the preposition "with" is the so-called articular infinitive, "verbal nouns" that communicate verbal action or movement. So, literally rendered, the first words of the prayer quoted above ask "that this holy-making water would . . ." The idea, then, is that there is a process, namely, "holy-making," that is underway in the context of the baptismal rite. When the text switches to the (present) perfect tense, using phrases such as "Blessed are you, O Lord God . . . who has given us . . . blessed purification" (158–9), it is natural to read it as claiming not that the process of purifying has been completed but that it has been initiated.

Let's take a moment to sharpen this "process" reading of the text. Suppose we say that a *state of an agent* is a non-episodic state that can be predicated of an agent insofar as that agent exemplifies—or is essentially disposed to exemplify—qualities of personal agency, such as being able to act under

---

[16] While the interpretation I have offered builds upon the idea, expressed by some of the Church Fathers, that the "seed" of virtue is planted in baptism, it is nonetheless considerably more modest than the views advanced by figures such as Mark the Monk, who maintain that once baptized, there is no "residue" from the "sin of Adam." See Ware (1972).

goals and entertain thoughts by employing concepts. Let's say, furthermore, that a *process-state* is a state of an agent that, when exemplified in an agent, consists in the unfolding of a process that is initiated at some point and is oriented toward the achievement of some end(s) or goal(s) at which that agent can intentionally aim. An example of such a state would be the process of forgiving. The process of forgiving is a state of an agent such that when it is exemplified it is, first, initiated in an agent, second, oriented toward a goal—in this case, achieving the state of *being such as to have forgiven*—and, third, this goal is one whose achievement at which the agent can intentionally aim.

For our purposes here, it is worth stressing that a process-state could be initiated in multiple ways, such as by one's own volition, by being struck by a realization, or by another's agency. Indeed, in principle, the process-state of forgiving another could be instigated by something as "external" as receiving a chemical injection. And it is also worth mentioning that a process-state can have multiple, complex goals. In the case of forgiving, it may be that the immediate aim of the process is to achieve the goal of *being such as to have forgiven*, while the mediate goal of the process is to achieve the goal of *being reconciled with the one forgiven*. When initiated, of course, a process-state can take a lifetime to reach fruition; sometimes this is true of forgiving, for example. And the process needn't proceed inexorably; it can be interrupted, short-circuited, subverted, or the like due to one's own agency, another's agency, or inhospitable circumstances.

Suppose, then, we think of the second alteration that is understood to occur by the performance of the baptismal rite as the initiation of a cluster of process-states in the one baptized. The processes in question are initiated by the activity of multiple agents. In some cases, they are initiated by the activity of the one baptized, such as when she enacts the decision to be baptized; in other cases, such as in the case of infant baptism, they are not. In all cases, these processes are initiated by both the activity of the ones baptizing and—as the baptismal rite makes evident—God.

What should we say about the character of these process-states? The text of the baptismal rite presents them not as quasi-mechanistic processes similar to the process of digesting food but as the exercise of personal agency, the *energeia* of the Holy Spirit. If this is right, the process-states in question are not simply initiated by divine activity but also consist in the exercise of divine agency. Admittedly, finding analogues to this sort of activity is not easy. We are familiar with cases in which one agent instigates a process-state in another, such as when my doctor injects me with antibiotics. But when my doctor instigates this state, the state itself does not consist in the exercise of my doctor's own personal agency. Rather, it consists in the antibiotics fighting off infection in my body. We are also familiar with cases in which an agent instigates a process-state in himself that consists in the exercise of his own personal agency. I might, for example, instigate the process of my reflecting on a philosophical issue, where the process of reflecting is very much an exercise of my own personal agency. What is much more difficult to identify is a case in which one agent instigates in another a process-state such that that process-state consists in the exercise of the first agent's personal agency. And yet, if I understand the text of the baptismal rite correctly, this is exactly how it presents the types of process-states instigated at baptism.

The best we can do to understand this, I think, is to imagine a case in which the normal barriers between persons break down, such as one in which by a neural wiring hookup, some of my reactions, feelings, thoughts, and attitudes become operative in you, initiating a process-state. In this case, you might become aware of reactions or tendencies in yourself that are the exercise of my personal agency, although you do not recognize them as mine. With time, however, you could become aware that these feelings, thoughts, and attitudes are indeed mine, and, if all goes well, they would be available to you in much the way that they are ordinarily available to me. Indeed, if all goes especially well, you might even identify with them, taking them, for all intents and purposes, as your own. The neural wiring hook up we are imagining, of course, might involve reciprocity. In that case, your reactions, feelings, thoughts, and attitudes would become available to me in much the way they are normally available to you. This would eventuate in a fusion of personal agency, which, I think, approximates the fusion between divine and human agency that is supposed to be instigated at baptism.[17]

When trying to capture the character of the transformation that this divine activity effects, the text of the Orthodox baptismal rite uses a remarkably wide array of phrases and images—a range that is a good deal wider than I have thus far indicated. Bring to mind, for example, a passage quoted earlier, in which the celebrant prays:

> Master of all, show this water to be the water of redemption, the water of sanctification, the purification of flesh and spirit, the loosing of bonds, the remission of sins, the illumination of the soul, the laver of regeneration, the renewal of the spirit, the gift of adoption to sonship, the garment of incorruption, the fountain of life. (155)

While these images are evocative, I do not read the text of the baptismal rite in such a way that, in the case of each image, there is some highly specific way to understand it and the state of the baptized that would correspond to it. Nor do I detect any attempt in the text of the baptismal rite to illustrate how the various regenerate states are related to one another. We are in the presence of something closer to poetry than systematic theology! Still, the text does

---

[17] I am here drawing upon William Alston's wonderful essay "The Indwelling of the Holy Spirit" (Alston [1989], 246).

provide clues about how to understand some of the process-states initiated by the baptismal rite.

Some of these states are epistemic. Take the state of being illumined, for example, which is predicated numerous times of the one baptized.[18] That this is an epistemic state is indicated by the text of the baptismal rite in various places: "Open the eyes of his/her understanding, that the light of your Gospel may shine brightly in him/her . . . that we may be illumined by the light of understanding by the outpouring of the Holy Spirit" (148, 152). This petition, in turn, echoes the prayer recited in the Divine Liturgy immediately before the reading of the Gospel: "Illumine our hearts, O Master who loves humankind with the pure light of your divine knowledge, and open the eyes of our minds to the understanding of your Gospel teachings . . . for you are the illumination of our souls and bodies, O Christ our God" (Liturgy of St. James). Understood as a process-state, being illumined seems to have as its immediate goal a trait-like state, a state of understanding and being disposed to understand the teachings of the Gospel. If this is right, baptism would have the function of instilling not character traits themselves but the processes that, when all goes well, eventuate in the formation of character traits.

In contrast, other images used in the text seem to stand for processes that produce not trait-like states but status-states, such as the status of being freed or loosed from the bonds of the sin-disorder. In some ways, we are now at a disadvantage when it comes to understanding the imagery used in some of the prayers of the baptismal rite, such as the prayer just quoted. For given the distance between ours and the ancient world, some of these images are not easily absorbed. This is probably true of the image and theme that is, in many ways, central to the rite, which is that of being made pure or clean. The presuppositions about ritual purity and impurity that seem to lie behind the imagery and which themselves have an ambiguous status in the New Testament are, for many of us, dark, alien, puzzling. What can be said, however, is that the imagery clearly has aesthetic overtones and that we continue to recognize the aesthetic dimensions of personal character. We speak, for example, of the ugliness of evil and the beauty of goodness and their tendency to both evoke and merit reactive states such as revulsion and awe in us. When viewed in this light, perhaps the thing to say about the images of purity is that they help us to understand the broadly aesthetic dimensions of the twofold transformation that is supposed to occur in baptism, a beauty that consists (in part) in the absence of a certain type of disorder.

While there is much more to say about the various regenerate states that are predicated of the one baptized, let me summarize the upshot of our discussion: the Intelligibility Puzzle raises pressing questions about the intelligibility of the

---

[18] Gregory of Nazianzus and others sometimes use the term "illumination" simply to mean "baptism." See his *Festal Orations* (2008), 100.

baptismal rite, specifically concerning the attribution of the regenerate states to the one baptized. But the puzzle has bite only when the regenerate states are understood to be product rather than process-states. When understood as process-states that are instigated by the performance of the baptismal rite, however, there is no deep puzzle, as there is nothing unintelligible about understanding these states as processes that are instigated in the one baptized by joint human and divine activity. Moreover, this understanding of what is accomplished at the baptismal rite is compatible with the empirical data, as the process-states instigated may fail to take root for various reasons. For the process-states to achieve—or even approximate—their ends, a lot needs to fall into place, including hard effort on the part of the one baptized.

Finally, the interpretation under consideration offers a pleasingly unified account of what occurs by the performance of the baptismal rite in two respects. For one thing, if the process interpretation is correct, the same dynamic is at work in the cases of both infant and adult baptism, namely, the instigation of an array of process-states. Since nothing depends on the one baptized being in one or another mental state for these process-states to be instigated, we have an explanation of why the church has seen fit to use the same baptismal rite when baptizing infants and adults. When interpreting the rite as it applies to infants, there is no need, then, to resort to the analogue of legal fictions, at least when it comes to the attribution of these states.

Moreover, the process interpretation allows us to see better how the two alterations that are understood to occur by the performance of the baptismal rite are related. The regenerate states initiated by the baptismal rite are neither initiated nor develop on their own. To come to fruition, these process-states require a community that conforms to its responsibilities, providing the conditions in which they can develop. Moreover, to the extent that these process-states do develop, it is through the one baptized and the community exercising their rights and conforming to their respective responsibilities. If the tradition is correct, it is (in part) by the one baptized exercising her privilege to partake fully in the eucharistic rite that the regenerate states conferred on her by baptism grow. And it is (in part) by the community conforming to its responsibility to enact this rite that this development occurs.

In a way, though, this is a misleading way of trying to capture the way in which the two alterations are related. It is not as if there were some process that, in the one baptized, develops more or less independently of the activity of the community in the sense that it is merely the community's job to help it develop, as a gardener helps a tomato plant to grow. The better way to view the matter, arguably, is that the process instigated by the baptismal rite consists, in part, in the community's conforming to its responsibilities. The process—which consists in the exercise of the *energeia* of the Holy Spirit—is extended in the sense of being "in" both the person and the activity of the community. Suppose, for example, that the process of being illumined consists in being exposed to the church's understanding of the Gospels. If that understanding and its presentation were the product of the exercise if the *energeia* of the Holy Spirit, then we could begin to see how the process in question might be present in both the community and the one baptized, moving from the former to the latter.

There are, then, multiple reasons to sympathize with the process interpretation of the baptismal rite. Toward the middle of our discussion, however, I mentioned that I find the process interpretation close to but not entirely satisfactory. Let me close by indicating why.

First, the view leaves important questions unaddressed. For example, although I raised questions about how to understand claims that the one baptized "partakes" in the death and resurrection of Christ, I offered no answer to them. It is not apparent to me that the process interpretation itself sheds light on this issue, although this interpretation might put us in a better position to address it.

Second, the process interpretation will strike some as overly modest and, thus, falling outside the arc of the church's understanding of the baptismal rite. Listen, for example, to what St. John Chyrostomos says in a homily to the newly baptized:

> You are not only free, but also holy; not only holy, but also just; not only just, but also sons; not only sons, but also heirs; not only heirs, but also brothers of Christ; not only brothers of Christ, but also joint heirs; not only joint heirs, but also members; not only members, but also the temple; not only the temple, but also instruments of the Spirit. Blessed be God, who alone does wonderful things![19]

Some of these words could, I suppose, be interpreted as being hyperbolic. But if they are not so interpreted, then I can understand why someone might feel dissatisfied with the process interpretation of the baptismal rite, for it is compatible with the one baptized enjoying rather few of the states that Chrysostomos mentions. In reply, I can only say that those who feel this dissatisfaction face a challenge, which is to interpret what Chrysostomos says in such a way that it fits with the reality of what does and could occur by the performance of the baptismal rite.[20]

Third, there are attributions of the regenerate states made in the context of the performance of the baptismal rite that do not easily admit of the process interpretation. At the end of the rite, for example, the celebrant addresses the newly baptized one, proclaiming: "You are justified. You are illumined. You are sanctified. You are washed in the Name of the Father, and of the Son, and

---

[19] Quoted in Kavanagh (1991), 143. Cf. Gregory of Nazianzus (2008).
[20] There was, in fact, a controversy—the so-called Messalian Controversy—over this very issue in fourth century Syria. See Ferguson (2010).

of the Holy Spirit" (160–1).[21] Unlike their Western counterparts, Eastern Christians have had very little to say about the topic of justification; it fails to figure prominently in their theological reflections. However that may be, given the major options for understanding the concept of justification—the best of which, I believe, is that although we have wronged God and each other, the charges against us have been dropped— I do not see a way to understand the concept of justification along process lines.[22] It is a status-state, and it would take some work to explain how it might coherently apply to infants and small children. Similar observations hold regarding claims that infants are forgiven of their sin.

A final concern about the baptismal rite is that it involves the imposition of a variety of states by the performance of speech acts. But in the paradigmatic case, speech acts are intentional: you assert a proposition in virtue of intending to do so. You issue a command because you intend to do so, and so on. But it is perfectly possible for those performing the baptismal rite not to intend to request of God that God impose on the one baptized the regenerative states, or bless the one baptized, or anything of the sort. The celebrant and the people could, in principle, be simply following the script of the rite, going through the liturgical motions. And yet it would seem that the one baptized is indeed baptized, inducted into the community. This raises the issue of what to make of deviant performances of the baptismal rite.

There are several ways of trying to handle this issue. One would be to appeal to the "ossification of intentions." In this case, the suggestion would be that what matters is that the script in some way expresses the intentions of its composers (or those of the church, which appropriated the rite from its composers) to petition God, bless the one baptized, and the like, and that these intentions are actualized by the performance of the rite. Another approach would be to emphasize the centrality of God's intentions in the performance of the baptismal rite, holding that they are sufficient for the locutionary acts performed to count as petitioning, blessing, and so on. I am not sure that either of these approaches, when worked out, is wholly satisfactory. But at least we see better where more needs to be said about the nature of the baptismal rite.[23]

[21] The proclamation lightly embellishes 1 Cor. 6: 11.

[22] For a defense of this understanding, see Wolterstorff (2011b), part IV.

[23] For their feedback on an earlier version of this chapter, I thank an anonymous referee, Robin Le Poidevin, David O'Hara, Luke Reinsma, Mark Usher, Nick Wolterstorff, and Phil Woodward.

10

Rites of Remission

The starting point of my reflections in this chapter is a prayer found in the script of the Divine Liturgy of St. John Chrysostomos. In the Litany before the Lord's Prayer, the liturgical script instructs the celebrant to pray:

> To You Master, Lover of humankind, we entrust our whole life and hope and we entreat, pray, and implore you: count us worthy to partake of your heavenly and awesome Mysteries . . . for remission of sins, for forgiveness of transgressions, for the communion of the Holy Spirit, for the inheritance of the Kingdom of Heaven, for boldness towards You, but not for judgment or condemnation.[1]

The line that interests me—and which is repeated no less than five times in the liturgy—is the one in which the celebrant requests of God that the eating of the eucharist be for the "remission of sins." What interests me about this line, at least initially, is that it does not simply echo Jesus's words in the New Testament. Although the Gospels of Matthew, Mark, and Luke all present accounts of Jesus's words at the Last Supper, only Matthew reports Jesus as saying anything at the Last Supper about the remission of sin. What Matthew reports Jesus as saying, however, is not that the partaking of the bread and wine is for the remission of sin, but that his *death* is for the remission of sin.[2] Likewise, when Paul reports Jesus's words at the Last Supper, Jesus says nothing about sin, let alone that partaking of the eucharist is for remission of sin (I Cor. 11: 23). By all appearances, then, when the liturgical script says

---

[1] I am using the Thyateira (1995) translation of *The Divine Liturgy of Our Father among the Saints John Chrysostom*. This translation is also available at <http://www.cappellaromana. org/DL_in_English_Booklet_Web.pdf> (accessed August 21, 2015). In what follows, I operate with a distinction between the liturgical script, which is a set of guidelines addressed to a group of people who might participate in the liturgy, and the liturgy itself, which is a sequence of act-types.

[2] This passage from Matthew is quoted in the Anaphora of The Divine Liturgy of St. John Chrysostom. The Gospel of John has no account of the Last Supper. Still, after the feeding of the five thousand, Jesus says that he is the bread of life and that only those who partake of him have eternal life (John 6: 55–8). While most Christians would affirm that there are interesting and intimate connections between having eternal life and the remission of sin, the two states are not identical.

that partaking of the eucharist is for the remission of sin, it goes beyond anything that is explicitly stated in the Gospels or the epistolary literature.

There might be an explanation for this. When blessing the waters during the baptismal rite, the celebrant prays several times that the water would be for "the remission of sins, the remedy of infirmities."[3] The content of this prayer, unlike the prayer quoted above, draws directly from scripture, echoing Peter's injunction in Acts to "Repent, and let every one of you be baptized in the name of Jesus Christ for the remission of sin" (Acts 2: 38). And yet, in the context of the liturgy, Peter's words about the function of baptism are understood in such a way that they apply equally to other liturgical rites, such as partaking of eucharist and anointing with oil. Why is that?

Perhaps a comparison will help. In American jurisprudence, certain constitutional provisions are understood to "incorporate" others, the most famous example being that in which portions of the Bill of Rights are understood to apply to the individual states, even though, when drafted, these sections were not so intended. In the case of baptism, a natural suggestion is that the liturgy articulates the church's understanding that, when Peter claims that baptism is for the remission of sin, his claim about baptism's function also applies to other liturgical rites, even though Peter's words make no explicit reference to these other rites. The idea is that, much in the way that the Supreme Court has held that certain constitutional provisions incorporate others, so also Peter's pronouncement regarding the purpose of baptism "incorporates" other liturgical activities, such as participating in the eucharist.[4] Under this understanding, a central aim of all these liturgical activities is to effect the remission of sin, even if the scriptures explicitly designate only baptizing and anointing for this purpose.

There appears, then, to be a way to explain why the liturgical script would go beyond the scriptural texts, denominating certain activities such as participating in the eucharist as being for the remission of sin. What puzzles me most about these liturgical pronouncements, however, is not the way in which they creatively extend the scriptural text, but what is said about the effects of these liturgical activities themselves. For it is difficult to see what the connection could be between the activities of participating in the eucharist, baptizing, and anointing with oil, on the one hand, and the state of enjoying remission of sin, on the other. When it comes to the remission of sin, wouldn't *repenting* be the relevant activity? Moreover, the effect that these liturgical activities are said

---

[3] *Service Book of the Holy Eastern Orthodox Catholic and Apostolic Church according to the use of the Antiochian Orthodox Christian Archdiocese of North America* (2002), 155. I will refer to this work as *Service Book* (2002).

[4] As for anointing the sick, see Jas. 5: 14–15. In the rite of the anointing of the sick, the celebrant entreats God to "send down your Holy Spirit and sanctify this oil; and grant that it may bring full pardon from sin to your servant who is anointed" (Meyendorff [2009], 136). The verb used in this prayer is ἀπολύτρωσιν, often translated as "release" or "redemption." In Col. 1: 14, it is used as a near synonym for the Greek verb that is translated as "remission."

to have—namely, the remission of sin—does not appear to hinge on whether the one who eats, is baptized, or is anointed understands what is being done. In the Eastern tradition, after all, babies and small children are both baptized and participate in the eucharist; those in advanced states of dementia and comas are anointed. If these activities do effect the remission of sin, they appear to do so (at least in part) at a sub-doxastic level. How they accomplish this, however, is something that is not easy to understand.

Those who wish to understand the underlying *ratio* of the various actions that constitute the liturgy face a task. The task is to try to uncover the rationale or justification for why the liturgy takes the shape it does—why certain things are said, certain actions are performed and are understood to have one or another type of significance. In the case at hand, the task is to understand how there could be a close link between taking eucharist, baptizing, and anointing, on the one hand, and enjoying remission of sin, on the other. My project in this chapter is to try to make headway on this task. I am going to suggest that the text and actions of the liturgy make sense given a certain understanding of our condition, an understanding that is controversial but deeply embedded in the Eastern Christian tradition. While I have no pretensions of dispelling the mystery of how rites such as taking eucharist, baptizing, and anointing could contribute to the remission of sin, I think some helpful things can be said on this score too. The key to making sense of these activities, or so I will suggest, is to work with a particular model of human and divine action.

Before diving into our topic, let me first enter a pair of caveats. Like biblical exegesis, interpreting liturgical texts and actions quickly plunges one into a set of complicated issues, in which philological, theological, historical, and philosophical questions intertwine with one another. Since my aims are broadly philosophical, I am not going to pause to explore or defend in detail claims that many of those with broadly philological, theological, or historical interests would, since doing so would often be beyond my competence and distract from my central project, which is to try to make sense of certain aspects of the liturgy. Sometimes it is best to present the model first and then return to defend its more controversial elements! In addition to not giving the full range of issues before us the attention they might deserve, I do not aspire to give anything like the complete story of how liturgical rites could plausibly be understood to have the effects that the liturgy seems to ascribe to them. I wish to present only the main lines of a certain understanding that could be supplemented, modified, and enriched in various ways.

10.1. DIAGNOSIS

What is being presupposed about our human condition such that it is intelligible to hold that eating, baptizing, and anointing are for the remission of sin? Let me begin with an observation about the phrase "remission of sin" itself. This phrase is an English translation of a Greek phrase (ἄφεσις ἁμαρτιῶν/*afesin amartion*) that belongs to a cluster of Greek terms and phrases that can have importantly different meanings and nuances in meaning, many of which are obscured (or even lost) in their English translations. When used in both the scriptures and the liturgy, the Greek terms that are translated as "life" and "death," for example, often communicate much more—and sometimes something entirely different from—physical life and death. Similarly for the Greek counterparts to other English terms such as "salvation," "flesh," "word," "world," and the like.[5] As I say, my aim here is not primarily philological; it is not to comb biblical scholarship for the purpose of uncovering and comparing the variety of meanings expressed by the phrase "remission of sin," but to make several observations that will guide our discussion.

Begin with the term "remission." The first observation is that, on linguistic grounds alone, when the liturgical text uses the phrase "remission of sin," this phrase is probably best understood not to mean "forgiveness of sin." That it should not is apparent from the prayer quoted in the opening paragraph. In this prayer, recall, the celebrant addresses God, asking that those present be:

> worthy to partake of your heavenly and awesome Mysteries . . . for remission [ἄφεσις] of sins, for forgiveness [συγχώρησις] of transgressions, for the communion of the Holy Spirit, for the inheritance of the Kingdom of Heaven, for boldness towards You, but not for judgment or condemnation.

Note that when this prayer lists the hoped-for results of partaking of the Mysteries—the Mysteries being the Eastern church's counterpart to the sacraments—it does not offer a list of states and activities that are simply slight variants or subspecies of the other. Instead, it lists a series of states— such as forgiveness of transgressions, communion of the Holy Spirit, inheritance of the kingdom, and boldness toward God—that are related in a variety of interesting but importantly different ways. Given that this is so, we should probably not interpret "remission" and "forgiveness," in this context, to be mere notational variants of one another, as some translators of biblical passages do.[6] These terms, after all, are the English translations of different Greek terms, which in this context appear to designate different states. To treat them otherwise would be to ignore the differences to which the liturgical script seems to be drawing our attention.

But if "remission of sin" does not mean "forgiveness of sin" in this context, how should we understand this phrase? In colloquial English, "remit" has

---

[5] When, for example, the prayers of the church address God as the "salvation of both humans and beasts," it's clear that they incorporate an understanding of the meaning of the term "salvation" that is much broader than is often thought. See McGuckin (2011), 118.

[6] The *New Zondervan Parallel New Testament in Greek and English* (1975), for example, repeatedly translates ἄφεσις as "forgiveness."

strong economic or legal connotations; we speak, for example, of being required to remit payment for a service provided. While present, these con- notations are not nearly as pronounced in the biblical and Patristic use of the Greek ἄφεσις, the term that is translated as "remission." In fact, my Greek- English lexicons tell me that the Greek term ἄφεσις admits of a broad range of uses, many of which are captured by a cluster of English phrases such as "letting go," "release," and "leaving."[7] Given this and a broader theological framework about which I shall have more to say in a moment, let me offer the following proposal: when used in the liturgy, the phrase "remission of sin" is best rendered as something along the lines of *being released or liberated from the grip of sin*. The phrase probably communicates a good deal more than this, but its focal meaning, I want to suggest, lies in this vicinity. I would immedi- ately add that whether this is the best understanding of the phrase is not something that can be settled simply by consulting Greek-English lexicons. It will only be vindicated by how well it comports with and makes sense of the rest of the liturgical script and the liturgical actions that accompany it. Holism, in this case, is the right approach.

The second observation I would like to make concerns the use, not of the term "remission," but "sin" (ἁμαρτία/*amartia*). Surprisingly often, sin is understood simply to be a derelict moral condition, something akin to state of moral guilt. In his book *Responsibility and Atonement*, for example, Richard Swinburne identifies sin with a "failure of duty to God."[8] George Hunsinger maintains that "sin is basically a matter of guilt and of the will's bondage consequent upon this guilt."[9] And in one of the most perceptive treatments of sin of which I'm aware, Cornelius Plantinga writes of sin "as . . . the *power* in human beings that has the effect . . . of corrupting human thought, word, and deed so that they displease God and make their authors guilty."[10]

I am not making a novel contribution by noting that these passages express an extraordinarily pinched understanding of what sin is. In the Eastern Christian tradition, the state is ordinarily understood much more broadly to be a state of deep disorder, which has moral, legal, aesthetic, and therapeutic dimensions, some of these dimensions being such that they needn't imply that an agent who suffers from them is morally guilty in virtue of suffering from them. The agent who suffers from this deep disorder might, for example, view the world in deeply distorted ways or desire what would be his destruction (even though he does not act on this desire). But that he views the world in these ways or is in the grip of these desires needn't imply that he is morally

---

[7] See, for example, Thayer (1996), Liddell and Scott (1996), and Lampe (1969). I thank Mark Montague for his help on these matters of translation.

[8] Swinburne (1989), 124.   [9] Hunsinger (2000), 250.

[10] Plantinga (1995), 13, n. 10.

derelict in virtue of viewing the world in these ways or being in the grip of these desires. Not all disorder is morally culpable.

A helpful way to appreciate these non-moral dimensions of sin is to bring to mind the positive counterpart of sin, which I take to be not innocence or goodness but *holiness*—a state that the liturgy repeatedly ascribes to God, which also has moral, legal, aesthetic, and therapeutic dimensions. As the Christian tradition describes God, God is the Holy One. The Holy One, in turn, is the one without guile, taint, or disorder—the one who is characterized by perfection that transcends all blemish, taint, disorder, and defilement.[11] Although some theologians have been keen to moralize holiness, viewing it simply as a moral quality, this tendency has not been strong; most have understood holiness to be a state with multiple normative dimensions. Why has the tendency to moralize its negative counterpart, sin, been so prominent in the Western Christian tradition? Nice question!

Suppose we pull together our reflections on the liturgical use of the term "remission" with those of the liturgical use of "sin." The conclusion to which we're led is that when the people pray that activities such as eating, baptizing, participating in and anointing be for the remission of sin, this should be understood as requesting that these activities be for the release from the sin-disorder in its various manifestations, including its broadly therapeutic dimensions. The petition, to say it again, is not a request to be forgiven for being in the grip of this disorder. It is rather a plea to be *delivered from* its grip.

That this is a helpful way to understand these prayers emerges, I believe, when one digs deeper into the liturgical texts themselves. For it is a striking feature of these texts that they highlight the broadly therapeutic dimensions of sin by repeatedly coupling the theme of sin with those of health and wholeness. For example, the text of the Trisagion Prayers, which are used extensively in the Eastern church, runs:

> All-Holy Trinity, have mercy on us. Lord, forgive us our sins. Master, pardon our transgressions. Holy One, visit and heal our infirmities for your name's sake.[12]

That these infirmities are not merely bodily is manifest when one consults other texts, such as the pre-communion prayers, in which participants in the liturgy pray that the Mysteries be for both "the remission of sin" and for "the healing of soul and body."[13] These prayers are, in turn, followed by the post-communion prayers, in which, once again, the themes of remission of sin and healing of the self are conjoined:

---

[11] This is the gloss offered by Wolterstorff (2015), 36.   [12] McGuckin (2011), 8.
[13] The same words are used in the baptismal rite; see *Service Book* (2002), 157, and the rite of anointing with oil; cf. Meyendorff (2009), 127.

O Lord Jesus Christ, my God, let your holy body be my eternal life, and your precious blood, the remission of my sins. May this eucharist be my joy, my health, and my gladness.[14]

And to quote more fully a passage cited earlier from the baptismal rite, the celebrant prays that the baptismal water would be "the water of redemption, the water of sanctification, the purification of flesh and spirit, the loosing of bonds, the remission of sins, the remedy of infirmities."[15] Finally, the prayers that compose the Lenten liturgies repeatedly and vividly employ therapeutic imagery. These prayers refer to the church as a "house of healing," speak of repentance as being like oil and wine for a soul that is sick, and present the sin-disorder as a type of wound or injury: "Bind up, O Jesus, the wounds of my soul, as the Samaritan bound up the wounds of him that fell among thieves, and heal me from my pain, I pray O Christ."[16]

The liturgical texts, then, repeatedly associate the sin-disorder with sickness and associate deliverance from the disorder with health.[17] In traditions in which participating in the eucharist and the practice of fasting are still alive, such as the Eastern tradition, these associations would be natural, especially in the context of the eucharistic prayers. For it is common in these traditions to understand the state of disorder from which human beings suffer in terms of a narrative in which food figures prominently. The falling away of human beings is presented as a matter of disordered eating, the refusal to fast, hungering for something other than God. Redemption, in turn, is achieved (in part) by "ordered eating," in which followers of Christ participate in the eucharist. It is no accident, then, that the eucharistic prayers are replete with imagery of sin, health, and food. For, according to the church's salvation narrative, it is by food that we have fallen and by food that we're redeemed.

The associations that one finds in the liturgy between the sin-disorder, health, and food, I believe, are rich and suggestive, so let me continue to explore them, as I believe they can help to shed light on our original question of how participation in liturgical rites could be for the remission of sin. When the tradition has addressed the issue of disordered eating, it has typically done

[14] McGuckin (2011), 160.
[15] *Service Book* (2002), 155. This rite contains various prayers of exorcism, including: "O Lord Sabaoth, the God of Israel, who heals every malady and every infirmity: Look upon your servant; prove him/her and search him/her; and root out every operation of the Devil" (147). As one might imagine, similar themes run throughout the rite of the anointing of the sick; cf. Meyendorff (2009), especially p. 123.
[16] Mary and Ware (2002), 360, 180, 408, and 691. Cf. also pp. 399 and 480.
[17] As do prominent figures in the tradition. To pick just one example, St. Cyril of Alexandria writes: "After Adam fell by sin and sank into corruption...nature became sick with sin.... Human nature in Adam became sick through the corruption of disobedience." Quoted in Hierotheos (2005), 37. In his homilies, John Chrysostomos airs similar themes, describing the church as a hospital. The word, says Chrysostomos, is like medicine to the soul. Hierotheos also (1996) addresses the theme of sin as sickness.

so by associating it with gluttony, which is often understood in the Eastern tradition as one of the "passions" and in the Western tradition as a deadly vice.[18] In the first chapter of his book *For the Life of the World*, the Orthodox theologian Alexander Schmemann also explores the connections between food and deliverance from sin, but approaches the discussion from a different direction. Schmemann writes that the scriptures begin with a portrayal of the human being "as a hungry being, with the man who is that which he eats.... In the Bible the good that man eats, the world of which he must partake in order to live, is given to him by God, and it is given as *communion with God*."[19] Continuing this thought, Schmemann says that "the 'original' sin is not primarily that man has 'disobeyed' God; the sin is that he ceased to be hungry for Him and for Him alone, ceased to see his whole life depending on the whole world as a sacrament of communion with God."[20] In these passages, Schmemann suggests that while the falling away is the manifestation of an eating disorder, the disorder is not so much a manifestation of gluttony as a failure to hunger—specifically, a failure to hunger for God.

The liturgical texts make bold and puzzling claims about the link between participating in liturgical rites and being released from the grip of the sin-disorder. What we're looking for is a way of understanding this disorder that sheds light on how it could be that we are delivered from its grip, as the liturgical texts claim, by participating in liturgical activities such as eating. Moreover, we are looking for a way of understanding these rites so that they could plausibly be understood to contribute to our deliverance even when those who eat, are baptized, or are anointed fail to understand their significance. Although Schmemann himself never developed the idea, there is, I believe, a way of understanding the disorder in question that might help us to answer our questions. And that is to take seriously the idea that the sin-disorder is akin to disordered eating in which we fail to hunger. The approach I want to explore, then, is one that flips on its head the traditional understanding between food and the sin-disorder. Rather than view the sin-disorder as manifested in the indulgence of appetite, view it instead as manifested in a lack of appetite.

A theme that repeatedly surfaces in Harriet Brown's riveting book *Brave Girl Eating*, which chronicles her daughter's struggle with anorexia, is that most of us operate with deep misunderstandings about disordered eating. It is commonly assumed that those who suffer from such a disorder choose, for various reasons, to suffer from them. Brown provides a powerful corrective to these misunderstandings. Those who suffer from disorders such as anorexia

---

[18] See Staniloe (2002), part I, for example. In *Paradise Lost*, Milton describes the Fall as the manifestation of gluttony.
[19] Schmemann (1973), 14.   [20] Ibid., 18.

do not choose them; rather, these disorders choose them.[21] Moreover, these disorders seem to be no respecter of persons; while those who suffer from anorexia in particular are often highly intelligent, curious, and perceptive, these qualities do not insulate them from the disorder. Those in its grip—and that is exactly how Brown describes anorexia, a power that grips—suffer from a baffling confluence of self-destructive behavior, loss of personal autonomy, and ruthless self-loathing, laced with the tendencies to isolate oneself from others, engage in deceptive behavior, and radically misperceive one's own state.[22] In one place, Brown quotes a therapist who describes the condition as a kind of "encapsulated psychosis": someone with anorexia suffers from a set of delusions just as powerful as those of the schizophrenic, but only with respect to food, eating, and body image.[23]

To illustrate the power of this disorder, Brown cites a researcher who describes a case in which he invited two anorexic women to his class and asked one of them to describe how much she weighed and how she looked. The woman said that she weighed seventy pounds and looked fat. When asked to describe her companion, she said that the other woman looked terrible, as if she were going to die. When the researcher pointed out that both women were the same weight and height, the first woman had no answer as to why she perceived herself as fat and the other as emaciated.[24] Apparently, suffering from the disorder is strongly correlated with not realizing that one suffers from the disorder or its effects. Distorted perception of this variety, as Brown herself stresses, has an important social component, for social feedback mechanisms, in countless and sometimes unintentional ways, reinforce it, presenting the bodies of anorexics as healthy, desirable, or attractive. In a passage intended to make readers wince, Brown describes a case in which a nurse inadvertently complimented her daughter for being so slim, even when her daughter's health was in grave danger.[25]

A moment ago I stated the obvious by describing eating disorders such as anorexia as being accompanied by self-destructive behavior. In truth, however, the tendency toward self-destruction among those who suffer from the condition is breathtaking. More people die from it than any other mental disorder,

---

[21] Brown (2010), 4.

[22] Although Brown describes herself as not religious, she often refers to the condition from which her daughter suffered as a power, indeed, a "demon." She even documents one case in which her daughter, who was in a trance-like state at the nadir of her condition, spoke with an unrecognizable voice while her tongue flicked like "a snake's forked tongue" (64).

[23] Ibid., 52–3. Describing her daughter, Brown writes: "On the subjects of food and eating and fat, Kitty's delusional. Obviously. On every other subject, though, she's the same girl she's always been, sharp-witted, insightful, quick" (62).

[24] Ibid., 52–3.

[25] Ibid., 28. During the course of her discussion, Brown cites Bynum (1987), which explores the ways in which the Christian tradition has failed to recognize anorexia as a disease, lauding it as the manifestation of the virtue of abstinence.

many from committing suicide. Only a third of those diagnosed recover from it. Particularly striking is that rational persuasion and therapy—on their own, at least—have almost no positive impact, despite the considerable intelligence of a large percentage of those who suffer from the disorder. In fact, on its own, therapy can be harmful. According to one expert whom Brown cites, what you end up with when you do intensive psychotherapy with someone with anorexia is "an insightful corpse," someone good at rationalizing but unable to alter her perception of food, eating, and the body.[26] But if rational persuasion, therapy—and for that matter, pharmaceuticals—tend not to help, at least on their own, where does the road to recovery lie?

Anorexics typically feel no hunger—indeed, the Greek word "anorexia" simply means "loss of appetite"—and appear to experience less pleasure from eating than others.[27] Still, the road to recovery lies in getting them to eat, the most effective environments for eating being ones in which they eat in community with those whom they trust, such as family. Reflecting on her daughter's case, Brown writes that it was not pharmaceuticals but food that acted as her daughter's "medicine," the cure for her "body and mind."[28] Still, Brown notes, the medicine works very slowly. Her daughter's recovery stretched out over months and years; there were no shortcuts. And, indeed, her daughter relapsed, as many who suffer from the disorder do. (The relapse rate among anorexics is staggeringly high.)

The parallels between the disorder that Brown describes in her book and the Christian understanding of the sin-disorder are telling. In both cases, we find ourselves describing the disorders in active terms, as powers to whose influence we do not choose to submit ourselves, but in some sense find ourselves under. Their manifestations are, moreover, baffling, often unintelligible, even to those in its grip. ("I do not understand what I do. For what I want to do, I do not do, but what I hate I do" [Rom. 7: 15]). Although their behavior is unintelligible in certain respects, those in the grip of these disorders are often highly intelligent; paradoxically, in the case of anorexia, the unintelligibility and the intelligence go hand in hand, although the latter often proves to be not particularly helpful in the recovery process. Moreover, the associations with death, self-destruction, self-condemnation, deceit, division, and misperception of oneself and others, which I only touched upon, are unmistakable. St. Paul's claim in Romans that death came into the world through sin (Rom. 7: 12) takes on a very different color when the latter is understood to be a disorder whose grip often drives us to self-destructive behavior.[29] Finally,

---

[26] Brown (2010), 179.   [27] Ibid., 130.

[28] Ibid., 194–5. Elsewhere, Brown describes her methods for helping her daughter as "exposure therapy" in which she slowly desensitized her daughter to the thing she feared most, namely, food (104).

[29] I realize that there is controversy regarding the correct translation of this passage from Romans.

to hearken back to Schmemann's observation, there is in both cases the failure to hunger. Taking Schmemann's original observation into account, *both* disorders manifest themselves as a failure to hunger—baffling from the perspective of the healthy—for that which we need most to live.

I began this section with a question, asking: What is being presupposed about our human condition such that it is intelligible to hold that liturgical activities such as eating, baptizing, and anointing are for the remission of sin? I suggested that we understand the phrase "remission of sin" to mean *being released from the grip of sin*, where the latter is understood to be a disorder of the self with multiple dimensions, including broadly therapeutic ones. To help us understand the character of this disorder, I worked with Schmemann's observation that it manifests itself as a failure to hunger, a condition that strikingly parallels the disordered eating that Brown describes in her book.

What most interests me, however, is not simply the ways in which these disorders are similar but also the ways in which they are addressed. In the case of Brown's daughter, recovery did not consist primarily in persuasion, therapy, argument, or the like. In fact, such efforts were typically futile and, at a certain stage, potentially counterproductive. Rather, recovery lay in the realm of the sub-doxastic, with eating; other modalities, such as therapy, which proved to be important, could take effect only when Brown's daughter had been "re-fed." The suggestion I wish to make is *not* that liturgical activities such as partaking of eucharist, being baptized, or being anointed with oil are to the person in the grip of the sin-disorder as ingesting a sufficient amount of calories is to the person with an eating disorder—at least not in the sense that there are some identifiable mechanisms for recovery that we could identify in each case. Rather, the line I wish to pursue is that deeply embedded in the liturgy is the conviction that deliverance from the grip of the disorder that afflicts us does not come exclusively—and perhaps not even primarily—through persuasion, argument, or hearing. Rather, deliverance comes in the form of participating in activities that operate on us on a sub-doxastic level.

Stated more broadly, the idea is that important elements that contribute to the loosening of the grip of the disorder do not consist in the presentation or acceptance of propositions about God or God's activity or experiences that aim to evoke beliefs about God or God's activity. The presupposition of the liturgy seems to be, instead, that there are important elements that contribute to the loosening of the grip of the sin-disorder that operate—at least in large measure—at a sub-doxastic level, below the level of understanding or belief. To the extent that it occurs, the presupposition seems to be that release from the disorder comes through doing bodily things in communion with others, such as eating, being baptized, and being anointed. Moreover, it may be that, for many, the temporal directionality of the process of being released parallels that described by Brown. First, one must do bodily things such as eat; only afterward are there shifts in perception, the ability to recognize one's illness and its effects, to hear what one could not previously understand, and so forth. At the very least, the conviction of the church seems to be that engaging in these liturgical activities must occur in tandem with actions that we would naturally identify as redemptive, such as praying or engaging with the texts of the Gospels.

I do not find it easy to articulate or understand this presupposition about the role of bodily actions that seems to be built into the liturgy. Most of us who identify with the Christian tradition are unaccustomed to thinking of that which contributes to the relaxation of the grip of the sin-disorder as bodily action that often operates, over time and gradually, on the sub-doxastic level, below the level of understanding or belief. We are much more accustomed to thinking about the cognitive dimensions of the sin-disorder and about the contributions that cognitive states, such as changes in beliefs and intentions, make to the loosening of the disorder's grip. Indeed, the liturgical life of huge swaths of Christians seems to be built on such "cognitivist" suppositions. However that may be, what we were looking for is an analogue—a model— of a deep disorder of the self whose grip is relaxed not, in the first instance at least, at the level of changing the beliefs or views of the person who is in the grip of the disorder, but in some other way, through bodily actions such as eating. And we have done that, even if we have little understanding at this point of how the relaxation of the grip occurs in the case of the sin-disorder. The thought is simply that, with the example of disordered eating and its treatment before us, we can point to them, noting that the sin-disorder and its treatment seem to be importantly like *that*.

10.2. MODELS OF RITES

When one consults the liturgical texts, a certain model of how the Mysteries or sacraments operate seems to emerge. Take, to begin with, texts from the rite of baptism in which the celebrant prays:

> That this water may be sanctified with the power, and effectual operation, and indwelling of the Holy Spirit, let us pray to the Lord.
> That there may come upon this water the purifying operation of the super-substantial Trinity, let us pray to the Lord.[30]

In the same rite (as well as the rite of anointing the sick), similar things are asked of the oil with which the baptized is to be anointed:

---

[30] *Service Book* (2002), 152.

Bless also this holy oil with the power, and operation, and indwelling of your Holy Spirit.[31]

And in considerably more poetic language, one of the post-communion prayers runs:

> O You who willingly does give your flesh to me as food, You who are a fire, consuming the unworthy.... Pass through all my body parts ... burn the thorns of all my transgressions.[32]

Under a fairly natural reading, these texts seem to express two related ideas: first, that in the rites of baptism, anointing, and eucharist, ordinary physical elements are endowed with new powers—powers to contribute to the remission of sin, among other things. And, second, that it is by coming into physical contact with these physical elements that we benefit from these powers.

For ease of reference, call this way of thinking of the Mysteries or sacraments the *contact model*.[33] Given a certain understanding of the Christian tradition, it is easy to see how the view might be attractive. It takes the role of matter very seriously, viewing it as a point of contact with the divine. It is, moreover, consistent with the traditional claim that the eucharistic elements are the body and blood of Christ. Finally, the model is well-situated to make good on the claim that liturgical activities can contribute to the remission of sin on a sub-doxastic level, as we could be entirely unaware of the powers of the water, the oil, or the bread and wine that operate on us.

That said, it is difficult to shake the impression—or, at least, I find it difficult to shake the impression—that this model traffics in magic. I make this observation not because I think it expresses a decisive objection to the contact model; perhaps there are ways to understand the model so that it looks much less as if it were describing something occult in which ordinary material stuff is endowed with supernatural powers. But I do think that the model is worrisome enough to encourage us to look for other models of how liturgical rites could contribute to the remission of sin. Are there any?

I believe so. In what remains, I would like to sketch an alternative model that captures what is attractive in the contact model, not—let me emphasize—for the

---

[31] *Service Book* (2002), 129. And elsewhere: "we beg you, O our God, to direct your mercy upon this oil, and upon all who shall be anointed with it in your Name, that it may be for the healing of their souls and bodies, for purification, and for the removal of every passion, every disease and infirmity, and every defilement of body and spirit" (148); cf. p. 152. Other translations, it is worth noting, run: "Bless also this holy oil *through* the power, and operation and indwelling of your Holy Spirit" rather than "with the power."

[32] *Service Book* (2002), 129.

[33] This is, arguably, the model with which the Council of Trent operated and that was attacked by Reformers, such as Calvin. As will become evident shortly, while I believe one can read the passages I have quoted as presupposing something like the contact model, I do not think that this is the best reading.

purpose of developing it in the detail that it deserves, but rather to try to make better sense of how liturgical rites could contribute to the remission of sin, when this is understood along the lines proposed earlier.

Like the contact model, the model I wish to develop has two primary components. The best way to present the first component is to remind ourselves that the Eastern tradition has tended not to think of the Mysteries or sacraments as "visible signs of an invisible grace," as the Western tradition has. Rather, the Eastern tradition has tended to think of the Mysteries as points of contact, means of communion with God. Schmemann articulates this understanding when he says that a sacrament is "a revelation of the genuine *nature* of creation."[34] As such, a "sacrament . . . is always a *passage*, a *transformation*." "Yet," Schmemann continues,

> it is not a "passage" into "supernature," but into the Kingdom of God, the world to come, into the very reality of this world and its life as redeemed and restored by Christ. It is the transformation not of "nature" into "supernature," but of the *old* into the *new*. A sacrament therefore is not a "miracle" by which God breaks, so to speak, the "laws of nature," but the manifestation of the ultimate Truth about the world and life.[35]

According to this way of seeing things, in rites such as baptism, eucharist, and anointing, matter is indeed changed. But the change is not that of endowing material stuff with supernatural powers, as the contact model would have it. Rather, the change is one of *function*. The new function is one in which matter becomes a means of communion with God. Schmemann puts this last point in various ways. Echoing the passage cited above, he writes that "Christ came . . . to restore . . . matter . . . and to fulfill it as the means of communion with God," which is its "original function."[36] And again: "such is the meaning of the baptismal blessing of water. It is the re-creation of matter, and thus of the world, in Christ. . . . It is the gift of the world as communion with God."[37]

In a moment, I will have something more to say about what it would be for something to be a means of communion with God. In the meanwhile, the point to stress, is that under this model, liturgical activities such as baptizing, participating in eucharist, and anointing incorporate a *normative* understanding of matter, an

---

[34] Schmemann (1987), 33.
[35] Schmemann (1973), 102. Schmemann continues: "Thus, for example, to bless water, making it 'holy water,' may have two entirely different meanings. It may mean, on the one hand, the transformation of something *profane*, and thus religiously void or neutral, into something *sacred*, in which the main religious meaning of 'holy water' is precisely that it is no longer 'mere' water, and it is in fact opposed to it—as the sacred is to the profane. Here the act of blessing reveals nothing about water, and thus about matter or world, but on the contrary makes them irrelevant to the new function of water as 'holy water' . . . 'sacramentality' has been replaced everywhere by 'sacrality,' epiphany' by an almost magical incrustation into time and matter (the 'natural'), by the 'supernatural'" (132). Cf. Schmemann (1987), 61.
[36] Schmemann (1974), 49, 42.   [37] Ibid., 51.

understanding not so much of what it is as what it is supposed to be, how it is supposed to function in our life together. As Schmemann himself indicates, this understanding of the liturgical rites in question and the role of matter look both backward and forward. They look backward insofar as, according to the Christian narrative, the original calling of human beings was to transform the world, including its material stuff, by transforming it into a means of communion with God. There is a sense, then, in which in the liturgical rites incorporate not simply a normative understanding of matter but also of human beings, inasmuch as by engaging in these rites, human beings return to their intended calling or vocation as the ones who are to transform the world—as Schmemann sometimes writes, the vocation of being the priest, offering back to God in thanks that which was given for our use.[38] These rites also look forward, however, having an unmistakable eschatological dimension. They anticipate—hence, Schmemann's use of the imagery of entering into the "kingdom"—and to some extent realize, what God is working toward, which is the restoration of creation.[39]

Liturgical rites of certain kinds, I have suggested, are helpfully understood as actions in which elements of matter acquire a normative function. While material things can acquire functions in various ways—we can, for example, construct or design artifacts in certain ways—often they do so by our *imposing* these functions on them: by treating pieces of paper in certain ways, we impose on them the function of being a dollar bill; by treating the rock on my desk in certain ways, I impose on it the function of being a paperweight, and so on.[40]

According to the first part of the model that I wish to develop, something similar is true of liturgical activities such as baptizing, eating the eucharist, and anointing; they, too, are activities in which we impose normative functions on matter. For when the assembled engage in activities such as baptizing, eating the eucharist, and anointing, they treat material things as points of communion with God; their following the liturgical script guarantees that they treat them in this way. If the model is correct, these scripted activities thereby impose a new function on these things: in virtue of treating these elements as points of contact, means of communion with God, they thereby become points of contact, means of communion with God. To be sure, these liturgical activities are also attempts on the church's part to fulfill commandments, issued by Jesus or by his followers, to baptize, to eat together in remembrance, and to anoint the sick. But that is not in tension with the model we're considering. For if what I am saying is correct, these injunctions would be

---

[38] Schmemann (1973), ch. 1 and p. 100.

[39] The "kingdom of God," Schmemann (1987) writes, "is the content of the Christian faith . . . unity with God, the source of life" (40–1).

[40] The most developed account of this phenomenon of which I'm aware is Searle (1995).

directives to impose normative functions on ordinary things such as bread, water, wine, and oil.

The first commitment of the model I am proposing, then, is to understand certain liturgical rites as ones that involve the imposition of normative functions. In this respect, I've suggested, these rites are similar to activities in which we impose monetary value on pieces of paper or metal. So, without too much distortion we can say that it is a social fact that elements such as bread, water, wine, and oil have the function of being a means of communion with God. That said, there is a crucial difference between the two cases. In the case of ordinary social facts, we can (all else being equal) impose a function on a piece of paper simply by treating it in a certain way. In the liturgical case, it is not that simple. For deep in the church is the conviction that if bread, water, wine, and oil are to become points of contact with God—means for liberation from the disorder that afflicts us—this is not simply up to us. God's activity is crucial.

The second commitment of the model that I am developing is to the claim that the normative function that is imposed on matter by way of liturgical activity is determined not simply by human but also by divine activity; that matter has such a function is a human-divine social fact, the result of a human-divine cooperative endeavor. In fact, I would say that the cooperative endeavor is a case of collective agency in which both God and the assembly share certain "we intentions" that have as their content the performance of certain joint activities—in this case, the activity of treating various material elements as points of contact with God.[41] In various places, Nicholas Wolterstorff has proposed that we can helpfully think of this sort of cooperation by employing the concept of *double-agency action*.[42]

Take a case in which I perform some action, such as promising to care for your children should you happen not to be able to care for them. Suppose the context determines that in promising this I speak for my entire family. In this case, not only have I promised you something but so also have the other members of my family. By one person doing something (in this case, promising), another person does something (in this case, an action of the same sort). In double-agency action, then, one agent acts by the actions of another such that the actions of the one count as actions of the other. In the case of liturgical rites, the thought is, when the assembled treat elements such as bread, water, wine, and oil as means of communion with God by following the liturgical script, God also treats these elements as means of communion, for God intends to act and acts by the actions of the assembled. Viewed from this angle, liturgical rites of

---

[41] Cuneo (2010) develops this theme. This essay is included as Chapter 6 in the present volume.

[42] Most prominently in his *Divine Discourse* (1995), ch. 3.

this sort would be a paradigmatic case of human-divine cooperative action in which human beings and God together impose normative functions on matter. Under this understanding, liturgical activity is genuinely creative action; it involves the creation of human-divine social facts.[43]

In the context of our discussion, this point strikes me as important for the following reason. Our overarching concern has been to determine in what sense liturgical activities, such as engaging in the eucharist, baptizing, and anointing, could be for the remission of sin—where this last phrase means *being released from the grip of the sin-disorder.* When one consults the liturgical texts themselves, however, it can seem as if they operate with the contact model: in the context of the liturgy, God endows material elements with powers such that, when a person comes into physical contact with these elements, they contribute to the loosening of the grip of the sin-disorder of that person. Given the almost occult features of the contact model, it would be good to have an alternative, one that helps us see how liturgical activity might contribute to the remission of sin. There is, I have suggested, an attractive alternative according to which certain liturgical rites impose on material stuff the normative function of being means of communion with God. And, although I haven't emphasized the point, this model seems to be consistent with the liturgical texts, sharing whatever virtues the contact model may have, such as being compatible with various understandings of the eucharistic elements as the body of Christ. The issue that remains to be explored is the way in which this model might account for how liturgical activities could contribute to the remission of sin, understood in the way suggested earlier.

Although I find myself with less to say about this matter than I'd like, let me make a few initial observations. In the first place, it would be a mistake, I believe, to attempt to identify a one-size-fits-all way in which liturgical activity contributes to the loosening of the sin-disorder; the disorder has multiple dimensions and, in principle, participating in liturgical rites could address its various dimensions and in various ways. Second, while the church has understood liturgical activity as a locus of divine action, it has not maintained that activities such as participating in the eucharist—to pick one example—are sufficient for the remission of sin. The best way to understand

---

[43] Richard Swinburne has called to my attention the similarities between this model and that developed by Dummett (1987). The primary difference between our views are these: first, Dummett wishes to offer a model for understanding how the eucharistic elements could truly be said to be the body and blood of Christ, whereas the model I develop endeavors to throw light on the nature of the Mysteries more generally. Second, Dummett maintains that divine action is implicated in the imposition of a new status on the eucharistic elements insofar as God has granted some agent the relevant authority to declare the eucharistic elements the body and blood of Christ. My view is consistent with but does not require this approach.

the liturgical script, I believe, is that, when all goes well, these activities contribute over time to the release of the grip of the sin-disorder—presumably in concert with other activities such as prayer and almsgiving. And, finally, it would, I think, be a mistake to think that the primary way in which these liturgical activities function as a point of contact with God is by evoking mystical experiences or beliefs about God's activity. A central task of the Christian life is, after all, to alter not so much our beliefs but our perception of—our "take" on—our environment, viewing it through eyes that see the extraordinary in the ordinary.

These points noted, let me call attention to the locution "means of communion" that I've borrowed from Schmemann to describe both liturgical rites themselves and the material stuff with which they work. The phrase is fecund. When thinking about human relationships, the means in question seem almost limitless: a spoken word, a letter, play, work, or an embrace can all be means of communion, ways of bonding. Moreover, the bonding between persons that occurs can range from coming to see something as someone else does, coming to appreciate something that someone else does, or learning to love something someone else does, on the one hand, to enjoying a sub-doxastic connection with another, such as that difficult-to-describe connection that parents share with their infants, or owners, with their pets, on the other. When it comes to speaking of something as being a means of communion with God, the best we can do is to start with these phenomena and extend our understanding of them analogically to God. We can speak, then, of an activity that contributes to our appreciating what God appreciates or of sensing the goodness of the Holy One, an experience that is no easier to describe than the experience of bonding that occurs between a parent and a child.

Suppose, then, we work with this fairly open-ended understanding of what it would mean for something to be a means of communion—a point of contact—with God. The next point to make is that to the extent that some activity is a means of communion with God—a way of bonding or joining together—it is thereby the sort of thing that can contribute to the loosening of the sin-disorder. The dynamic is familiar: union with one thing contributes to the release from another. Joining one alliance means releasing oneself from the other. If this is right, there is no need to think of liturgical rites or matter as having some special function of loosening the grip of the sin-disorder. They accomplish this simply by bringing us into communion with God in one or another way—this communion being the upshot, in part, of our treating certain acts and objects as points of contact with God. The point that I have been eager to press is that this communion is not exhausted by cognition. It has important—if difficult to understand—sub-doxastic dimensions, similar perhaps to that effected by the touch of another human being.

10.3. CONCLUSION

Not long ago, I listened to a radio program in which the respected poet Christian Wiman spoke of the role of poetry during a time in which he was suffering from an extremely rare form of cancer and was near death. Wiman found that the experience re-kindled a faith that he had abandoned decades earlier. In a state that he describes as one in which he could feel death "sniffing" him over, he found abstract poetry and descriptions of God empty, even "poisonous." Only poetry full of concrete images and descriptions, such as the vivid description of peeling a grapefruit, resonated with him.

Wiman's experience isn't universal; some find comfort in abstractions. It should be conceded, moreover, that the liturgical script is full of fairly abstract depictions of God. Still, what Wiman's experience points to is the power and importance that the particular can have. And, in the liturgy, the particular abounds. For the liturgy is not a series of propositions or a philosophical meditation on God's greatness. It is rather a sequence of actions composed of particular bodily rites—rites such as baptizing, participating in the eucharist, and anointing—that engage with material stuff. Even when we are children, these rites often shape our sensibilities without our realizing it, helping us to associate God and God's activity with the concrete, the particular, the material, the communal. This is not a capitulation to our failures of imagination; on the contrary, it is a testament to divine immanence, to the "One who fills all things." And to the extent that these rites do this—so the assumption of the tradition seems to be—these actions could be the sort of thing that brings us into communion with God in ways that are difficult to articulate and that we sometimes do not understand.[44]

---

[44] Thanks to David O'Hara, Mark Montague, Luke Reinsma, Gregory Tucker, Nick Wolterstorff, and an anonymous referee for their help with this chapter.

11

Entering through Death,
Living with Doubt

I remember well the moment I decided to become Orthodox. I was standing in front of the kitchen sink washing dishes, turning over in my mind the recent experience of attending Orthodox services. I had a lot to think about. I was at a point in my life in which I had attended Orthodox services for some years. There were elements of the tradition that I found extremely attractive, such as the beauty of its liturgy. But there were other elements of the tradition with which I struggled, such as its radical apophaticism about God. At that moment, however, I was not doing a mental cost–benefit analysis, trying to determine whether it made sense to become Orthodox. Rather, as I stood there, I found myself struck by the following realization: I wanted to die Orthodox. I wanted to die not as an outsider but in the arms of the church. Although I wouldn't officially be received into the church until years later, it was on the basis of this realization that I decided to become Orthodox. It is probably worth emphasizing that, in my case, the experience was that of *resolving* to become part of the church. Mine was not an experience of being overwhelmed by a realization, but of deciding to act on the basis of one.

To this day, I am not sure why this thought about death made such a strong impression upon me. In one of his essays, Metropolitan Antony Bloom recounts his experience of being at a soldier's deathbed and asking the dying soldier whether he was afraid of death. The soldier's response to Bloom was to say that he was afraid not of death but of dying alone. I suspect that something like this fear was operative in me that day while washing dishes. I had been part of many groups and social organizations: universities, philosophy departments, ski clubs, rock bands. I knew that none would be of any help in preparing for death. None was equipped to lead a person through the process of dying. None, in all likelihood, would keep alive the memory of a person who had died.

The Orthodox Church, I recognized, was different. It did not counsel avoidance of the subject of death. To the contrary, built into the very fabric of its daily prayers were prayers for a good death—"painless, blameless, and peaceful." In its prayers and rites, the church offered the means by which one could keep death in mind as something the preparation for which needed to be worked out on a daily basis. It was, moreover, in its various ministries, equipped to help a person face the ambiguity and suffering that so often accompany death, offering whatever strength and comfort it had to give to the dying. Finally, it was difficult not to be impressed by the church's memory. Unlike nearly all the other branches of Christendom with which I was familiar, the Orthodox did not forget the dead but kept the memory of them alive in their daily prayers and regular commemorations, especially on Sunday, the day of resurrection. Years later, when my father died, I found great comfort in this. Not only did the church provide the words and actions to remember him, the memory of him was also kept alive in a public way. In its words and actions, the church was telling me that his life mattered. Commemoration is honoring; in its paradigmatic forms, it is the remembrance of a person's worth. The church seemed to understand this.

In some implicit way, then, I knew that to die in the arms of the church was to die in the midst of a community that understood the significance of death and whose purpose is, in part, to help us die. Yet the full explanation of why the subject of death played such a prominent role in my decision to become Orthodox is more complicated than I have indicated. To present the fuller explanation, however, I need to turn back the clock and fill in some autobiographical details.

I was baptized Roman Catholic. When I was very young, however, my parents became acutely disaffected with the church and, consequently, I do not remember attending mass with them. So, although nearly our entire extended family was Catholic, I was raised Protestant. From my fifth to my tenth year, our family attended a local Evangelical Free Church. While I have some fond memories of these years, they were tumultuous; it was during this time that our family was more or less blown apart by my parents' divorce. I do not exaggerate when I say that both the divorce process and its fruit were extremely bitter. It resulted in brothers being pitted against brothers and children being pitted against their parents. For eleven years I had limited or no contact with my father, sadly, of my own volition. I am extraordinarily grateful that he was so patient with me.

Having my world fractured as a young boy did not result in a loss of religious faith. If anything, it intensified it. The intensification was, in large measure, a result of being immersed in the charismatic movement in Protestant Christianity, which heavily emphasized the centrality of a personal experience of God. Initially I found this electrifying, but as I grew older, disillusionment crept in. What I saw and heard in church made less and less sense. A typical service seemed to me semi-chaotic. I had, moreover, questions about God and the world around me that no one in or outside the church seemed either willing or able to address. And, perhaps most importantly, I was struck by the dark side of religion as I knew it: my parents had divorced (at least in part) because of their very different religious sensibilities and the Assembly of God Church of which we'd been a part had split because of scandal. The net result was that, by the time I went to college, I had almost entirely checked out of Christianity. Nearly twenty-five years after having been part of the broadly charismatic tradition, it is very difficult for me to assess it with any degree of objectivity. I know I owe a debt to it. But I also find myself shrinking from it in nearly all its manifestations.

This period of non-religiosity as a young adult, however, did not last very long, for during my second year of college I made a twofold discovery. The first was of philosophy. It is difficult for me today to convey properly the exhilaration I felt of having discovered a whole new world, one in which people were asking and addressing questions that were both fascinating and important. When I took my first philosophy course, I didn't know whether I would be any good at it, but I was completely smitten nonetheless. The second discovery was realizing that philosophy did not avoid questions of religion. It asked hard questions about God, evil, and the nature of faith— questions about which I was intensely curious. Nor was philosophy, as such, hostile to religion. (It wasn't until much later that I encountered how deep the hostility toward religion can run among contemporary philosophers.) In fact, I soon discovered that several of my professors were Christians who engaged in the discipline as Christians; they were asking questions about God and the religious life without pretending to be neutral observers. This deeply impressed me. My Christian formation had been so deeply anti-intellectual that I had never dreamt of engaging in the life of the mind and also being a Christian. I now saw this was possible and I pursued it with eagerness. I know that for many studying philosophy has been the occasion to reject religion. It had the opposite effect on me. Philosophy reinvigorated my interest in Christianity.

Ironically, the branch of Christianity that I found most impressive was Roman Catholicism. I say "ironically" for two reasons. In the first place, my primary exposure to Christian philosophy was through my teacher, Nicholas Wolterstorff. Nick, however, identified himself with not the Catholic but the Reformed tradition. While I couldn't help but feel the tug of the Reformed tradition because of Nick's influence, my primary interests were in ethics. And in comparison to the Catholic tradition, it seemed to me that the Reformed tradition had contributed relatively little to ethical theorizing. (Those who know Nick's work also know that he has written extensively on the Christian liturgy. These writings—which are the most perceptive of any I know—later proved to be enormously influential in my journey toward Orthodoxy. This remains a source of amusement to us both.) Second, I had grown up in a household that was deeply hostile to Catholicism. It was a complete epiphany to me to learn that the tradition had so much to offer. The more I learned about its intellectual richness, the more I felt its allure. So, I went to graduate school with the purpose of seriously exploring Catholicism and studying philosophy in the Catholic tradition.

For various reasons, however, things did not go to plan. On paper, I found important aspects of the Catholic tradition attractive. And I tried my best to immerse myself in Catholic life by doing such things as attending mass regularly. But something seemed to be missing; Catholicism just didn't take. This was frustrating to me because I admired many of the Catholics I knew enormously. While they could be very critical of their tradition, they none-theless seemed to have a deep sense of belonging to it. And this I envied. When I compared my situation to theirs, I felt displaced. I felt so displaced, in fact, that I stopped attending church altogether. The average Sunday during the first years of graduate school consisted in my listening to tapes of sermons from Protestant pastors whose preaching I thought was particularly good.

It was during this period of feeling displaced that I first encountered (in any sustained way) the Christian East. Unlike my encounters with Catholicism as an adult, which were largely through the study of texts, my first exposure to the East was through its liturgical life. Two events leap to mind.

A few paragraphs back, I mentioned that, while I was raised Protestant, most of my extended family was Catholic. But not all of it was. My mother's family primarily consisted of Russian immigrants, many of whom, including my grandfather, were Russian Orthodox. Immediately prior to starting gradu-ate school, my grandfather died. Although he was not what I would describe as a religious man, he was, naturally enough, given an Orthodox funeral. There are details of that funeral service that I vividly remember. I remember, for example, not knowing what to do upon seeing a throng of people at the funeral forming a line to kiss my grandfather's body to say their final goodbye. What has remained with me, however, is not so much the details of the service as its ambience: it was a swirl of smoke, candlelight, and chant. The air was raw with emotion. The emotional tone, moreover, was that of thick, heavy grief. But the grief, I discerned, was not despair. The emotional tonality of the service was deep lament, deep sadness, shot through with hope.

Like most my age, I have attended my fair share of funeral services. But very rarely have I attended a service that seemed to me to be a fitting response to death. Some of the services I have attended have been little more than extended eulogies in which photographs of the person who had died were projected on screens while music played. Other services have been muted, even flat in their tone; there were hardly any words on which to hang grief, any actions to perform to express it, even when the death in question was tragic. These services were the liturgical equivalent to what psychologists call flat affect. Still other services attempted to strike a tone of optimism, intentionally focusing on the fact that the person who had died was now with Jesus. (I often would wonder whether the Christian tradition really gives license for such optimism.) As a whole, these services either gave the impression of not knowing exactly how to respond to death or of having a ready response, but getting the emotional tonality all wrong.

This issue gnawed at me over the years. It gnawed at me not simply when I attended the funerals of friends, acquaintances, and relatives but also upon the death of one of my own children. Early in our marriage, my wife and I found ourselves faced with what seemed like an impossible situation. My wife was pregnant with twins, we discovered, but the pregnancy was extraordinarily complicated. The complications meant that the probability of even one baby surviving was very low. In the end, after extensive medical intervention, one child did survive, while the other died. This experience, as you might imagine, was heartrending; both my wife and I found ourselves having to navigate that strange experience of simultaneously feeling both intense joy and grief, sometimes being overcome by one and then the other. The image that comes to mind of that period is that of being on a moving train: at one moment, you are plunged into complete darkness as you head underground; the next moment, you are brought again into the light. Whether in darkness or light, you are at the whims of forces over which you have no control.

There was no funeral for our baby daughter. In principle, my wife and I could have planned one. But our strength was gone, so we dedicated our remaining energies to caring for our surviving daughter who was born two months premature. The (non-Orthodox) church community of which we were a part, while incredibly supportive during this time, seemed uncertain about what to do upon the death of a baby. My sense was that there was no expectation that there should be a funeral. (That, I say, is how it seemed to me. It may be that what seemed to me like uncertainty on their part was simply a desire to "give us space.") And, so, my wife and I grieved privately. There were no words, no communal rites for us collectively to express our grief. In the subsequent years, we had no available rites, beyond those we manufactured ourselves, to commemorate the little one who we had lost.

After this experience, questions that I had previously not considered began to press themselves upon me. Christians, it struck me, were prone to evaluate their own confessional tradition and that of others by asking a set of stock questions: How do we (or does that other tradition) interpret the scriptures? What is the role of the eucharist and how do we (or they) understand it? And what sort of ecclesiastical authority structure does our tradition (or that other tradition) incorporate? These are worthwhile questions to ask. I have asked them myself. But in addition to these commonly raised questions there are, I came to believe, other important questions to ask, among which is this: How does a given tradition, in its liturgical practices and theology, understand and respond to death? I had learned that the Orthodox response to death is not a eulogy for the deceased, a giving of thanks for the life lived, or a celebration of the fact that the deceased is in heaven. It is a prayer, a cry for mercy, a lament in the face of the awfulness of death, mixed with hope. And this response seemed to me not only strikingly different from those with which I was familiar, but also profoundly correct.

A moment ago, I noted being struck by how fitting the tone of my grandfather's funeral service seemed, even though my liturgical sensibilities had not in any sense been shaped by the Orthodox tradition. Years later, when I consulted the text of the service, I saw there was also a beautiful fit between its tone and its words. The text, written in large measure by John of Damascus, consists (in part) of sections in which a reader voices themes from Ecclesiastes while the people respond with the Beatitudes. Here is a taste of the service's text:

> I mourn and weep when I ponder death and see our beauty made in the image of God laid in the grave, disfigured, dishonored, and lacking form. O wonder! What is this mystery that comes to pass for us? Why should we be given over to corruption? And why should we be wedded to death? . . .
>
> Blessed are those who hunger and thirst after righteousness, for they shall be filled . . .
>
> I remembered the prophet who said: I am earth and ashes. And I thought of those in the tombs and saw their bones laid bare. Then I said: "Who is the king or the soldier? Who is the rich man or the beggar? Who is the just man or the sinner?" But give rest to Your servant with the Saints, O Lord.
>
> Blessed are the pure in heart, for they shall see God . . .
>
> With what may we compare this life? A flower, a vapor, an early morning mist? Come, O people, let us look at the grave! Where is the beauty of youth? Where are the eyes that we knew? Where are the hands that we clasped? So soon we perish like the grass of the fields. Let us therefore bathe the feet of Christ with our tears!
>
> O Christ, in the sweetness of Your beauty, give rest to him whom You have chosen, for as much as You love humankind.

What I find so striking about these passages is not so much the tension the text creates by juxtaposing Ecclesiastes with the Beatitudes, pressing the hard actuality of death against the promise of that which is not yet. It is rather the emphasis the text places on the beauty of the body. The awfulness of death consists, in part, in the destruction of beauty—eyes that we knew, hands that we clasped. And yet in the last line quoted above, the destruction of beauty is answered with redemption by beauty. In this case, it is the beauty of Christ, the one whose feet we bathe with our tears. The sheer physicality expressed in these passages—not to mention the physicality of the actions expressed in the funeral service itself—resonated deeply with me.

My decision to become Orthodox, I wrote earlier, was driven by the recognition that I wished to die in the arms of the church. I noted that this desire itself was rooted in the desire to die as part of a community, one that equips us to cope with death's grim reality. Evidently, however, there was more lying behind the decision than these desires. In that moment before the kitchen sink, I was not simply recognizing a deep-seated desire. When it came to death, I had also come to believe, the church had got things right. It fully recognized just how much is lost in death. And it gave us the words and actions, both beautiful and fitting, to express this.

In many ways, attending my grandfather's funeral is the prehistory to that period in which I seriously engaged Orthodoxy. That period began in graduate school when I considered myself a Christian but had stopped attending church altogether. It was during this time that my roommate, without saying a word to me about it, converted from Anglicanism to Orthodoxy. He probably recognized that it would be better if I did something to celebrate Easter rather than listen to cassette tapes of sermons. So, he invited me to attend a Paschal liturgy with him at St. Vladimir's Orthodox Seminary. Although I knew nothing about how the Orthodox celebrate Pascha, I accepted.

To this point in my life, I had more or less despised the Easter services that I had attended; they all seemed to me anticlimactic, strangely out of kilter with the significance of what was being commemorated. Indeed, in some traditions with which I was familiar, Easter seemed almost an afterthought. When I later taught at Christian colleges, you could tell immediately if it was the Christmas season. There in the public space were the Christmas trees and the gifts. But when Easter rolled around, you would almost not know it. Almost nothing changed in the space in which we worked. There were no parties, no exchanging of gifts. There was nothing particularly festal about it. The idea that the Easter season might extend beyond Easter Sunday was, apparently, totally foreign. Easter left as stealthily as it had come.

There really was no way for me to prepare for what I saw and heard that night during my first Paschal liturgy. The Orthodox call Pascha the Feast of Feasts. It is an apt title: the liturgy I attended was if nothing else a feast for the senses—the eyes, the ears, the hands, the nose and, when it was all over, (to switch to a non-sensory modality) the stomach too. The post-liturgical feast— you have to picture it being accompanied by a great deal of singing and vodka—extended into the early morning hours, until everyone was too exhausted to carry on anymore. When that time came, everyone went home to sleep only to return later to reconvene the celebration.

While standing during the Paschal liturgy, I sensed, for the first time ever, a fit between the actions being performed in an Easter service and the significance of that which was being celebrated. The service itself was highly scripted; but it was not at all stiff. I suppose the best analogue would be to a group of musicians or dancers who are following a score but are so comfortable in doing so that their performance is nothing less than structured fluidity. Interestingly, like my grandfather's funeral, the theme of death was all around; but, unlike that service, the Paschal service was not a lament. It was a celebration, a proclamation of a great living hope that death—and here it helps to recognize that the term "death" is multivalent in the mouth of the church, also signifying despair, emptiness, and darkness—does not have the final word. The message of the liturgy was clear: death is the enemy. Its bitterness should not be underestimated. But God has been actively at work in the world. The creation has not been abandoned but is being rescued, redeemed through the life, death, and resurrection of Christ. Not Ecclesiastes but the Beatitudes have the last word. The trope used throughout the liturgical texts is that death has been defeated by death. Perhaps putting the phrase in the continuous present —"death is being defeated"—more nearly captures the sense of the liturgical text, as the use of the liturgical present is ubiquitous in the Paschal liturgy. The liturgy announces that *today* Christ is risen. Apparently, the Paschal liturgy is not supposed to be simply the commemoration of an historical event, but the occasion for us here and now to absorb the life-altering significance of the resurrection.

Jubilant and reverential, serious and beautiful: that first Paschal liturgy made quite an impression on me. Still, it would be misleading to describe my first serious encounter with Orthodoxy as love at first sight. It would take years until I felt as if I'd "lived into" and reconciled myself with various aspects of the tradition, for there were dimensions of Orthodoxy that struck me as dark, exotic, alien, and problematic. Indeed, a central part of becoming Orthodox was learning to accept the fact that there would be elements of the tradition with which I would simply have to live. It was far from perfect. (When I married my wife, I recognized something similar: while remarkable, she was not perfect. That, however, did not seem to me a sufficient reason not to marry. Why should it be different here?) Despite all this, something kept pulling me back. I was magnetized.

The magnetism of Orthodoxy consisted, at least in part, in the effect that participating in the liturgical life of the church had on me. While I often found the services very long, I noticed that I found myself praying during them. Prayer had never come easily to me. The recipe I had been given growing up was that it took place primarily in "quiet times," when one would lock oneself away in a private space with a Bible. That had never worked for me. I found huge stretches of the scriptures absolutely baffling. And left to my own devices, I'd sooner fall asleep than pray. But somehow being in the space of an Orthodox Church and participating in the liturgy enabled me to pray. Not only was I able to pray, I found the prayers and hymns of the liturgy reaching me at a level of my being that none other had. They spoke to me.

I do not know how to explain this. The best I can say is that I was slowly experiencing something like a gestalt switch. The comparison that comes to mind is that of a person who has, throughout most of his adult life, been fed a literary diet that almost exclusively consists in such things as novels, newspaper articles, and academic essays. Then, at some point, he is introduced to very good poetry. At first, the nuances and even the meanings expressed by this poetry tend to escape him. With increased exposure, however, he latches on. He finds that the poetry speaks to him in ways rather different from prose; there is something about the poetic use of images that has an entirely different effect on him. The images themselves, he has to admit, are in many ways elusive; they often resist any sort of systematic unpacking or formulation, as the tensions and ambiguities they introduce remain unresolved. And were he not to exercise care, this person would attribute to the poets silly and incompatible views, blurring over important distinctions such as what the poets are saying and what they are showing him. Eventually, however, he finds that not only does the poetry have a different effect on him than prose, but also that the poetry speaks to him—and allows him to speak—in ways that prose cannot. The two are not, for all intents and purposes, interchangeable. He has a new window to the world.

Something like the transition I have just described is how it has felt to enter into the liturgical life of the church. The experience has been that of being presented with a new set of images—images tumbling over one another in ways that were sometimes baffling, resisting in many cases any sort of systematic unpacking—that speak to me in ways that are difficult to articulate. Most importantly, I have often sensed that the icons, bodily movements, and hymnody were showing to me things about God and the world that are not easily said. The task has been to look where they are pointing.

Anyone who has studied poetry knows that it is often very hard work to interpret it well. One of the more startling discoveries upon immersing myself in Orthodox life was learning that the Christian life is similar inasmuch as it too is a difficult road. In his book *Great Lent*, Alexander Schmemann writes that "Christianity is above everything else expectation and preparation."[1] My earlier exposure to Christianity had taught me virtually nothing about preparation. I knew nothing about the role of such things as fasting and confession, for example, in the Christian life. I soon learned, however, these two things: first, that for the Orthodox all these broadly preparatory activities are oriented toward Pascha. Pascha is both the highlight and center of the entire liturgical calendar; everything done during the church year revolves around it. How different this was from the Christianity I knew according to which Easter was more or less an afterthought! And, second, I learned that the Pascha is itself as much about preparation as it is about celebration. Repentance, confession, and fasting are the entryways into the feast. Moreover, they are, for different reasons, activities that are demanding and difficult. The athletic images that St. Paul employs in his letters to the early Christians are not idle!

Appreciating this dimension of Orthodox life has taken time. There are days in which I do not feel up to the challenge. And, frankly, I often struggle to immerse myself into the flow of Orthodox life. I find it helpful to bring to

---

[1] Schmemann (1969), 85.

mind, however, that while the Orthodox emphasize that we work out our own redemption and that of the world, the model is that of a divine-human cooperative endeavor. God and human beings together work for the redemption of human beings and the world together. Although Orthodox spiritual life requires that we learn to discipline ourselves by doing such things as engaging in regular prayer and fasting, these activities are not particularly self-concerned. The idea is not that each of us is to undertake certain disciplines to achieve enlightenment or personal holiness. Rather, the idea is that, by engaging in the disciplines, we become the types of agents that can, to use Schmemann's imagery, play the part of the priest: offering back to God in thanksgiving and gratitude that which God has given to us. The goal is not self-realization but being in right relation with God, each other, oneself, and the rest of creation.

My grandfather's funeral had impressed upon me that the Orthodox understood death's bitterness. The Paschal liturgy (and engaging in its preparatory activities) impressed upon me something different, a different vision of death. As I wrote earlier, I do not understand why that thought about death by the kitchen sink years ago struck me with such force. I suspect, however, that it was because (in part) I had come to view the Orthodox vision of death as not only attractive but correct. Christianity is nothing if not a defiant expression of hope.

My theme has been death and the ways in which it has been the entryway for me into the Orthodox Church. My relation to this topic is, however, more complicated than I've indicated. Let me elaborate.

I know people—some whom I deeply admire—who have a vivid sense that our lives extend beyond the grave. I recently listened to an interview with an Athonite monk in which he explained that he was not troubled about not having been with his father before his father's death; he was certain that they would meet again. I, by contrast, have never had a vivid sense of there being an afterlife. In fact, I am fairly confident that whatever attitude I hold toward the Christian doctrine of the resurrection of the dead, it is not belief, at least as contemporary philosophers tend to think of it. It is not that I *dis*believe this component of Christian doctrine. It is rather that I find myself not believing it. And, were I to speak with complete candor, I think something similar is true of how I view nearly all the central claims of Christianity itself. I find myself neither believing nor disbelieving them—although at different points of my adult life I have found myself decidedly leaning one way and then the other concerning them. Having said this, I can imagine being pressed about it in the following way: "You identify yourself as a Christian. Surely, then, you believe that Jesus is the Christ? And, surely, you believe in the resurrection of the dead?" My answer to these questions would probably be this.

I do not think that what Christianity teaches is false (or even probably false). I believe, moreover, that there are plausible considerations in favor of the central claims of Christianity, perhaps on balance rendering them more plausible than their alternatives (although perhaps not more so than the disjunction of all their alternatives). While I feel the force of considerations that call the central Christian claims into question, I continue to be impressed by the degree of cohesiveness that these claims exhibit: the central claims of Christianity seem to me to hang together fairly well, on the whole. Perhaps more importantly, I find myself deeply impressed by the tradition's ethical vision, its understanding of justice, love, and forgiveness and the particular way in which these ethical values mesh. Unlike most other ethical visions with which I am acquainted—such as those articulated by Aristotelians, consequentialists, and Kantians—the Christian ethical vision is one that commands my allegiance, my devotion. Were someone to tell me that I could extricate the true kernel of this ethical vision from its theistic context, I wouldn't know how to begin. I have no idea how to extricate what the Christian tradition teaches about justice, love, and forgiveness from its theistic commitments.

Yet on most days I find myself not believing many of Christianity's core claims. This is not because I fail to hold beliefs. I believe countless propositions about mundane matters. I believe, for example, that jazz is one of the finest musical genres invented and that grapefruits have fiber. I also believe certain philosophical positions, such as metaphysical realism or the view that there is a ready-made external world. A good sign that I believe these things is that I would be very surprised were I to learn that they are not so. The attitudes I hold toward many of the central claims of Christianity seem different, though. I would not be overcome with surprise were I to discover that the central claims of Christianity are false, that there is no resurrection of the dead. At least I wouldn't be surprised in the way that I would be were I to discover that grapefruits do not contain fiber or that metaphysical realism is false.

I would, however, be *dismayed* if the central claims of Christianity were false. For I want these claims to be true with all my heart. I find the Christian vision of the world, especially as it is expressed in the Orthodox tradition, incredibly attractive: here there is beauty, forgiveness, redemption, and meaning. I hope, then, with all my being that what the tradition says is true. Moreover, and perhaps most importantly, I am committed to the central components of Christianity, as they are understood in the Orthodox tradition. These components play a central part—arguably, the most central part—in how I view the world and what sort of practical structure my life takes in its rhythm of prayer, fasting, and celebration. The tradition structures my intellectual and practical world. I do not rule out for a moment that this non-doxastic commitment might be transformed into belief. I would welcome that. But, I have become convinced, there is little to recommend a view according to which a certain high level of credence is a prerequisite for authentic Christian commitment. Admittedly, I have often been tempted to engage in a type of internal monitoring wherein I check to see whether

I hold such and such level of credence in Christianity's central claims, as if maintaining such a level were a prerequisite of genuine faith. But, I have learned, monitoring of this sort bears no fruit.

I suppose, then, that when it comes to religious matters I am a doubter (in one ordinary sense of the word), but not a skeptic (in another, darker sense of this word). Although I have often found this stance uncomfortable, my adult years have been ones in which I have learned not to take my doubts too seriously. For I realize that it would be pure fantasy to hold that, on the whole, my doubts accurately track the evidence. More often than not, they track such things as my own unhealthy tendencies to fixate on certain issues to the exclusion of others, my tendency to be moved by certain events and not others, my social environments (which at present is highly secularized), and my own inability to see how things fit together. How often I have been wrong in my assessment of others, misinterpreting their words and actions! It would be entirely unsurprising to me if the same were true of my assessment of God. In my darkest moments of doubt, when I have worried that what I hold dear is false, I have often asked myself whether there is anything better on the other side.

As best I can tell, the answer is no. I do not see how a life in which I drink coffee on Sunday mornings instead of participating in the liturgy is better. I do not see how a life that has no rhythm of fasting and feasting, no structure in which one can communally express grief and hope is better than one that does have such a rhythm and structure. I do not see how a life in which on Easter I do little more than collect chocolate-filled plastic eggs with my children is better than one in which I sing the hymns of the church with my children, expressing defiant hope in the face of death. On this matter, I wish not to be misunderstood: the secular life does not seem to me meaningless. But the secular life does seem to me considerably less rich than that offered by Orthodox Christianity; in comparison to what I know, it looks to me empty. When I have "tried on" the secular life that is how it has felt at least.

At this point, however, I can imagine being pressed further: "But you do recite the Nicene Creed during every liturgy, don't you? You do say that you believe in God the Father, maker of heaven and earth, and of all things visible and invisible? Given what you've said above, wouldn't it be bad faith on your part to say during the liturgy that you *believe* these things?"

I do not think so. It is, first of all, not at all apparent that the word "believe" as it appears in the Creed expresses the same concept as that on which contemporary epistemologists have their eye. Arguably, "belief" is plausibly rendered as something more similar to what I called above "commitment."[2]

---

[2] On this matter, William Alston's comments on the biblical use of *pisteuo* are instructive. Alston notes that biblical translators often render this Greek term as "believe," arguably because there is in English no verb cognate of "faith." But, Alston suggests, *pisteuo* is probably more

But even if the concept of belief expressed in the Creed were more robust than mere commitment, my response would be to say that the Creed functions for me as something like a regulative ideal. It is what I aspire to live into, even if at present I do not: "Lord I believe. Help, thou, my unbelief."

And this brings me to the final observation I would like to make about the Orthodox tradition. The intuitive picture that many people have of Orthodoxy is that it is fossilized, stiff, and archaic: it is a world of black robes, long beards, and elaborate rites. The tradition appears redolent of a bygone age. For the most part, I myself find these idiosyncrasies charming. (I do not find all the traditional Orthodox practices charming. The tradition's resistance to healthy change can be frustrating. Still, by contrast, I find the tendency of other Christian traditions to appropriate the trappings and tendencies of twenty-first century American life totally off-putting.) What I have found, however, is that there is little correlation between Orthodoxy's being deeply committed to traditional Christian practice, on the one hand, and its being a tradition in which there is limited freedom, on the other. To the contrary, my experience has been that the opposite is true. The tradition has provided space to breathe.

Let me explain what I mean. Consider the issue of how Christians interpret the scriptures. I know many intelligent Christians who bend over backwards trying to square fairly literal readings of Genesis, Job, the New Testament genealogies, and the like with what we know about the world (such as what evolutionary theory tells us). As a result of this approach to the text, tensions arise, strained readings are advocated. Early on, I learned that the Orthodox tend to approach and read the scriptures in ways very different from this. Certain questions are closed, to be sure. The main theological issues, for example, regarding the triune nature of God and the nature of Christ are settled. Because the church's understanding of these issues is settled, it provides the boundaries within which we interpret the scriptures, the hermeneutic playing field. On the playing field itself, however, the interpretations available are not only various but often highly creative, even playful. There are some who have told me that the ways in which the Orthodox approach the scriptures remind them of the ways in which liberal Protestants approach the scriptures. There is some truth to that. Neither is shy of emphasizing the

accurately translated as "have faith that." See Alston (1996), 22. Fr. Andrew Cuneo has pointed out to me that even this rendering may not be entirely felicitous. In the Creed, pisteuo is part of an accusative case construction implying *motion*: "pisteuo eis" is literally rendered as "I believe *into* one God." Arguably, the phrase "committed to" better captures the motion and continuity of the Greek in a way that locutions such as "having faith" or "believe" often do not. I should note, finally, that what I have referred to as *commitment* is a fairly close analogue to what Alston calls *acceptance*. Alston says that to accept a proposition is to "take it on board" as true, even when it does not seem clearly correct. Commitment, as I understand it, is different. To commit oneself to a proposition needn't be to take it on board as true. One can commit oneself to a proposition even when one views it as only modestly more likely than its denial.

metaphorical, or in the Orthodox case, the typological meanings of the text. The crucial difference, of course, lies in the fact that, for the Orthodox, not everything is up for interpretation. The parameters within which these interpretations play out are, well, thoroughly Orthodox.

Then there is the issue of how to understand fundamental theological issues in the Christian tradition, such as the atonement. Long before I was Orthodox, I would wince at broadly Augustinian understandings of original sin, the atonement, hell, and God's providence. I felt trapped. I found these understandings so deeply problematic that I increasingly felt myself pushed toward the outer boundaries of traditional Christianity, even though I found the work of the figures that occupied that space, such as Barth and Tillich, generally unappealing. Eventually, however, the shape of the Orthodox understanding of doctrines such as the atonement came into focus for me. It became clear to me that, although the church is happy to operate with various models of the atonement, the fundamental model is one according to which the atonement has nothing to do with the appeasement of divine wrath or the punishment of a scapegoat. Rather, the atonement is achieved via God's full identification with humanity in the life of Christ. It is through this process that the major impediments that mar the divine-human relation are removed, including the fear of death. More breathing room!

As a practical matter, however, the most important realization for me has been that the church's emphasis is not on the issue of whether its members mentally assent to certain propositions. Rather, it is on the practice of becoming a follower of Christ. The fact that a person harbors doubts makes no difference to his status within the church. He is not on that account a second-class citizen. For, if the church is to be believed, it is by authentically engaging in the practices of prayer, fasting, and giving that a person is transformed, redeemed. It is no accident, I believe, that the Sunday after Pascha in the Orthodox calendar is St. Thomas Sunday. In this service, the church celebrates a doubter. Thomas is not chastised or vilified or held up as second best. To the contrary, on Thomas Sunday we sing:

> As the disciples were in doubt, the Savior came on the eighth day to where they were gathered and granted them peace, and cried unto Thomas: Come, O Apostle, and feel the palms in which they fastened the nails. O good unbelief of Thomas, which has led the hearts of the faithful to knowledge! Hence, he cried out with fear: O my Lord and my God, glory be to You.

"O good unbelief of Thomas"! The church is perfectly clear that Thomas's unbelief is *good*; it is what ultimately leads his heart and those of others into knowledge. (In fact, it is often noted that Thomas is deeply committed to Christ. He is the one disciple who is willing to go with Jesus to Lazarus's tomb, even though he knows that Jesus will probably receive a violent welcome.) If one has been to an Orthodox liturgy, one cannot help but be struck by the degree to which the modality of touch is employed: those attending do such things as kiss the icons, kiss the Gospel, and take the eucharist into their mouths. According to the Gospel, it is by Thomas's touching something—the wounds of Christ—that he comes to knowledge; the employment of the body is the means to knowledge of God. Some of us find ourselves in something like Thomas's predicament—committed to Christ but also with doubts (cf. Matt. 28: 17). The church invites us to follow Thomas's example. We are invited into the richness of the church, to touch, taste, and see.[3]

Friday, Bright Week, 2011

[3] In one way or another, Fr. Andrew Cuneo, Tyler Doggett, Matt Halteman, Dan Howard-Snyder, Rico Vitz, and Lori Wilson helped me with this chapter. I am grateful for their help.

Bibliography

Adams, Marilyn. 2006. *Christ and Horrors*. Oxford: Oxford University Press.

Adams, Robert M. 1986. "The Problem of Total Devotion." In Robert Audi and William Wainwright, eds., *Rationality, Religious Belief, and Moral Commitment*. Ithaca, NY: Cornell University Press: 169–94.

Adams, Robert M. 1999. *Finite and Infinite Goods*. Oxford: Oxford University Press.

Alston, William P. 1989. "The Indwelling of the Holy Spirit." In his *Divine Nature and Human Language*. Ithaca, NY: Cornell University Press: 223–52.

Alston, William P. 1992. *Perceiving God*. Ithaca, NY: Cornell University Press.

Alston, William P. 1996. "Belief, Acceptance, and Religious Faith." In Jeff Jordan and Daniel Howard-Snyder, eds., *Faith, Freedom, and Rationality*. Lanham, MD: Rowman & Littlefield: 3–28.

Alston, William P. 2000. *Illocutionary Acts and Sentence Meaning*. Ithaca, NY: Cornell University Press.

Anderson, E. Byron and Bruce T. Morrill, S. J. 1998. "Introduction." In E. Byron Anderson and Bruce T. Morrill, S. J., eds., *Liturgy and the Moral Self*. Collegeville, MN: Liturgical Press: 3–14.

Auerbach, Erich. 2003. *Mimesis*. Princeton, NJ: Princeton University Press.

Baber, H. E. 2013. "Eucharist: Metaphysical Miracle or Institutional Fact?" *International Journal of Philosophy of Religion* 74: 333–52.

Bell, Catherine. 1997. *Ritual: Perspectives and Dimensions*. Oxford: Oxford University Press.

Bell, Catherine. 2007. "Religion through Ritual." In Catherine Bell, ed., *Teaching Ritual*. Oxford: Oxford University Press: 177–94.

Bengson, John and Marc Moffett. 2011. "Nonpropositional Intellectualism." In John Bengson and Marc Moffett, eds., *Knowing How: Essays on Knowledge, Mind, and Action*. Oxford: Oxford University Press: 161–95.

Brandom, Robert. 1998. *Making it Explicit*. Cambridge, MA: Harvard University Press.

Bratman, Michael. 2009. "Shared Agency." In Chrysostomos Mantzavinos, ed., *Philosophy of the Social Sciences*. Cambridge: Cambridge University Press: 41–59.

Brown, Harriet. 2010. *Brave Girl Eating*. New York: HarperCollins.

Bynum, Caroline. 1987. *Holy Feast, Holy Fast*. Berkeley, CA, and Los Angeles: University of California Press.

Carroll, Noël. 1992. "Art, Intention, and Conversation." In Gary Iseminger, ed., *Intention and Interpretation*. Philadelphia, PA: Temple University Press: 97–131.

Carroll, Noël. 2001a. "Art, Narrative, and Moral Understanding." In his *Beyond Aesthetics*. Cambridge: Cambridge University Press: 270–92.

Carroll, Noël. 2001b. *Beyond Aesthetics*. Cambridge: Cambridge University Press.

Carroll, Noël. 2011a. "Narrative and the Ethical Life." In his *Art in Three Dimensions*. Oxford: Oxford University Press: 373–95.

Carroll, Noël. 2011b. "Narrative Closure." In his *Art in Three Dimensions*. Oxford: Oxford University Press: 355–72.

Casel, Odo. 1962. *The Mystery of Christian Worship*. London: Darton, Longman & Todd.

Cath, Yuri. 2011. "Knowing How without Knowing That." In John Bengson and Marc Moffett, eds., *Knowing How: Essays on Knowledge, Mind, and Action*. Oxford: Oxford University Press: 113–35.

Crisp, Oliver and Michael Rea, eds. 2009. *Analytic Theology*. Oxford: Oxford University Press.

Cuneo, Terence. 2010. "If These Walls Could Only Speak: Icons as Vehicles of Divine Discourse." *Faith and Philosophy* 23: 123–41.

Cuneo, Terence. 2012. "Entering through Death, Living with Doubt." In Rico Vitz., ed., *Turning East: Contemporary Philosophers and the Ancient Christian Faith*. Crestwood, NY: St. Vladimir's Seminary Press: 157–76.

Cuneo, Terence. 2013. "Another Look at Divine Hiddenness." *Religious Studies* 49: 151–64.

Cuneo, Terence. 2014a. "Liturgical Immersion." *Journal of Analytic Theology* 2: 117–39.

Cuneo, Terence. 2014b. "Protesting Evil." *Theology Today* 70: 430–44.

Cuneo, Terence. 2014c. "Ritual Knowledge." *Faith and Philosophy* 31: 365–85.

Cuneo, Terence. 2014d. "The Significance of Liturgical Singing." *Res Philosophica* 91: 411–29.

Cuneo, Terence. 2014e. *Speech and Morality*. Oxford: Oxford University Press.

Cuneo, Terence. 2014f. "Transforming the Self: On the Baptismal Rite." *Religious Studies* 50: 279–96.

Cuneo, Terence. 2015a. "Liturgy and the Moral Life." In Christian Miller, ed., *Character: New Directions from Philosophy, Psychology, and Theology*. Oxford: Oxford University Press: 572–89.

Cuneo, Terence. 2015b. "Rites of Remission." *Journal of Analytic Theology* 3: 70–88.

Cuneo, Terence. 2015c. "Love and Liturgy." *Journal of Religious Ethics* 43: 587–605.

Cuneo, Terence. forthcoming. "St. Isaac's Dictum." In Stewart Goetz and Joshua Seacharis, eds., *Theism and the Meaning of Life: New Essays*. New York: Bloomsbury.

Currie, Gregory. 1994. "Imagination and Simulation: Aesthetics Meets Cognitive Science." In Martin Davies and Tony Stone, eds., *Mental Simulations*. Oxford: Blackwell: 151–69.

Deiss, Lucien. 1967. *Springtime of the Liturgy*. Collegeville, MN: The Liturgical Press.

Dix, Dom Gregory. 1945. *The Shape of the Liturgy*. London: Dacre.

Dummett, Michael. 1987. "The Intelligibility of Eucharistic Doctrine." In W. J. Abraham and S. Holtzman, eds., *The Rationality of Religious Belief*. Oxford: Oxford University Press: 231–61.

Fagerberg, David W. 2004. *Theologica Prima: What Is Liturgical Theology?*, 2nd edition. Chicago, IL: Hildebrand Books.

Ferguson, Everett. 2010. "Baptism in the Messalian Controversy." *Studia Patristica* 46: 353–8.

Finn, Thomas. 1976. "Baptismal Death and Resurrection: A Study in Fourth Century Eastern Baptismal Theology." *Worship* 43: 175–89.

Florensky, Pavel. 1996. *Iconostasis*. Crestwood, NY: St. Vladimir's Seminary Press.

Florovsky, Georges. 1972. *Bible, Church, Tradition*. Belmont, MA: Nordland.

Florovsky, Georges. 1975. *Aspects of Church History*. Belmont, MA: Nordland.

Florovsky, Georges. n.d. "Baptismal Symbolism and Redemptive Reality." Available at <http://www.holytrinitymission.org/books/english/theology_redemption_florovsky_e.htm#_Toc104243112> (accessed July 13, 2012).

Gregory of Nazianzus. 2008. *Festal Orations*. Crestwood, NY: St. Vladimir's Seminary Press.

Gregory of Nyssa. 1979. *From Glory to Glory: Texts from Gregory of Nyssa's Mystical Writings*, selected and with an introduction by Jean Daniélou S. J. Crestwood. New York: St. Vladimir's Seminary Press.

Guroian, Vigen. 1985. "Seeing Worship as Ethics: An Orthodox Perspective." *Journal of Religious Ethics* 13: 332–59.

Guroian, Vigen. 1990. "Bible and Ethics: An Ecclesial and Liturgical Interpretation." *Journal of Religious Ethics* 18: 129–57.

Harris, Paul. 2000. *The Work of the Imagination*. Malden, MA: Blackwell.

Harrison, N. V. 2008. "Introduction." In Gregory of Nazianzus, *Festal Orations*. Crestwood, NY: St. Vladimir's Seminary Press: 11–56.

Hierotheos, Metropolitan of Nafpaktos. 1996. *Orthodox Spirituality*. Translated by Effie Mavromichali. Levadia: Birth of the Theotokos Monastery.

Hierotheos, Metropolitan of Nafpakos. 2005. *Orthodox Psychotherapy*. Translated by Esther Williams. Levadia: Birth of the Theotokos Monastery.

Horn, Stacey. 2013. *Imperfect Harmony*. Chapel Hill, NC: Algonquin Books of Chapel Hill.

Hunsinger, George. 2000. "Baptism and the Soteriology of Forgiveness." *International Journal of Systematic Theology* 2: 248–69.

Hütter, Reinhardt. 2010. "Transubstantiation Revisited: *Sacra Doctrina*, Dogma, and Metaphysics." In Reinhard Hütter and Matthew Levering, eds., *Ressourcement Thomism: Sacred Doctrine, the Sacraments, and the Moral Life*. Washington, DC: Catholic University of America Press: 21–79.

Jasper, R. C. D. and G. J. Cuming, eds. 1987. *Prayers of the Eucharist*, 3rd revised edition. Collegeville, MN: The Liturgical Press.

John of Damascus. 2003. *Three Treatises on the Divine Images*. Crestwood, NY: St. Vladimir's Seminary Press.

Johnston, Mark. 2009. *Saving God*. Princeton, NJ: Princeton University Press.

Kavanagh, Aiden. 1991. *The Shape of Baptism*. Collegeville, MN: Pueblo Books.

Kavanagh, Aiden. 1992. *On Liturgical Theology*. Collegeville, MN: The Liturgical Press.

Kivy, Peter. 1997. *Philosophies of Arts*. Cambridge: Cambridge University Press.

Lampe, G. W. H., ed. 1969. *A Patristic Greek Lexicon*. Oxford: Oxford University Press.

Levitin, Daniel. 2006. *This Is Your Brain on Music*. New York: Penguin.

Liao, Shen-yi. n.d. "Becoming Immersed."

Liddell, H. G. and R. Scott, eds. 1996. *A Greek-English Lexicon: With a Revised Supplement*, 9th revised edition. Oxford: Oxford University Press.

Lipton, Peter. 2007. "Science and Religion: the Immersion Solution." In Andrew Moore and Michael Scott, eds., *Realism and Religion*. Hampshire: Continuum: 31–46.

Mantzaridis, Georgios. 1996. *Time and Man*. Canaan, PA: St. Tikhon's Seminary Press.

McGuckin, John A., trans. and ed. 2011. *Prayer Book of the Early Christians*. Brewster, MA: Paraclete Press.

Mellema, Gregory. 1997. *Collective Responsibility*. Amsterdam: Rodopi.

Meyendorff. Paul. 1984. "Introduction." In St. Germanus of Constantinople, *On the Divine Liturgy*. Crestwood, NY: St. Vladimir's Seminary Press: 9–54.

Meyendorff, Paul. 2009. *The Anointing of the Sick*. Crestwood, NY: St. Vladimir's Seminary Press.

Mother Mary and Kallistos Ware, trans. 2002. *The Lenten Triodion*. South Canaan, PA: St. Tikhon's Seminary Press.

New Zondervan Parallel New Testament in Greek and English. 1975. Grand Rapids, MI.

Noë, Alva. 2011. "Ideology and the Third Realm (Or, a Short Essay on Knowing How to Philosophize)." In John Bengson and Marc Moffett, eds., *Knowing How: Essays on Knowledge, Mind, and Action*. Oxford: Oxford University Press: 196–214.

Nussbaum, Martha. 1990. *Love's Knowledge*. Oxford: Oxford University Press.

Oupensky, Leonid. 1992. *Theology of the Icon*. Crestwood, NY: St. Vladimir's Seminary Press.

Palmer, G. E. H., Philip Sherrard, and Kallistos Ware. 1979. *The Philokalia*, Vol. 1. London: Faber and Faber.

Pelikan, Jaroslov. 1974. *The Spirit of Eastern Christianity*. Chicago, IL: University of Chicago Press.

Pelikan, Jaroslov. 1990. *Imago Dei: The Byzantine Apologia for Icons*. New Haven, CT: Yale University Press.

Plantinga, Alvin. 2000. *Warranted Christian Belief*. Oxford: Oxford University Press.

Plantinga, Alvin and Nicholas Wolterstorff, eds. 1983. *Faith and Rationality*. Notre Dame, IN: Notre Dame University Press.

Plantinga, Cornelius. 1995. *Not the Way It's Supposed to Be*. Grand Rapids, MI: Eerdmans.

Pruss, Alexander. 2009. "The Eucharist: Real Presence and Real Absence." In Thomas Flint and Michael C. Rea, eds., *The Oxford Handbook of Philosophical Theology*. Oxford: Oxford University Press: 512–40.

Ramsey, Paul. 1979. "Liturgy and Ethics." *Journal of Religious Ethics* 7: 139–71.

Richardson, Cyril, ed. 1996. *Early Christian Fathers*. New York: Touchstone Books.

Rischin, Rebecca. 2003. *For the End of Time: The Story of the Messiaen Quartet*. Ithaca, NY: Cornell University Press.

Rorty, Richard. 1989. *Contingency, Irony, and Solidarity*. Cambridge: Cambridge University Press.

Ryle, Gilbert. 1949. *The Concept of Mind*. Chicago, IL: Chicago University Press.

Saliers, D. E. 1979. "Liturgy and Ethics: Some New Beginnings." *Journal of Religious Ethics* 7: 173–89.

Saliers, Don. 1998. "Afterward." In E. Byron Anderson and Bruce T. Morrill, S. J., eds., *Liturgy and the Moral Self*. Collegeville, MN: Liturgical Press: 208–24.

Schellenberg, J. L. 2007. *The Wisdom to Doubt: A Justification of Religious Skepticism*. Ithaca, NY: Cornell University Press.

Schmemann, Alexander. 1966. *Introduction to Liturgical Theology*. Crestwood, NY: St. Vladimir's Seminary Press.

Schmemann, Alexander. 1969. *Great Lent*. Crestwood, NY: St. Vladimir's Seminary Press.

Schmemann, Alexander. 1973. *For the Life of the World.* Crestwood, NY: St. Vladimir's Seminary Press.

Schmemann, Alexander. 1974. *Of Water and the Spirit.* Crestwood, NY: St. Vladimir's Press.

Schmemann, Alexander. 1987. *The Eucharist.* Crestwood, NY: St. Vladimir's Seminary Press.

Schmemann, Alexander. 1990. *Liturgy and Tradition.* Crestwood, NY: St. Vladimir's Seminary Press.

Searle, John. 1969. *Speech Acts.* Cambridge: Cambridge University Press.

Searle, John. 1995. *The Construction of Social Reality.* New York: The Free Press.

Searle, John. 1990. "Collective Intentions and Actions." In P. Cohen, J. Morgan, and M. E. Pollack, eds., *Intentions in Communication.* Cambridge, MA: MIT Press: 401–16.

Service Book of the Holy Eastern Orthodox Catholic and Apostolic Church according to the Use of the Antiochian Orthodox Christian Archdiocese of North America. 2002.

Shaughnessy, James D., ed. 1976. *Made, not Born.* Notre Dame, IN: University of Notre Dame Press.

Smith, J. K. A. 2009. *Desiring the Kingdom.* Grand Rapids, MI: Baker.

Staniloe, Dimitri. 2002. *Orthodox Spirituality.* South Canaan, PA: St. Tikhon's Seminary Press.

Stump, Eleonore. 2007. "Beauty as a Road to God." *Sacred Music,* 134: 11–24.

Stump, Eleonore. 2010. *Wandering in Darkness.* Oxford: Oxford University Press.

Surrin, Kenneth. 2004. *Theology and the Problem of Evil.* Eugene, OR: Wipf and Stock Publishers.

Swinburne, Richard. 1989. *Responsibility and Atonement.* Oxford: Oxford University Press.

Swinburne, Richard. 2005. *Faith and Reason,* 2nd edition. Oxford: Oxford University Press.

Thayer, Joseph. 1996. *Thayer's Greek-English Lexicon of the New Testament.* Peabody, MA: Hendrickson Publications.

Thiessen, Gesa Elsbeth, ed. 2005. *Theological Aesthetics: A Reader.* Grand Rapids, MI: Eerdmans.

Thyateira. 1995. *The Divine Liturgy of our Father among the Saints John Chrysostom.* Oxford: Oxford University Press.

Tilley, Terrence. 2000. *The Evils of Theodicy.* Eugene, OR: Wipf and Stock Publishers.

Toner, Patrick. 2011. "Transubstantiation, Essentialism and Substance." *Religious Studies* 47: 217–31.

Trakakis, Nick. 2008. *The End of Philosophy of Religion.* London: Continuum.

von Allmen, J. J. 1965. *Worship: Its Theology and Practice.* London: Lutterworth Press.

Waldron, Jeremy. 2000. "On the Road: Good Samaritans and Compelling Duties." *Santa Clara Law Review* 40: 1053–103.

Walton, Kendall. 1990. *Mimesis as Make-Believe.* Cambridge, MA: Harvard University Press.

Ware, K. T. 1972. "The Sacrament of Baptism and Ascetic Life in the Teaching of Mark the Monk." *Studia Patristica* 10: 441–52.

Ware, Kallistos. 2000. "The Theology of Worship." In his *The Inner Kingdom.* Crestwood, NY: St. Vladimir's Seminary Press: 59–68.

Ware, Kallistos. 2004. "God Immanent yet Transcendent: The Divine Energies according to Saint Gregory Palamas." In Philip Clayton and Arthur Peacocke, eds., *In Whom We Live and Move and Have Our Being*. Grand Rapids, MI: Eerdmans: 157–68.

Wettstein, Howard. 2012a. *The Significance of Religious Experience*. Oxford: Oxford University Press.

Wettstein, Howard. 2012b. "Theological Impressionism." In his *The Significance of Religious Experience*. Oxford: Oxford University Press: 78–102.

Wolterstorff, Nicholas. 1980. *Works and Worlds of Art*. Oxford: Clarendon Press.

Wolterstorff, Nicholas. 1983. *Until Justice and Peace Embrace*. Grand Rapids, MI: Eerdmans.

Wolterstorff, Nicholas. 1984. *Reason within the Bounds of Religion*, 2nd edition. Grand Rapids, MI: Eerdmans.

Wolterstorff, Nicholas. 1990. "Remembrance of Things (Not) Past." In Thomas Flint, ed., *Christian Philosophy*. Notre Dame, IN: University of Notre Dame Press: 118–61.

Wolterstorff, Nicholas. 1995. *Divine Discourse*. Cambridge: Cambridge University Press.

Wolterstorff, Nicholas. 1998. *Justice: Rights and Wrongs*. Princeton, NJ: Princeton University Press.

Wolterstorff, Nicholas. 2010a. "Are Religious Believers Committed to the Existence of God?" In his *Practices of Belief: Selected Essays*, Vol. 2, Terence Cuneo, ed. Cambridge: Cambridge University Press: 350–71.

Wolterstorff, Nicholas. 2010b. *Practices of Belief: Selected Essays*, Vol. 2, Terence Cuneo, ed. Cambridge: Cambridge University Press.

Wolterstorff, Nicholas. 2011a. *Hearing the Call*. Mark R. Gornik and Gregory Thompson, eds. Grand Rapids, MI: Eerdmans.

Wolterstorff, Nicholas. 2011b. *Justice in Love*. Grand Rapids, MI: Eerdmans.

Wolterstorff, Nicholas. 2015. *The God We Worship*. Grand Rapids, MI: Eerdmans.

Index

Printed and bound by CPI Group (UK) Ltd, Croydon, CR0 4YY